INCA-KOLA

MATTHEW PARRIS

INCA-KOLA

A Traveller's Tale of Peru

WEIDENFELD AND NICOLSON
London

First published in Great Britain in 1990 by
George Weidenfeld & Nicolson Limited
91 Clapham High Street
London SW4 7TA

British Library Cataloguing in Publication Data
Applied for

ISBN 0 297 81075 8

Printed in Great Britain by
Butler & Tanner Ltd
Frome and London

Contents

The account of the Peruvian bandit attack has appeared in *The Spectator* and is published in *Views from Abroad: The Spectator Book of Travel Writing* (Grafton). The account of the episode at the 'Cross Keys' bar in Cuzco has appeared in *The Times*.

For my mother, Theresa

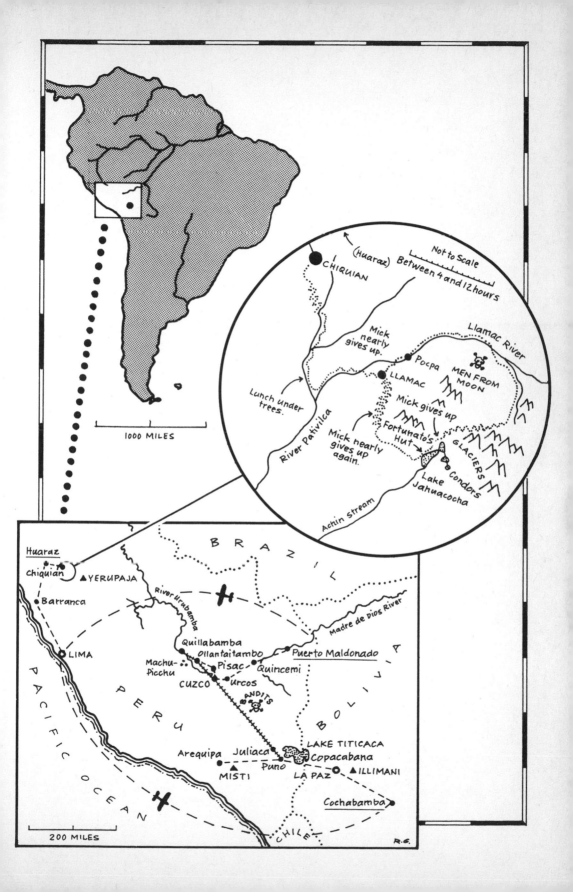

Atrocious Lima

'This is my company card,' said glamorous Rosa, the car-hire woman at Lima airport. We noticed the Playboy bunny badge on her lapel. 'If you have any problems while you are in Peru you can telephone.'

She smiled, hesitated ... 'And this is my home number. I would like to service you personally when you return. Please contact me' – she winked, in case Ian had missed the point – 'big boy ...'

Ian, fresh-faced, sharply dressed and newly graduated in geography from Sheffield Polytechnic, had only fifteen hours ago detached himself from a passionate farewell kiss with his latest girlfriend, at London's Heathrow airport. He was in no mood for a fling with a Peruvian bunny-girl.

'Or any of your friends ...' Rosa added. She glanced at Mick, John and me.

John glanced shyly down, avoiding her eyes and returning to his book, the book he carried with him everywhere. It was a bird watchers' manual, and he had been committing the chapter on torrent ducks to memory. These ducks, he had explained during the long flight, 'are specially streamlined to shoot the rapids, you know – spend all day shooting up and diving down. Ever seen one? I'd give anything to! Lots in the Andes.'

John had celebrated his last evening with his young wife by taking her to sit on some rocks near a hole in the ground to watch in case badgers came out. By 2 a.m. none had, and he had returned to pack, leaving her with a flask of cocoa to continue her observations alone. Rosa had little chance here.

And Mick? He had already telephoned his wife twice: once (at Heathrow) to ask about some unlabelled pills and liniments from his huge collection, and once (during a stopover in Bogotà, Colombia) to remind her to water the tomatoes. He was a church warden at his local village church. Here, too, Rosa's chances were slim.

We thought of her, later, in Lima's Museum of Erotic Art (adults only): a collection of ancient Inca sculptures and carvings, mostly of men and women coupled in the dog position. Rosa would have been more inventive.

We took from her the keys to the little Japanese car we had hired, and set out.

Lima is an atrocity. Ankle-deep in urine and political graffiti, the old Lima rises from the middle of the largest expanse of wet corrugated iron in the southern hemisphere: the new Lima.

'*Ah! Que lindas las tardes de Lima!*' ('How lovely those Liman afternoons!') runs the old Spanish song, recalling an elegant past, long faded now. The old Lima died, our hotelier told us, 'when the slum-people came'.

But the old Lima is still discernible: the colonnades and avenues that have survived a series of horrific earthquakes to stand, cracked and peeling monuments to their imperial past.

At the core of the city, then, lies the decaying hulk of a great colonial shipwreck. In flaking baroque these relics gaze, stained and weary, over the tin and concrete and electric wires. They are waiting for the next earthquake to do the decent thing.

'DRINK INCA-KOLA!' screamed the neon through the filthy air as we piloted our tiny car between the pot-holes and dogs' corpses which adorn the Avenida Elmer Faucett leading into town. The foggy grey dawn turned into a grey morning drizzle, a grey afternoon and a damp grey twilight.

So it was until we quit, so it was when we returned, and so it remains all winter. The Pacific coast lies beneath a great bank of cloud, permanent and solid, its top surface basking flat and still in the sun, pierced by the Andes which emerge as from a sea. Its underbelly heaves gently up and down, loosing a thin and intermittent drizzle over a sombre city. It never quite rains and it never quite shines.

The rich escape for weekends up the side of the mountains where you climb into the sunlight and look out over a white ocean of cloud. The poor are consigned to Lima. The place is purgatory.

Lima's traffic must be seen to be believed. It is a war between cars and pedestrians in which there are no rules, and many casualties on both sides. Motorists prefer to drive on the right but it is only a tendency. A bare majority of cars have headlights, far fewer have tail-lights, and there is a general amnesty on traffic-lights. No signals at all are used, in any circumstances.

Into this assault course we were immediately plunged. John took the wheel. He showed a flair and ingenuity which no one had suspected. A man with a passion for wild birds and flowers and who complains noisily about the uselessness of foreigners, seemed the last person to dive happily into Lima's traffic. Once – only once – he complained, 'Bloody Latins!' – as a taxi came at us head-on, driving on the wrong side of the road to avoid pot-holes. Then a dead animal (we did not have time to see what kind) loomed into vision, blocking our path. John did not hesitate, nor did he complain. Without touching the brakes or making any kind of a signal he swerved straight over the carriageway, dodged an oncoming bus and – with a triumphant blast of the horn – returned to the right side, downstream of the corpse.

There was a jaw-clenched silence in our car. 'I think I could learn to enjoy this,' John said. After that there was no stopping him.

One thing saved us from real tragedy: cars in Peru do not, in fact, move very fast. They can't. Go to any scrapyard in Europe and command the wrecks to rise like Lazarus from the slab: you will have launched a fleet of the finest and newest that Lima has to offer! Chevrolets that are barely post-war; Dodge pick-ups that are not; boots and bonnets missing, windscreens entirely absent or with peep-holes punched through the shattered glass, chassis twisted and steering awry, they stagger honking along the road, seldom firing on all cylinders, and belching smoke. But slowly. Lima's traffic is a sort of limping mayhem.

Through it, we were heading for a hotel whose address we had been given in England. The best route appeared to be across the centre of Lima, so that was our first destination. 'We could do some sightseeing while we drive,' said the optimistic Ian. Soon, John was traversing one of Lima's widest highways, across five lanes of angry buses.

These buses must be seen to be believed: symphonies in blistered rubber, ripped metal and smashed glass, each with its own name – Jesus, for instance, or Fifi – painted above the windscreen. They compete vigorously for custom. Packed to bursting they will dive across each other's paths to pick up new passengers.

Their competitors up-market are the *colectivos*, battered little windowless vans which ply a set route for a set fare. Up-market of the *colectivos* are the taxis. Some of these are actually identifiable as taxis. Others are simply private motorists with time spare to make a quick buck. Never wink, blink or twitch a finger on the streets of Lima, lest the nearest car plunge for you in the hope of negotiating a fare.

We would have done better to travel that way. That much became clear when we reached the centre.

It is hard to say at what point the street John was driving down became the Central Market, and ceased to be a street, for it all seems a blur now. Nor is it clear how we got between the peanut barrow and the record stall, though we smelt the roasting nuts and heard the needle jump. Memories of the clothes and dressmaking section of the market are confused and our drive through the religious and devotional kiosks was a nightmare only half-remembered. All we know is that – often tempted to ditch the car – we were impelled onward by the thought that it must surely end, somewhere. And by the fact that nobody outside seemed in the least taken aback to see us.

The old Indian lady in bowler hat and acres of pink skirts, whose roaring kerosene stove almost set fire to our front offside tyre, seemed surprised only that we continued without buying any of her fried sausages. The money-changer whose calculations we almost upset called out his rates as we passed. It was like driving through Woolworths on a Saturday morning without so much as a raised eyebrow from customers or staff.

In the end we did reach our hotel. Lima was best explored on foot.

Chapter Two

Skulls, Feathers and Dollars

La Alameda was a small, pleasantly quiet hotel, in a place of fading elegance called Miraflores, which means Look-at-the-flowers. This had once been the real Lima, but no more.

The real Lima lay some way off. But, in Miraflores, never out of mind: to keep the real Lima at bay, there were security guards everywhere. Down an avenue of torn and dying trees ran the toxic life-blood that even the healthy parts of a body must share with the diseased: a stream of broken vehicles belching filthy smoke and carrying, to the doorsteps of the rich, the poor men, beggar-men and thieves from the poorer quarters.

These we needed to see, but first money had to be changed. Our experience so far with South American currency exchange had been slight, and bizarre. Needing a little local currency during the stopover in Bogotà we had been directed to a hawker selling condoms and pistachio nuts. He was also the money-changer.

In Peru the position was no less strange, but it took on a manic quality. Peruvians were desperate for dollars. Their own currency was inflating so fast that savings lost their value almost as you watched. The national banks' interest rates were 48 per cent but inflation was more than 100 per cent, so – as one shopkeeper told us – the best thing to do with your money was buy dollars, or gems, 'or alcohol'.

The government, in a futile attempt to keep money in the country, had fixed the international value of their currency artificially high (so that foreigners would have to bring more dollars into Peru and get fewer Peruvian *intis* in exchange). To stop their own citizens from switching out of local currency, the government was limiting the amount they were permitted to change to a tiny sum.

Of course the result was a black market. We never once saw or heard of any foreigner changing money in a bank. Peruvians would offer you a huge premium to change it with them, illegally, on the street. *Bureaux*

5

de change had just been closed and locked, by law, but on the street you could get twice the official rate for a dollar.

The money trade flourished in Miraflores. You were importuned on every corner by little men clicking pocket-calculators at you. The police seemed to turn a blind eye.

The game was to find the best rate. Competition between touts was fierce; and we were warned to watch out for cheats who offered the old, worthless notes to unsuspecting foreigners. We decided to split up and try our chances independently.

Ian failed spectacularly. Standing outside the Centro Pediatrico Higgins he saw a well-dressed, elderly gentleman, in cravat and sunglasses, staring significantly at passers-by. Ian stopped in his tracks and engaged eye-contact.

'You want some business?' said the man, in broken English. Ian nodded enthusiastically. '*Bueno*. How much?'

'A hundred and fifty dollars,' replied Ian, thinking he might as well change plenty.

'*Qué*? A hundred and fifty dollars? You think just because you blond boy, I pay a hundred and fifty dollars? I get fucky-fucky with much cheap boys. Dollars no. *Intis*.'

Ian scarpered.

John got closer. A young chap with alcohol on his breath, dressed Peruvian-cool (fake UCal T-shirt and ski shades – it was night) tugged his sleeve. He offered a rate markedly more favourable than we had been told to expect.

At the last minute, John spotted red numbers on the notes he was being handed. These, we had been warned, were the duds. Mick was nearby and John called to him. The rascal grinned and sauntered off. He didn't even run.

Still, Mick got a good rate from a little oriental-looking tout. The other money-changers called him 'Chino'; they flocked around as soon as we joined Mick's negotiations and started trying to outbid – first Chino, then each other. Eventually we four were able to stand back, hiding our amusement, while Chino and his competitors bid each other downwards in a furious private auction. Once the bid reached some kind of floor we accepted the best – still Chino's – and changed all we needed.

En route, triumphantly, home, John suggested a meal. He nipped up some stairs to inspect the first (as it turned out, the only) Hindu Peruvian vegetarian restaurant we were to encounter. He returned unimpressed: 'Asian waiters. Peruvians eating yoghurt.' We moved on.

The place we settled on proved adequate, though their menu had been eccentrically translated and none of us was tempted by 'cattle consommé'. Only gradually does one come to realize there is really only one menu in Peru; and that, without rice, potatoes, scraggy beef and fried eggs – all seared by fiery red pepper sauce – most restaurants would close. First courses are no more varied: avocado stuffed with egg-and-potato salad (good) and chicken-claw soup predominate; but on the coast *ceviche*, which is raw fish marinated in lime juice, is served everywhere. Coffee is vile, and there is no milk anywhere.

One of us tried the *ceviche*. It tasted better than it sounded. We tramped wearily back to the hotel, past the gates of a huge cinema whose lights trailed (translated), 'THE MONSTER CLUB. A COLLECTION OF RICH VAMPIRES, SNAKE MEN AND WOLF MEN. EVERY KIND OF CREATURE WHO LIKES ROCK MUSIC. LUMINOUS PHANTOMS!'

Where the London barrow-boy may deal in flowers, bananas or post-cards, his equivalent in Lima hawks volumes on molecular physics, Chilean maritime law or the Bolivian constitution. These nestle side by side with Ingrid Bergman's memoirs and the Marxist interpretation of Inca imperialism. Nowhere can so many or such varied book stalls, book barrows or book carts ply their trade in such unlikely streets. Dogs, beggars and prostitutes pick their way through this outdoor library, as comfortable with anthologies of pictures of girls' bottoms, on one side, as they are oblivious of Plato and Wittgenstein on the other.

As we jostled among this throng, on our first morning in downtown Lima, the crowd parted to allow the passage of what must be the most striking book display unit ever devised. A wizened man staggered forward, barely able to lift two massive sandwich boards on which was written (in uncertain crayon), 'IN THIS LITTLE BOOK ARE COLLECTED ALL THE SAYINGS OF ALL THE GREAT MEN. UNFORGETTABLE EPIGRAMS! CELEBRATED PHRASES!' And, swinging on little strings hanging from all around the rim of his hat – like corks on an Australian swagman's hat – were the books themselves! Dozens of copies of a volume so tiny yet plump that it was nearly cubic in shape.

We watched while he made a sale. He cut a book off his hat with a pair of scissors strung to his wrist, and stuffed the money into his hatband. Even Peruvians marvelled.

But we could not stop. Mick wanted to see the Museum of the Inquisition, and we hoped to fit in the Museum of Gold and the Erotic Museum too; as well as the catacombs. 'Don't forget the catacombs!' people kept telling us.

Peru was not the only place to have had an Inquisition, but they seem to have had it more, worse and longer than anyone else.

Our young lady guide to the Hall of the Inquisition spoke English, softly, confidingly. 'The purpose of this procedure,' she said tenderly, as one might advertise lingerie, 'was to make the veins burst.' She knelt beside her waxwork victim, strung with little cheese-wires in a mock-up of the torture, as though herself preparing to administer the final twist. She was pretty, delicate. 'It's my first time,' she told Mick, when he complemented her on her English.

We passed on, into the Inquisitors' Hall. As a mock-up, this seemed rather unimaginative: a bare room with a baroque ceiling, unfurnished except for a polished table. A human skull graced its centre, where a modern hostess might put flowers. But it was not a reconstruction, we discovered. It *was* the Inquisitors' hall, for the Inquisition only ended in 1820.

We left, passing an entire class of Peruvian schoolgirls on a visit to an exhibition of Peruvian constitutions. The girls' history teacher showed the flair of history teachers everywhere. He had ordered his class to spend the morning copying out the names of all the signatories to all the constitutions, in longhand. He was enjoying a cigarette. 'There have been at least eleven constitutions,' he boasted, as if that were a proof of Peru's affection for constitutional government. He nodded in the direction of his feverishly scribbling students: 'This helps young people feel a sense of identification with their history.'

Outside the hall, there was some sort of show of military strength going on in the square. Armoured cars, a brass band, and soldiers in a variety of uniforms marching up and down. Perhaps Peru was due for its twelfth constitution – but we did not stay to enquire. We were bound for the Gold Museum via the Erotic Museum.

But first the catacombs. Beneath the Church of St Francis lay about a cricket-field's extent of dismembered human skeletons. It seems that Lima buried her dead here for some centuries. When space grew short, they started dismantling the corpses, for ease of storage. Thus, for instance, one encountered a pit of forearms, bones bleached white, neatly stacked in parallel; a pit of skulls, arranged in concentric circles; and a pit of miscellaneous foot bones, like a box of assorted biscuits. We had been warned to watch out for the tribe of scorpions which scuttle among them, but we saw none.

The mood of the day was growing macabre and – sadly – the Erotic Museum failed to cheer, as might have been hoped. The carvings and sculptures – hundreds of them, almost all of couples on each other's backs – were neither art nor pornography. They were not beautiful, for no grace or appreciation of the human form illuminated them; nor were they sexually titillating – the opposite, in fact: like children's comic strips they had been carved with a cartoonist's instinct to mock or poke fun. The overall effect, after an hour's browsing through them, was deadening. It was like staring into a pond of toads coupling in the spawning season.

Perhaps the Gold Museum would lighten the air? Far from it. The gold itself – tons, seemingly, of weaponry and decoration – might as well have been brass. The main impression was that this was a poor sort of metal, hopelessly soft, upon which the natives had relied, there being no steel. Far from sharing the conquistadors' amazement that the Indians could be so ignorant of gold's value, one began to understand the Indians' amazement that their conquerors were so obsessed with this inferior yellow metal. And *they* had iron!

One exhibit, though, stayed in the mind, and it was not gold at all. Among a scattering of mummies, leather faces twisted variously into expressions of rage or pain, stood a feathered skull: a bleached, detached human skull to which had been glued thousands of tiny, soft, blue and yellow parrots' feathers. It was covered – upholstered – in a carpet of sky-blue and acid-yellow. Though centuries old, the feathers' colours had kept all their brilliance. Eyeless, two black holes stared out through this gaudy fringe. The old teeth grinned, as through a bank of flowers.

Sometimes (as with African art, for instance) it is hard for a European to know whether the feelings of fear, or beauty, that some mask or carving excites are a European reaction only. Perhaps the object was created for quite another purpose: perhaps it is not really 'art' at all? But to feather this skull, so richly to ornament so grim a symbol of decay – the juxtaposition was timeless in its inspiration, transcending race and culture. It was supposed to be spine-tingling. It was supposed to be grotesque, chilling, beautiful ... like their haunting flute music. And, like the music, it was.

We left the Gold Museum with enough light remaining to sample one of the poorer quarters, a strange pink slum: pink because all the walls had been, well, 'pinkwashed' is the word.

The people looked very poor. There was a smell of urine everywhere and the houses were tiny, segmented by corrugated iron partitions.

Ian explored a bit, even venturing into a funeral parlour. There were literally hundreds of these in Lima. With the hat-shops and banks, they stood out as the only businesses as prosperous and extravagantly fitted out in the poorest of quarters as in the rich. He noticed the prominent display of children's coffins – from schoolboy size down to pathetic baby-coffins in polished wood, adorned with little plastic bunches of flowers, and a place for a photograph of the infant. The cost of one of these, to a poor family, must have been almost unimaginable. Yet poor families would have been this parlour's only customers.

Peering through the iron gates of a state primary school, Mick saw some five hundred children, dressed in a tawdry but discernible uniform and standing in military formation. They were singing the Peruvian national anthem, accompanied by a crackling brass band on a tape recorder. Their headmaster was beating time: '*Somos libres: seamos lo siempre*' ('We are free: let us always be') – '*Antes nieges las luces del sol …*' ('You would deny the light of the sun, before denying that …')

They had shoes of a sort, and you saw none of the obvious, pathological signs of malnutrition you see in Africa. Just the hard-bitten, pinched, worried little faces of the children of the poor: old before their time, alert to know from which direction the next blow may fall. 'We are free …' they sang.

The whole quarter was dominated by a vast and imposing modern beer brewery, steam whistling from its aluminium chimneys, and sirens intermittently announcing the labour shifts. It, too, was painted pink. It must have been the source of much local employment – and some local solace …

At its feet and in its shadow were the run-down remains of a park. It had once been a fine place, a place to see and be seen in. At one end was a convent, pink, like the brewery at the other end. Between them, laid out on classical lines, was what had been the promenading ground of the grandest people in colonial Lima. An avenue of trees – half of them now dead – was interspersed with solid white marble benches and noble stone statues in the Greek style.

You could stand in front of one of these figures – still dignified though her nose was missing, her arms long gone, and political slogans decorated her legs – and look past the statue, past the dying hibiscus bush behind her and past the brewery … past the sharp little hill beyond, hundreds of tiny tin houses clinging to its mud slopes … past all that, outward and upward to where – faint in the polluted air – hung a huge cross on a distant mountaintop.

For those for whom the human misery at its feet offered an insufficient prospect, the brewery rumbling among them an inadequate escape, perhaps the cross gave some sort of comfort. Only once did we see an Indian crying, and that was in the cathedral: an old woman sobbing to a gaudy painting of the Virgin Mary.

The poverty, the children, the religious devotion … it all brought to mind a prayer which Anthony Daniels found pinned by a small icon of the baby Jesus in a corner of that church of San Francisco. He translates it in his book *Coups and Cocaine*:

'*Small Child of my heart, I come before you to ask for yet more favours. Pour your grace on me, give me health of body and soul. Oh my sweet Child! Send down on me a rain of flowers, flowers of your grace, enraptured in their own perfumes. Give me the smile of your lips and the sky of your eyes. Your caresses are worth more to me than all the joys of the world. With your little hands extended, press me tight in your arms. Take me along the way, and never depart from me, I beg you. Amen.'*

Night had fallen when we made our way back across the city. John bought some chocolate from a peasant woman.

Her day's commerce was just ending. Her meagre assortment of wares – chewing gum, cigarettes, some dyed cloths, dog-eared magazines and knitted children's jumpers – were stacked in little piles laid out on newspaper around her, hung on her arms, and pinned to her clothes. She was just a human display rack.

She sold nothing that you could not get from a thousand such hawkers, standing or squatting at the road's edge.

The volume of business she could hope for must have been tiny and the four bars of chocolate, for her, an important sale. But she agreed a price, gave the chocolate and took the money with no hint of triumph or even pleasure: with no trace, in fact, of any kind of emotion. Then she began to pack her goods to go.

She had no barrow and nobody but her little girl to help her; and the little girl was already carrying her baby sister on her back and all the cares of the world across her thin face. Their mother folded and packed every item. The display rack became now a beast of burden. All her stock on board and her two children in tow, she humped and dragged her way back towards wherever home was.

How old was she? It was impossible to say. In this place people's faces turn to leather soon after adolescence; and adolescence comes soon after learning to walk. Boys horse around as boys everywhere do, but little girls seem to have no childhood at all. A twelve-year-old can look soft and virginal. A fifteen-year-old can look worldly-wise, flirtatious and pretty. At thirty-five she is already turning into an old witch, indistinguishable from all the others shuffling their way down the road – as our chocolate seller now was.

'But she's still moving,' said Mick. 'It's the ones who have stopped moving who are finished, in Lima.'

Chapter Three

To The Mountains

Everyone had told us that bus stations are the worst places for thieves. But we forgot. Bright lights, bustle and noise seem so unthreatening. Besides, we were excited for we were going to Huaraz.

The town of Huaraz lies north of Lima and high in the mountains, between the spectacular ranges of the Cordillera Blanca and the Cordillera Huaywash. That was where we wanted to go – walking in the Huaywash mountains. So, first, we had to reach Huaraz.

Peru consists of a long Pacific coastline and, behind it, an equally long narrow desert strip. Behind that rise the Andes, which run the whole length of the country. And on the other side of the mountains lie the jungles of the Amazon basin. Wherever you start, if you start from the sea and head inland, your cross-section of Peru will be the same: desert, mountains, jungle. But there are relatively few points on Peru's long coastline where it is possible to find an easy passage up into the mountains.

Only one spectacular railway makes the ascent direct from Lima itself (and it is one of the railway wonders of the world). But once you have climbed up behind the city, winding your way all day to the high Andes, it becomes a slow and complicated matter to journey further. Easier by far to follow the coast up or down until you are within striking distance of whichever part of the Andes you want, then head inland and up.

So almost all lines of communication from Lima start by going north (up the Pacific coast) or south (down it): and buses to Huaraz were no exception, though the town lies well inland from the coast and high above the sea. That was the way our route started: due north by the Pacific, a route followed by the bus company Empresa Rodriguez.

Long-distance transport in Peru almost always travels by night, leaving after dusk. It was at nightfall, then, that we reached the premises of the Empresa Rodriguez.

Each company has its own offices, 'terminus' (usually a cramped, walled yard) and waiting room. Tickets purchased, we sat among scores of peasants in a scruffy room. It felt safe after the unlit streets of the run-down quarter where buses bound for northern destinations start.

Our heap of rucksacks, hold-alls and plastic bags looked no richer pickings than the flour-sacks and cardboard boxes which the Indian families were guarding; and it seemed natural for three of us to leave the fourth keeping watch while they shovelled down gristly meat and fried eggs in a verminous eating-house nearby.

And when hunger overcame the fourth – well, why not get a respec-table-looking grandmother on the next bench to keep an eye on our belongings? She agreed; but the others were doubtful and Mick and John gobbled their meal, returning fast. Everything was still there, and a little later the woman left to catch her own bus. That left two of them to keep watch.

Mick hurried back to where we were still eating to warn us that it looked as though our bus, too, would soon be leaving. He left John with the bags, chatting with another woman who spoke some English. After a moment, and with Mick gone, she asked John to help her move some boxes. How – as he said to us later – could he have refused?

No doubt that was when the bag with Mick's passport in it disappeared.

Chaos reigned. Mick stared wildly about him while the rest of us searched mindlessly and repeatedly through the remaining baggage and beseeched the other passengers (in broken Spanish) to help. They seemed as bewildered as we were.

At that point the departure of our bus was announced.

It was one of these frozen moments when whoever fills the void with a suggestion – any suggestion – is likely to be followed. If anyone had said, 'Back to the hotel: it would be crazy to go on without a passport. Foreigners have to carry them and the British Consulate must make a start on preparing a replacement. We can see a little more of Lima while Mick arranges things … then that is certainly what we would have done. As it was, somebody said, 'Fuck the passport; let's go!'

And that is what we did.

As we pulled away, Mick realized that his bus ticket had been stolen too. Curiously, the conductor accepted this without question – just as, previously, the grandmother had accepted our baggage and we had accepted her honesty. Thieving and honesty, suspicion and trust … they live side by side in Peru. In Europe everything mingles and dilutes into a higher level of mistrust – and a lower level of thieving.

'Bloody Peruvians,' said John. 'Of course tourists like us are their natural prey.' He said it as though the whole waiting-room had been in a conspiracy against us, and Peruvians never robbed each other. He voiced the mood of all of us.

*

Our bus was about Ian's age. A couple of decades (perhaps) of service had left it battered, tired, but still pretty much in one piece, mechanically. The seats smelled of mouldy cloth, vomit, biscuits, mango and old leather. We settled back to peer through grimy windows as the elderly machine lurched and roared through the endless miles of rickety telegraph poles, breeze-block cabins, dead dogs and iron-roofed shacks that stretch north of the city.

Not long after we had started, a middle-aged peasant woman discovered that her own small bag had gone too. She had stowed it in the rack above her seat.

Her grief was enormous. It seemed the more poignant for the soft, insistent voice in which she appealed directly to each row of passengers, one after the other. 'Sister,' she would say – or 'Brothers,' – 'my name is Isadora Fernandez. I beg you – there is nothing of value in that bag – no silver. Just old clothes. My own belongings ...'

People looked embarrassed and avoided her eyes. But she continued, softly, insistently. A bus careered past us, overtaking. Caught momentarily in our headlights, the motto emblazoned across its tailboard announced, 'MY NOBILITY PARDONS YOUR IGNORANCE'. For a moment her voice was drowned in the roar of its exhaust, but she carried on, pleading.

Eventually the conductor asked her to sit down. She did so without resisting. At this point she simply gave up – completely – and began to cry. Nothing more was said. She just sat there sobbing quietly, it seemed for hours.

All was black outside. We were in fact travelling north along the desert coast where the road was straight and fast, and towns were few. To our right, a few miles inland, loomed the great dry fingers of the Andes. Wave upon wave of desolate foothills, each higher than the last, reached back and up towards a land which was unbelievably high – another world, a world of ice and wind and flowers.

But the desert at its feet gave no trace of that other world towering on our right hand. Moonlight, white on the bony ridge of foothills, showed nothing of what lay behind. Black streams, littered and stagnant-looking, seeped through the sand and stones, betraying no memory of the glaciers from which they had descended.

To our left, the caps of great Pacific rollers far out to sea flashed silver in the same moonlight. How far to New Zealand? Seven thousand miles?

This was the edge, a thin line between two great emptinesses: the ocean and the mountains. Looking out towards the ocean rollers on one hand, the dunes and foothills on the other – things magnificent in themselves yet unnamed and uncelebrated, only the fringes of what lay out of sight – you had a sense of something no English landscape can inspire. It is the feeling that what lies within vision is only just the beginning of what waits beyond.

Before we started the climb, the bus paused ('For your comfort and refreshment,' as the driver announced, waking us up). What time was it? We had lost all sense of time. Almost everyone had been asleep. We tottered out: peasants (some of the Indian women in their own dress: bright skirts in scarlets, oranges and crimsons, worn over many layers of petticoat; most of the Indian men in shabby western clothes), whiter Peruvians, and us. We were the only foreigners on board.

All stumbled, blinking into the harsh glare of the security lamp that lit the yard. It was our first chance to size each other up.

Few Peruvians own cars. People of all walks of life (bar the richest) must use buses; and for most they are the only means of reaching distant places.

Nor do the poorer people travel often. Long bus journeys have an aura of great occasion for passengers: hampers are packed, cardboard boxes and old flour-sacks are laced intricately up in what looks like weeks of preparation. The fares – ludicrously small to us, a few dollars for hundreds of miles – may have been carefully saved over months.

And, where travellers in Europe find themselves among people for whom the journey is routine, in Peru the coaches streaming into and out of Lima are filled with individuals for each of whom the occasion is exciting and strange. We noticed as we wandered bewilderedly from our bus that many of our Indian fellow travellers were equally baffled, with just as little idea where we were or what we were supposed to do.

How did they react to us? With wary, sidelong interest.

Strangers seldom stared and almost never confronted us with direct enquiry or even eye-contact. It almost seemed that the presence of foreigners had not even been noticed. Then a look, a glance hastily averted when returned, discussion overheard (unintelligible in itself, but how easy it is to tell when someone is talking about you!) – and curiosity was betrayed.

There was a warehouse-like canteen nearby, where it seemed that in exchange for a little square of scissor-cut notepaper bought from an old lady at the door, you would be served with thin soup, bread and tea. Many made their way in.

Outside, on the side of the bus facing the lighted canteen, the men were carefully pissing on its wheels. On the dark side of the bus, shadows of Indian women, squatting to face the deserted road, moved dimly.

The air was hot and still. Flying insects buzzed around the glaring light high above.

From another building, some hundreds of yards away, came the sound of Latin music. On closer inspection this appeared to be the last stages of a celebration dance night. A score of couples shuffled to a slow dance on a scratched recording played through a distorting amplifier. They clung to each other in that alloy of passion and fatigue characteristic of the last half-hour of late-night dance parties anywhere in the world. One needed no watch to reckon that the time was about half past three.

A convoy of trucks thundered past, blaring horns and wrecking the calculations of the squatting women. They scattered in dismay, and were further disturbed by a flurry of activity from our own bus; for it was time to go. The driver revved the engine and flashed the lights. Skirts were hitched up in panic. Some of the passengers started screaming to friends and family still outside.

It was now that Ian made what seemed at first a most unlucky move.

It started when our bus drove off without one of the passengers.

They had nicknamed him El Gordo (The Fat One). He was a grossly overweight, middle-aged travelling salesman (we never quite worked out in what) whose shabby suit was literally bursting at its seams, and who perspired continuously. He was probably on his third helping of soup as the bus pulled away. '*Falta El Gordo*' (El Gordo is missing), Ian shouted. Other passengers took up the cry. '*Falta El Gordo,*' yelled the whole bus.

We shuddered to a halt. Far back, in the dust, El Gordo could be seen, waddling desperately behind us, calling for us to wait. He caught up – panting – and heaved himself up the steps, soaked with sweat, to general laughter.

What happened next seemed so unfair to Ian. El Gordo was standing at the front of the bus, Ian sitting (with us) in the back seats. But El Gordo's own seat, which should have been waiting for him, seemed to have disappeared. This was not surprising. Ever since our departure from Lima, no one had wanted his huge bulk next to them because he overflowed hopelessly into surrounding seats.

But he had eventually established a place next to an Indian mother. Mothers can be ruthless. She was the dog who hadn't barked when he failed to board, leaving Ian to announce that he was missing. She it was who had made quick use of his absence and conjured children out of nowhere to fill his seat.

El Gordo lurched, still perspiring, down the gangway, eyeing every slight gap between passengers. But as fast as he spotted gaps, passengers moved to close them. 'No! No! El Gordo no!' they chanted. The women shrieked with laughter as The Fat One ran the gauntlet of their inhospitality, row by row. Moving down from the front of the bus, still searching, he neared the back.

A look of alarm grew on Ian's face as the inevitable became clear. He was at the very back, the terminus of El Gordo's hopeless search. And there was a tiny space just next to him. As relief spread across El Gordo's plump features, there was horror in Ian's eyes.

Into the gap crashed El Gordo, shirt dripping. Did the offending hulk realize that it was his saviour whom he now almost crushed? Probably not. Ian groaned. The whole bus grinned.

We lurched forward again, on into the darkness. One by one, each of us fell asleep. El Gordo snored peacefully; the woman who had evicted him was comfortable now, her children around her. Señora Fernandez had stopped crying and was calm. Mick and John dozed. Even Ian drifted off, as one pinned helplessly underground in a mining disaster might drift from consciousness.

That we started to climb, and climbed continuously until dawn, we knew more as you know it on an aeroplane than on a bus. We could see almost nothing outside; but it was easy to tell that the road was winding up the side of the Andes. Through a fitful sleep we were conscious of the whole dead weight of the bus heaving regularly, left to right, then back again. The springs creaked and the luggage piled on the roof above shifted heavily. The moon swung wildly across the windows as we hairpinned upwards – not for ten minutes as in Scotland, or twenty as in Switzerland: but for the whole of the rest of the night ... left, right, left ...

The slope of the bus floor, steeply uphill, stayed constant while the stars outside spun crazily in the sky. From time to time a child cried, but mostly there was silence, and darkness without. Little clusters of lights down on the coast, now so far below us, were sometimes visible, and the spines of mountain ridges showed white and skeletal in the moonlight, like the bones of hands reaching down towards them. We seemed to be climbing through thin air.

Once the bus stopped, rather before dawn. When we got to our feet to stretch our legs, we found ourselves breathing hard in the rarefied atmosphere.

It was getting very cold. The bus had no heating at all. All around us the peasants produced blankets, ponchos and shawls – from nowhere, it seemed, as conjurors produce silk scarves – and disappeared beneath them. The windows, already misted over, froze on the inside.

John shivered and felt sick. Mick's feet were so cold that he put all his socks on, planted his legs in a plastic bag, then placed the whole bundle into a travelling bag. This completely immobilized him.

It was then that we noticed Ian. No longer recoiling from El Gordo he had now snuggled right up close, almost enveloped by one fatty flank. El Gordo himself, a warm, slumbering mound, heaved rhythmically with gentle snores. Alone among us, Ian was warm, his face a picture of peaceful repose. Virtue had had its reward.

*

Dawn was a steely-grey affair. It came when we finally stopped climbing and emerged upon a bleak scene: a treeless, windswept plateau strewn with black rocks and frozen ponds.

There was a science-fiction look about the place. Clusters of snowy peaks needled high into streaks of ice-cloud. There was absolutely no colour.

It was a dispiriting landscape. With the dawn, John woke up, looked out and started to retch. Mick gave him his plastic bag, and John clenched his teeth and stared grimly around at the harsh world about us.

The sun edged above the rocks.

Quite suddenly, a distant mountaintop caught its rays and burst into flame. A yellow-orange streak fell across the monochrome scene. In the thin and freezing air every line, every colour was sharp. All was jagged. There were no curves, no fading, no blurring. It looked like a different universe, in which our bus moved like an alien capsule from a softer, fleshier world. You felt that if you left the bus and walked in this new world you might cut your feet even on a blade of grass. It was beautiful.

A peasant woman near me murmured '*Cristalina*' (Crystalline). It was said almost reverently and I looked across at her. She was old and withered: like a potato baked too long in its jacket, leathery-tough against a harsh world. You would have thought that she had long lost any capacity for tenderness. Yet she was staring out now at a scene with which she may have been familiar since birth – still lost in wonder.

There is an idea that physical hardship dulls the sensibilities or somehow thickens the skin; that the poor are hard-bitten emotionally, too; that they lose the capacity to see and love beauty.

But perhaps that is just an illusion with which the rich have always comforted themselves. I remembered a Jamaican woman to whom my mother often gave a lift as she tramped her way every day through miles of blistering heat from her cleaning job in Kingston to her shack up in the hills. She had had a hard life, her man had left her and she was trying to raise seven children.

She became pregnant – in her fifties – when it was the last thing she wanted. The child was stillborn. A blessing, we all thought.

But she cried for days, almost without ceasing. You would see her toiling up the hill, her eyes red with weeping. The sun had burned her skin but had dried nothing that was within.

Could it be that what we are never changes, but is only overlaid, scar on scar, by what comes after? My friend Colin Welch once recalled that at his mother's death he had an impression of the ruined hulk of an old ship sinking beneath the water, dragging down with it a little girl, screaming from the vessel's heart, trapped.

*

The old Indian woman began to sing, quietly. Passengers started to talk, exclaiming, pointing. You would expect a sense of wonder at the natural world from foreigners to whom this was new and strange, but South American Indians – even the humblest or most downtrodden – seem to love their environment. Reserved about expressing other feelings, their love of beauty goes quite unhidden.

Even John awoke and cheered up. 'Classic torrent-duck country,' he whispered weakly, peering out at the stream we were following.

And now we began to descend again. Not steeply or far, but winding down beside a stream which flowed along a broadening, deepening valley. We bowled down the road, warming in the first rays of the sun, passengers chatting excitedly, babies clamped to breasts. And outside, too, the bleakness was giving way to small fields, green crops, donkeys laden with produce, children waving, and from many hearths the thin plumes of breakfast fires.

Brush-stroke by brush-stroke the morning was being painted in. The grey-and-black outlines of the night ride receded. It began to seem as though everything had been a strange dream.

With much honking and revving of engines, we arrived in Huaraz.

Chapter Four

A Small
Riot

It was very early in the morning and still frosty. Behind the town mountains rose up so vast and high and white that Huaraz seemed to nestle at the foot of things – and you forgot its own great elevation above the sea.

Until, that is, you tried to do anything. Running, lifting, or walking uphill quickly left you breathless; and a persistent, thin headache reminded you that at an altitude of 10,000 feet it was best to take things slowly at first: to find the centre of town, perhaps, and look for somewhere to stay, and rest. John still felt pretty ill, and after the bus ride a room with beds was the first thing on all our minds. None of us was hungry.

Morale improved as we shook off the travel-shock and began to drink in the morning air and to feel part of the place where we were.

Huaraz was just waking up, emerging from the long blue shadows of the mountains into thin yellow sunshine.

With sacks of animal fodder and green foliage on their backs, boxes of eggs, chickens and bicycle spares in tow, people and donkeys moved through the street towards the market. We followed the tide.

Huaraz is a modest town which gives little hint of its horrific history. In 1941 much of the town was swept away when a lake in the mountains above broke in an earth tremor and 6,000 people died. Then, in 1970, came a terrible earthquake which all but wiped out the town, killing half of its inhabitants. This earthquake went wider than Huaraz. In total it killed some 80,000 people, and days passed before rescue workers could even reach the region. It was one of the worst natural disasters in the history of mankind. Curiously, it seems to be largely forgotten, today. For the second time this century, the people of Huaraz set to rebuilding their town.

Its buildings are low – mud-brick and breeze-block – and its architecture undistinguished. There is nothing spectacular about the place: just a breathtaking backdrop and a feeling of quiet local sufficiency. It is the hub of a sheltered valley, comfortably farmed. To the poorer Indians, riding down from the mountain slopes, it must have seemed a land of milk and honey.

At an altitude where the air is thin, sunlight is hotter and shadow colder. We stood on the sunny side of the road by a little tin shack. Its kerosene pressure cooker roared while they made us tea: hot, weak and sweet, with no milk. We watched the shadows of the rooftops traced out in frost on the dust. As the shadows moved, so the frost melted – maybe ten seconds behind. It gave each retreating shadow a thin edge of frost exposed to the sunlight: a temporary etching, brilliant white, following the shadow backwards.

Stalls were opening and the town was coming to life. Longhaired auburn pigs, polka-dotted pigs and pigs with tortoiseshell patches rootled around among stalls which sold underpants, herbal medicines, little tubs of aniline dye in acid colours, soap, condensed milk – and hats. Every second stall seemed to be a hat stand.

Everyone wore a hat. The local fashion seemed to be for a sort of white straw hat of the type that elderly gentlemen in the British Legion wear for bowls matches. Ian tried a couple on for himself. The young woman selling them screamed with laughter.

A very, very old man shuffled past, bent double beneath a bundle of branches three times his size. A woman in high heels with matching suit and handbag promenaded by at a quickstep, as if tugged by some outside force. At second glance, she was: a pet racoon strained at the end of a scarlet leash. It was neatly brushed and wore an expression of utter determination. The pair of them stormed onward, slaloming between pot-holes.

John was suffering badly from diarrhoea. Twice he had dived behind the nearest hut, in the nick of time. Now he felt a sudden hunger. Seeing this as a hopeful sign (he had not eaten since Lima) we bought him a hardboiled egg, still warm from the market and wrapped it in our second purchase: a pair of underpants to replace those which diarrhoea had taken beyond recall. The new ones were purple with a green portrait of Charlie Chaplin on the front. This design seemed the most popular with the Indians.

Ian finally chose a dashing broad-brimmed straw hat, and found a card for his girlfriend. John, despite his illness, began what was to become an epic search for a jumper suitable for his wife. It had to have llamas on it, and had to be in alpaca wool, coloured in pastel blues and pinks, and of the right size for a girl who was six inches taller than most Peruvian men. Huaraz was the first place, but not the last, to fail to produce jumpers possessing all these qualities at once. Yet somehow John never lost heart.

Mick's Spanish turned out to be near-perfect. Equally important, he had an almost saintly willingness to translate everything for everyone else. It worked well for him today, for he found what we never found again, a street telephone-kiosk from which you could make international telephone calls, using special tokens which you had to toss in at an alarming rate. Mick rang his wife.

We caught his last words to her before he ran out of tokens: '... and have you remembered to water the tomatoes?' Then he was cut off. The tomatoes had been worrying him since he had last phoned home from Bogotà.

Mick stared blankly for an instant, returning mentally from the old familiar world to this bewildering place of rootling piglets, soldiers in toytown uniforms and sad-eyed old peasant women.

We regathered. We were tired. The bus ride and the altitude were catching up with us. It was getting hotter; and our bags were heavy.

A mestizo in an oily shirt filling kerosene drums had heard of the hotel our guidebook recommended. A lighted cigarette hanging from his lip, he wiped the kerosene from the top of the drum, pointed the way, and warned that it was a steep walk.

It didn't look steep, and we could see the building we were aiming for. But John barely made it, and the rest of us were glad to have him as the excuse for pausing breathlessly along the way. Morale improved when we reached the hotel. It was clean, pleasant and unbelievably cheap. The six-bedded room that Mick negotiated for us had a magnificent view straight over the town and up to the ice-peaks beyond. From one you could see a thin stream of snow blowing from the top in an apparently motionless line – sharp and straight as an architect's drawing – shining in the midday sun. John collapsed on to a hard bed.

It was a day before he could walk again. John was an uncomplaining type, and quite tough. If he said he was ill, then it was bad.

It was harder to tell with Mick. His health was important to us, for not only was he an expert interpreter, but he seemed to have an ability to strike up with people we met. He was often our bridge with Peruvians. Complaining already of diarrhoea and nausea, he showed a lively interest in the symptoms. We had yet to learn that it was when he stopped talking about illness that his companions needed to start worrying.

Ian was our ambassador towards children. It did not seem to matter that he spoke no Spanish: young people were immediately drawn towards him, and he to them. Already, in the market, we had left him a few minutes and returned to find him playing street football with a gang of youths with whom he was quite unable to converse. After that he had been mobbed by a little bunch of adoring boys and girls, who had started to teach him Spanish. Something about his open face and fair hair attracted and fascinated the Indian people, and infants would babble excitedly to him, baffled but not deterred by his failure to understand or respond to a word they said.

But the football had left Ian with a sick headache which grew as the day wore on. To a greater or lesser degree, we were all affected by the altitude, and glad of the security lent by our room. Burning already from our first day in the Andean sun, we lay around, feebly discussing what we might do once John recovered. 'If,' said Mick.

We wanted to begin at a village called Chiquian. From there we could take a ten-day walk in the Cordillera Huaywash, an isolated and (it was said) magnificent range. We had the maps and equipment needed for a hiking expedition right through the range.

But how to get to Chiquian? It looked about a day's truck journey away, back south in the direction of Lima, but further inland.

Mick had found out that there were occasional local buses, but advice about them was conflicting. The most confident opinion we had received came from a kerosene stove repairer ('Gas Fitero' was the description above his shop) who said buses were uncertain, but trucks left every morning from outside his shop. If we turned up in time, he said, we could negotiate a ride to Chiquian. Other people did.

We resolved to try.

Then John was sick again. Mick became convinced that this was pulmonary oedema, an illness (he had read) afflicting those unused to altitude, leading often to death: an illness of which we were to hear much more from him. The rest of us thought it more likely that it was something John had eaten. Mick reacted to this frivolously irresponsible diagnosis with a reproachful stare.

In any case, we all agreed that it was best to wait for at least another day, and hope that John recovered sufficiently.

By the following day, he was well enough to join us in observing a small riot.

We thought at the time that this was rather sensational. Were we, perhaps, witnesses to the triggering of another South American revolution? Only with time did we come to understand the matter-of-fact disregard with which onlookers treated this, and other, public demonstrations.

The Peruvian economy was falling apart. A relatively democratic government, of centre-left ideology, had been doing its best for some years to please most of the people for most of the time. It had spent more than it could find and inflated the currency to do so. It had defaulted on some of its international debts and lost the ability to raise new ones. It had promised more reforms than it could deliver and tried to control and nationalize more of Peruvian life than it could competently handle.

Gravest of all, it had pretended that the country's chronic Maoist terrorist problem would simply go away now that a leftist government was in power. In fact, the terrorists had sneered at compromise, redoubled their activities, and left a bankrupt administration relying on military suppression which they could not afford and which was not working.

Inflation was halving the value of money every few months. Private commerce was desperate; saving and investment had become a nightmare. State employees were hopelessly underpaid and the state unable to raise their pay as fast as inflation undermined it. Many were now little short of frantic.

Schoolteachers were a case in point, and the cause of the riot we were now to see. It seemed that teachers were on strike for a doubling of their salaries; a reasonable-sounding demand when you realized that it was a year since their last raise, and inflation had halved its value in a far shorter time. But the strike had dragged on for weeks and nobody seemed to care. Children stayed at home or played in the streets. So the strikers had gathered with placards in the main square for a demonstration. We watched.

It was all pretty low-key, at first. Teachers marched around waving pieces of cardboard with their demands written on them. The rest of the populace stared with mild interest at the scene.

Then the local police, backed by the army, piled in. They arrived in armoured cars, and advanced on the demonstrators with riot shields.

At this the strikers felt obliged to riot, which they did by shouting and throwing a few stones rather half-heartedly at the police. The police responded by dragging a few of them off, and drenching the others with water-cannon. This seemed to satisfy honour on both sides, and uninvolved spectators – the citizens of Huaraz, who had watched politely until now – moved off to do something else. The riot was over.

Something about the reaction of the spectators would perplex any European: you could not tell whose side they were on. Like commuters in an English railway carriage, nobody wanted to draw attention to themselves by shouting – or even talking. Nobody joined in. A few – just a few – of those watching looked utterly absorbed. Others were just amused. Yet on all sides the approach was – again – like that of railway passengers you catch peeping over the top of sheltering newspapers: not involved, not wishing even to register an interest, but curious. Such reserve does not fit the popular image of South Americans; but it is very marked among Peruvians.

That night, however, we did get some sense of popular protest.

It was about ten o'clock. John had decided to try eating again, and after a reasonable meal we came out onto the square by the church.

Something seemed to be going on, so we joined a large crowd to find out what it was they had gathered around.

It turned out to be impromptu street theatre, not the self-conscious Arts Council-sponsored sort of thing one sees in England: just two men – one more Indian, the other more Spanish in appearance – with a handful of shabby props and a non-stop flow of hilarious mimicry and banter. The crowd roared its approval.

Even Mick could not get all the nuances, but he translated as best he could. The men were lampooning the government, the police and the armed forces.

In one sketch the more Indian of the pair joined the army. He was given a uniform. As he put it on his whole demeanour – and finally his whole personality – changed. He began to high-step around, haranguing members of the audience.

Then he was given orders to kill strikers and demonstrators; this he mimed in such a flashy display of bravado that – as 'soldier' – he almost gained the audience's regard. But this spell was broken when his partner brought him news of trouble at home: death and hardship in his own village. It stopped him in his tracks. He looked down, ashamed, at his uniform, and began to take it off, piece by piece, changing back into his ragged peasant clothes, and weeping. For the second time, his whole character changed.

It is impossible to convey how funnily, and how movingly, this was done. Looking back, it is hard to explain how such a comic-strip performance could spellbind a hard-bitten street audience. Undeniably the performers had talent: but they had the sympathy, and the whole attention, of three or four hundred people. This was what made the performance work.

The peasant-turned-soldier-turned-defector now joined the revolutionaries. Here, you could sense that the act began to lose a few of its audience, and to discomfit others: but for the bulk of them the effect was to move them, emotionally and politically, just a little further than they had intended down a road they were already disposed to travel.

It was the cleverest kind of propaganda because it used the emotions that ideologues (particularly on the left) so often fail to engage: humour and sympathy. Just when the groundlings and the children in the audience were getting impatient with the serious message, the actors deftly switched back into comedy.

They did so after this sketch, passing round the hat with the announcement that 10,000 *intis* (not much) would secure one more act. 'Fifty *intis* each' they said – then, realizing that there were four foreigners in their audience, rounded on the most embarrassed, John. 'That equals one hundred dollars, Gringo!' they said to him. The audience roared with laughter, but it was good-humoured laughter.

The hat was quickly full of money. If there were more than the 10,000 *intis* demanded, the Spanish-looking actor said, they would return the balance. They started to count the money out, aloud.

It takes a skilful comic (and a receptive audience) to create a hilarious stage routine out of the counting, on stage, of 10,000 *intis* in notes of small denominations. But an uninterrupted flow of wisecracks kept the audience in the actors' hands. Then, at precisely the point when it became clear to the audience that there was a great deal more than 10,000 *intis* in the hat, but just before that figure was actually reached, our two entertainers announced that the target had been met – *just* – and stuffed all the rest of the money into their pockets. There was a great shout of laughter from the crowd.

A slight enough joke. To see it engage a crowd of hundreds on a piece of ragged turf in a noisy square, with no seats, no special effects, no sound amplification, and no illumination but the street lamp, gave a sense of what Elizabethan theatre might have been like. It made it easier to understand why so many of Shakespeare's comic scenes – hopelessly unfunny when studied for examinations and scarcely better when performed by the Royal Shakespeare Company – were put there.

'Revolutionaries' were mentioned often. The word 'terrorist' never was. Nor was the Shining Path. But a tension in the humour and in the audience's reaction to it pointed to what nobody needed to say: that the Shining Path *were* the revolutionary challengers.

We did not at that time know much about the *Sendero Luminoso* – Luminous Pathway or (as the western press style them) Shining Path. They are perhaps one of the most bizarre – and macabre – terrorist groups in history. Attributing their ideological birth to a half-caste with a falsetto voice (long dead) and led by a mysterious university don called Dr Abimael Guzman who is widely believed to have been killed but is still rumoured by some to be alive, the *Sendero* now operate among the Indian peasants and in the poorest parts of Peru.

One province was almost entirely out of the government's control, and the revolutionaries were active in many other regions and cities. Their areas of operation were, we were told in tones that were half-excited and half-alarmed, spreading. Their ideology was said to be a gothic amalgam of unreconstructed Maoism and ancient Inca belief.

Their methods were utterly ruthless. Animals were driven into market stuffed with explosives, and detonated. A little girl had been used in the same way – to walk into a crowded hotel lobby in Lima.

Guzman's doctoral thesis was on the eighteenth century German philosopher Immanuel Kant, a man so ordered in his habits that it was said you could time your watch by his leaving his house each morning. Kant might be surprised to see his student Abimael's donkeys exploding all over Peru. Villages or communities were 'turned' to the *Sendero* cause by intimidation (their critics claimed), whereupon government troops employed the same approach to 'punish' the community and regain its loyalty.

The revolutionaries differed from many other groups in that they seemed to have little interest in their international standing. They had not aimed to attract attention outside Peru. And, even within the country, they hardly seemed to be spreading the ideological word, publicizing their aims or trying to win support or sympathy by argument. Their purpose seemed to be simple: to destroy, to spread fear.

The very mention of their name in Peru sent a nervous chill down the spine: whether of excitement or dread depended upon the audience, and was often very difficult to tell.

So it was, we noticed, with the crowd we now found ourselves among.

And something else Mick noticed. The importance of uniforms. It strikes you again and again in South America. In this street theatre it had really been the central theme. The soldier changed from human into monster when he put on his uniform. But he also changed from fearful to fearsome, from shabby to macho.

Mick contrasted the type of stiff-necked official we had already encountered – and they do not come more stiff-necked or official than in the Latin countries – with the warm and easy going natures that are otherwise a pleasant general rule. Yet these are usually the same individuals: two sides of the same personality.

How can people who are normally so relaxed be so different behind a desk or a sub-machine gun? The change follows upon the assuming of an official position, and the outward sign is a uniform.

Perhaps some races find the tension between the human and the official irreconcilable? The wearing of a uniform may be a sign that the attempt has been abandoned, and the two halves of the personality allowed to split and go separate ways.

We English would pride ourselves, perhaps, on a steadier personality. But maybe that just means we need no uniform to be officious. We are perfectly capable of dressing casual and acting formal at the same time: we slip naturally into behaving like traffic wardens, at home or at work. But never with the manic inhumanity of a South American official! The on-duty and off-duty sides to an English nature – if they are at war at all – have usually met half way in some sort of truce.

It may mean that we will produce neither the world's best traffic wardens nor the world's best lovers, but at least we have traffic wardens who are not impossible to love, and lovers who are not impossible to control.

We walked home, much affected by the street theatre and the riot we had seen that day.

*

We awoke early and were packed and waiting at the kerbside spot to which we had been directed, far earlier than we needed to be.

The truck was called Divine Light. It had rampant tigers painted on to the rear mud-flaps. Across the front, on the wooden panel above the cab's windscreen, where every truck bore its name, was written *Luz Divina*, and, beside this, a picture in original oils of a condor, couchant, with her chicks.

Divine Light waited for an hour or more outside the Gas Fitero's shop while the driver sorted out the cargo. He was a little man, with more Spanish than Indian blood, called Lazarus.

Truck drivers are a special breed in Peru, carrying status in society. Often they will have a much younger assistant who himself rarely drives, generally acting as overseer of cargo and passengers and collector of fares. Most drivers seemed to be small, cynically good-humoured men. Lazarus was both. Most are middle-aged and stoical. Lazarus was both. Middle age, perhaps, was the time when your apprentice years were served and you moved into the driver's seat. Stoicism was the quality needed to face the daily peril sent by your job. The daily peril was no doubt the reason few got much beyond middle age!

He asked us to keep watch over his cab while he made a few calls on foot in the town. John, who was still weak, rested in the shade. Ian sweated it out in the sun because he had promised his girlfriend a suntan. Sporting his new hat and leaning against a battered classic car – a 1958 Ford Zephyr – he looked the part. He always did. It was just that it was never quite clear what the film was. Before long he was scoring in a street football game with a gang of youths.

Mick, still worrying about his tomatoes, sloped off in search of oranges and biscuits for the journey.

From some shack around the corner, crackling over a street vendor's loudspeaker, came the sound of Andean, Indian music. The emotional power of this music is hard to explain: it has to be heard. One can only describe the most common instruments: a sort of lute-like guitar more jangling in sound than our guitars, a wooden flute and an instrument which looks like the stacked pipes of a church organ constructed in miniature out of bamboo sticks, and sounds like someone blowing over the top of a Coca Cola bottle.

The important difference between their flute and ours is that theirs is played with fluid, sliding notes, like a man whistling. When two or more of these flutes are played together there will always be a slight dissonance between them, as occurs when people whistle in harmony, because each is wavering fractionally above and below the desired note, hunting the mark. This causes a curdling discord at the very high frequencies which a flute (or whistle) emits. The result is a spine-chilling edge to the sound.

It is extraordinarily poignant: enormous emotional power yet with a strange cold streak.

After some time, Lazarus returned to say it would be an hour or more before Divine Light was ready to depart. So we wandered off to see if this music could be bought, on cassette. It could. We returned later, after some more weak tea in tin mugs, with our musical souvenirs.

But while we were away, Lazarus, who had been supervising the loading of the truck, had been robbed. A quick-witted thief had got into his cab and removed his tape-player while he was behind the vehicle. Lazarus took it philosophically. We were quietly relieved it had not happened while any of us was in charge.

It was time to claim space in the back of the truck, on top of the cargo among the other passengers now starting to arrive. Ian wore his straw hat tied under the chin with a woven ribbon a little girl had given him. Mick was modelling a bright orange deerstalker-type cap with 'TOYOTA' printed across the top, bought from another stall. John, stretched out in a little pit immediately behind the cab, peered wanly up at the magnificent peaks that soared above the mud walls and tin roofs and dusty streets of the little town.

He said: 'When you look at how beautiful the background of mountains is, and compare it with how shabby and filthy this place of Huaraz is, the two don't seem to go together.'

Brought up, like all of us, on picture books of Alpine peaks and neat Swiss chalets, flower-boxes spilling over with geraniums, and clean looking lads and lasses dancing on green meadows, it was easy to forget that the power of those mountains was beyond 'clean' or 'dirty'. Later we would see the corpses of mountaineers being brought down from the slopes that now glistened so hygienically in the sun.

Three blasts of the horn and off we went, rocking and rattling down the main street leading out of Huaraz. Narrowly we avoided a large uncovered sewage shaft, gaping in the middle of the road. A concerned citizen had placed a huge rock beside it as a warning.

As the truck lurched, John groaned. 'To me this is hell,' he said.

I stood at the front with the wind in my face. To me it was paradise.

Chapter Five

Divine
Light

In Peru, people with any position in society do not travel in the backs of trucks. In the unlikely event that they would need to visit a place served only by trucks, money (or influence) would secure them a place in the cab, with the driver.

Trucks, in short, bring you into contact with the humblest Peruvians.

Divine Light was a twenty-ton, two-axled truck. She was in moderate condition. Outside Lima, and wherever really rough road conditions were common, vehicles might be elderly and battered, but mechanical condition was usually basically sound. Whatever the look of a truck or bus, you could be fairly sure that the things that mattered – engine, transmission, suspension – were there. Rather less attention was paid to brakes, and none at all to tyres.

Our truck's chassis and body were built in Lima, the engine and gearbox imported from the USA. She ran twice weekly from Chiquian, bringing in produce to the market in Huaraz. The return journey (carrying us) offered less cargo: a consignment of wooden poles, four 44-gallon drums of diesel, one of petrol and one of kerosene, some spare parts for Chiquian's diesel-powered electricity generator and ten crates of Coca-Cola.

But we had our full complement of passengers. The team was dominated by four fine-looking Indian men, in traditional ponchos and hats, blind drunk. Alongside them, but keeping her distance in an elaborate frock and hat and a good deal of dignity, was a middle-aged lady and her infant granddaughter – all dressed up for the great expedition.

Then there was a teenage boy, thin as a rake, who helped the driver. He had a mischievous face and a keen ability to spot the passenger who was avoiding paying his fare. With the agility of a gibbon, he clambered up and down the sides of the truck, and over and into the cab through its windows, while we were moving.

It was for most of us our first truck ride in South America. We learned fast.

The first thing we learned was that, for the truck-rider, almost everything depends on the place he manages to corner for himself in the back. There are one or two key sites. In these, a comfortable and secure nest may be built. At the other end of the scale, there are sites where the occupant is in danger of his life – from shifting cargo or from being lurched overboard. Most other positions lie somewhere in the purgatory between these two extremes.

There is no standing upon courtesy or seniority in getting the best positions. Nor must you think that, once won, territory is secure from invasion. Fellow travellers will edge (or pounce) into unguarded places; and, whereas a little extra consideration is given to mothers with babies, there is no precedence for women (as there might be in Europe) or for men (as there might be in Africa) or for the elderly.

The elderly seem to be more than capable of looking after themselves. There was an old man on our truck who was a demon at this.

He was a farmer; and from the moment we set off he talked of money. His money. How much he had, how much he expected, and how much his property would realize were he to sell it. We pretended not to understand him, so after a while he pushed his way sideways along the uncomfortable bench towards a sheltered corner where, with her knees up, the middle-aged lady was dozing gently.

Her dress was the typical mixture of squalor and finery: mauve skirts and pink calico knickers (winter-quality). The wily old farmer, under cover of an animated inventory of the entire contents of his farm and their approximate value, moved in close to her, pushing one of the drunken Indians off his perch.

Like his fellow farmers the world over, his clothes defied our era's preference for 'casual-smart': they were formal rags, and filthy. 'Take a look at my spectacles,' he was saying, to nobody in particular. 'I had them made in Lima. The best. Very expensive. I think I have the receipt with me ...' and he fumbled through the pockets of what had once been a blazer to produce a grubby stack of dog-eared papers.

All the while, he was inching towards the middle-aged lady. But it was not passion which drove him. It was an ambition to share her comfortable corner, which she showed no sign of yielding, nodding boredly as he barked on, his metaphorical finger – like farmers everywhere – poking you in your metaphorical chest as he spoke.

'Of course I do not need to travel by public truck. I have my own truck but my son-in-law is running it down to Lima this week. Bought it for 300,000 *intis*. I think I have the receipt ...' He observed that she had nodded right off to sleep. Stealthily he shifted his old buttocks off the hard bench onto the cosy patch just next to her, in one swift movement lifting her little granddaughter off the space the child had occupied and depositing her on to the nearest thing – Ian's knee. So quickly was this done that she did not even properly awake. Ian, mildly surprised, took the new arrival with his usual good nature. Our Peruvian yeoman carried on talking.

'... And I'm expecting my son – the eldest one, in the 300,000-*inti* truck – and he's worth a lot more himself – and that's without counting his wife's fortune – back in Chiquian with the new kerosene refrigerators. I reckon they'll fetch 20,000 *intis* each. Maybe more. What do you think?'

This was fatal, for the lady opened her eyes momentarily, saw him all but snuggled up against her and realized what was taking place. She did not hesitate. One powerful knee emerged suddenly from a sea of petticoats, knocking him violently sideways into an oil drum. He resumed his place on the bench, wordlessly. The drunken Indians laughed.

Meanwhile, the little girl, Lis, had awoken to find herself on a strange lap: the lap of a huge creature she had never seen before with fair hair such as she had only seen in pictures or at a distance on tourists, speaking a language she could not understand.

As if it were all the most natural thing in the world, she started talking to him, babbling away non-stop, careless of the fact that he appeared neither to respond nor understand. His broad smile was enough. Her name was Lis, she told him, and she was four.

Now the old farmer tried a new trick. John's position on the bench was better than his. John was right up under the lee of the cab, and well-placed beneath the horizontal pole that truckers run like a central spine from the back of the cab roof to the rear tailgate. Passengers can cling on to this; and if it rains or snows, the pole becomes the ridge for a canvas awning. John, therefore, had both shelter from the wind, and security. He was weak enough to value both, and the old boy knew it. So his method was cunning.

He waited for a rough patch of road, rough enough to make us all bounce a little in our seats. He bounced too, but exaggeratedly – amplifying the force of each bump (as a horserider might) so that his body yo-yoed up and down on the bench. And each bounce moved him fractionally sideways, towards John. The appearance was of a feeble old man being thrown along the bench until he was knocking against John: the *reality* – well, John was not too weak to understand the reality. He was not about to yield.

His response was brilliant. He waited for a particularly big bump, rose (with it) at least a foot into the air, and came down violently sideways, knocking his challenger right back along the bench to where he had started, like a billiard ball. One of the drunken Indians noticed this manoeuvre and nodded approval at what – for a foreign novice – was an intermediate if not advanced piece of truck-gamesmanship.

We pulled into a roadside settlement for soup and to change a wheel, Lis still talking to Ian.

There must be a shortage in Peru of rubber or of the foreign exchange to buy it, for tread on tyres was something you almost never saw, and few journeys were completed without at least one puncture. Nobody seemed to travel without spare wheels and the means to change them. Extra wheels were available at places like this – a tin shack by the road. The problem was that there seemed very little to distinguish the tyres put on from the tyres taken off.

Mick came out of the soup-shack and was surprised to see a detached wheel leaned against Divine Light's side with great chunks of rubber missing from the tyre-walls and shafts from its steel ribbing sticking out sideways like spikes on Boadicea's chariot. He was even more surprised to see them putting this wheel *on*.

We sat on a rock in the yard. On another rock sat a passenger from another truck reading an old newspaper. You could just discern its lead story: 'ANTONIO DIAZ MARTINEZ, ONE OF THE IDEOLOGICAL LEADERS OF THE SHINING PATH, CAPTURES FOUR CEMETERIES TO THE SOUTH OF LIMA.'

A little dog, white – like Tintin's dog Snowy in the French cartoon – chased an auburn pig with black polka-dots over the ditch. We saw other dogs and other pigs in this village, the dogs all identikit copies of Snowy, the pigs all auburn with spots. A great-grandfather Snowy and a very senior polka-dotted boar must have been active at some early stage in the settlement's history. Equally clearly there was little inter-village tourism in the dog or pig world.

Wheel changed, Divine Light tooted her horn and we rushed aboard. Someone had stolen our oranges, but who cared?

Now our route took us up and out of the broad valley where Huaraz lay, and over the plateau beyond, retracing the last part of our journey from Lima before plunging off the main road, towards Chiquian. Once, when the truck stopped for a moment, Ian summoned up just enough Spanish to ask Lis's grandmother where we were. From her lair on the truck floor she could only see the encircling rim of the distant mountaintops – nothing closer. She peered around, judged their distance and position relative to each other, and told us unhesitatingly how long it would be before we left the main road. Lis was still babbling away to Ian.

The old lady's estimate was right; and at a frozen grey marsh called Conococha we rattled off down a rocky road towards the highest of the mountain ranges in view. Soon we were climbing again, gently, through low brown hills, treeless and covered in stones and tufts of yellow grass.

Here and there, Indians had scratched out shallow little fields to plant some weedy cereal crop. The fields were irregular in shape and the crop desperately poor, petering out completely wherever the rock came to the surface.

By now our arms and faces were burning in the sun, while the wind grew bitterly cold. In these hills we passed only one human settlement, but its huts had long been abandoned and the straw roofs stove in.

Once we saw in the distance a small fenced circle of stone or mud huts, with people and goats. It was a harsh, windswept scene, a near-desert, cut by icy streams running down from the peaks.

Once we passed a dead horse, lying by the road. Later, a dead mule.

Once we passed a woman walking slowly, with a moth-eaten sheep on the end of a piece of string. Her direction was diagonal to ours – a broad angle across the road as if in her scheme of things the road did not exist. It seemed we did not exist either, for she kept her head and eyes down, never once looking at us.

Neither in the hills from which she had come, nor across the plateau over which she was heading, could you make out any feature – any hut, or bush, or group of sheltering rocks, even – which might have been a provenance or destination, a reason for her journey. She followed no discernible path – just straight across the stones. Wrapped in a dusty brown cloth with a flash of scarlet lining, her whole head was muffled against the sun and wind, her face down to the earth.

Her sheep had one crimson tassel in its left ear. On she plodded, through the cloud of dust raised by our truck. Where was her home? Where had she come from? Where was she going? Why?

You could see why the girls aged so fast, why even thirty-year-old women had begun to crumple and wither. Childhood for these people was over in a flash.

For Lis it was not yet over. She had been talking at Ian ever since she woke up on his lap. He had been inventing games for her, swapping hats, hiding sweets and mimicking Spanish and Indian words.

She had huge brown eyes. Tassels were tied in her hair and she was all dressed up for the journey in a mauve and scarlet dress, with patterns embroidered around the hem. Her grandmother watched, tolerantly.

We shuddered to a halt by a single, ruined mud wall. Two of the four Indian men made their drunken farewells to the others and clambered down. We pulled away, leaving them standing in the road. Why? What were they going to do next?

John was more or less comatose by now, after three days of being unable to keep food down (or up). But Mick, in his 'TOYOTA' cap, stood clinging on to the central pole, peering out from the top. Now he signalled us to look, too.

The road had reached the very edge of the plateau and was about to descend into a vast, steep valley. Far, far below was the thin white ribbon of a mountain river, and you could just discern Chiquian perched on a hill above it. The road wound precipitously down, all the way to Chiquian. Above and across the other side of the great canyon towered the ridges and peaks of the Cordillera Huaywash – our chosen range – blinding white in the afternoon sun. Mick recoiled from the side of the truck closest to the sheer edge, and sat down. It was breathtaking.

Just before beginning this descent, we passed another truck – the first we had encountered – coming up, across its front panel the name: Lion Of Route No. 4. It stopped abreast of us for the drivers to exchange news. Two youths who looked like Europeans – wild, tanned, dirty, windswept versions of us, a sort of 'before' and 'after' advertisement – hailed us.

'What's it like – the Huaywash?' Mick shouted.

'Terrific! It's ...' But the trucks began to move again. 'Look out for the dogs!' was all they had time for, then all was lost in the roar of engines. John groaned, Ian translated 'dogs' into Spanish for Lis, and Mick mentally inserted rabies to his list of likely health problems: between 'oedema (pulmonary)' and 'tetanus'.

It was unlucky that one of the two remaining drunk Indians, perhaps sensing Mick's anxiety, chose this moment to intervene. He was magnificently dressed in a yellow and brown poncho woven in alpaca wool, and a broad-brimmed leather hat. He looked like something from a child's picture book of Indian tribes. He poked Mick in the ribs.

'The Cordillera Huaywash,' he said, in broken Spanish. 'Peril. Death. Go never.'

Mick blanched. A look of panic entered his eyes. This encouraged the Indian.

'Bodies,' he said, then added for good measure: 'Cadavers.'

Mick crouched, his strength gone, against the non-precipice side of the truck.

The valley into which we were descending in the evening sun was a different world from the bleak plateau behind us. As soon as we came off the top and into the shelter of the hillside, a sort of gentle magic entered the air.

It was cool, but the biting wind was gone. Blue lupins crowded the banks of the road and little streams crossed it. The scent of flowering bushes mingled with the kerosene from the oil drums. We passed donkeys and children; and the sighting of a tiny hummingbird – a green flash – lifted John's spirits.

As we entered Chiquian's modest square, a brass band was playing a sort of ragged military samba. It was dusk, and as the town's electric generator rumbled into action, lighting flickered on in the little bars and shops.

There was only a handful of vehicles in the whole place, and our arrival was an event of its kind. People glanced up curiously as Divine Light trundled down a narrow street to the town's edge. There it stopped.

Lis's grandmother lifted her from Ian's arms, where she had eventually fallen back to sleep. She left him as she had arrived, slumbering.

Would she remember this episode – rounded by a sleep – as some kind of a dream? Is there now, somewhere in the Andes, a pretty girl who once dreamed that she awoke in the arms of a spaceman, a man from the moon, a strange albino sort of man, who couldn't speak properly; and that they played children's games, and he tried to teach her his language, before she again drifted off, to awake in the morning in her own bed, in her grandmother's house in Chiquian? Such stuff as dreams are made on!

We picked up our now-dusty bags, thrown down from Divine Light, and made our way through the small town in the gathering darkness.

Chapter Six

A Mislaid
Soul

Hostales in Peru vary greatly. Usually they have individual, private rooms, often with up to five or six beds. Some sort of bed-linen is provided, and payment is made for the whole room, not for a place within it. Some are cleaner, some filthy. Some serve food, most do not. All are cheap, and for the most part safe and friendly.

Only a few have hot water. Washing facilities are pretty basic, and toilets – which are always shared – can be unbelievably primitive. The chamber pots usually found under the beds become an attractive alternative. But then Peruvians spend a lot less of their time thinking about lavatories than we do. They often prefer to use the streets (discreetly) to urinate – particularly the men. Some of us took easily to this practice; but Mick, being English, always felt that it was cleaner to go somewhere dirty.

The Hostal San Miguel presented no more than the usual problems in this respect. The rooms, in fact, were unusually clean. The mud-brick building formed a courtyard on two rickety floors around a luxuriant little garden. When we awoke next morning, the painted tin roof, the encircling wooden veranda on the top floor – its wooden balustrades newly coated in shiny blue paint – and the bright flowering bushes in the garden made a lovely sight.

It had been almost dark when we arrived, sweaty, dusty and tired. We were also a little anxious. Mick was worrying about the climbing and walking which lay ahead, and John was still unwell.

'Calm yourselves,' said the proprietress, Maria-Carmen. She was a tiny middle-aged lady. Boundlessly energetic, she fussed over us, full of concern. One just sensed that she was a spinster.

There was a 'restaurant' she could recommend, she said. It was called Tio Sam (Uncle Sam's) and she gave us directions, writing out for John the name of a maize porridge they would cook for him, to settle his stomach.

Just the thought of porridge brought back John's stomach cramps, and he made his excuses to Maria and rushed for the lavatory.

Five minutes later we heard a thud, a splash and a yelp. Ian ran to investigate, ready to break in if necessary. But John had already broken out, staggering from behind the black plastic binliner which formed the door to what was really just a plywood cupboard marked '*Baño*'.

His trousers were around his knees and he was drenched from the head downwards, as though he had been caught in a flash thunderstorm.

In fact he had. The toilet, it seems, doubled up as the shower. There being no room for both side by side within the confined space, they had been placed one on top of the other instead. The shower (cold water only) was suspended on some coathanger wire, immediately above and just to the front of the toilet-bowl. The toilet was flushed using a blue plastic bucket which was filled from the shower.

The tap to the shower was on the wall beside the toilet bowl. A sign (in Spanish and hilarious broken English) reminded guests that toilet paper was not to be placed in the toilet, but in a 'wicker bucket' nearby. This turned out to be a basket, cunningly concealed behind the toilet.

John had read the sign but failed to see the basket. Therefore he concluded that the plastic bucket was for toilet paper. That left the problem of how to flush the toilet. He assumed this was done by turning on the adjacent tap.

Expecting to be on the lavatory for some time, he had decided to sweeten the air by organizing an interim flush of the toilet. He opened the tap, vigorously.

The shower (which was not really a shower, but a sawn-off pipe-end) was an especially effective spouter. A massive jet of icy water under high pressure shot straight down on to John's head. As students of psychiatry will recognize, this episode may point the way to a promising aversion-therapy treatment for stomach complaints whose origin is psycho-somatic. But John's wasn't.

The porridge at Tio Sam's, though, did seem to help. It was made from maize flour, sickeningly over-sweetened and flavoured with cin-namon, with the consistency of wallpaper glue. It looked revolting; but that soon became immaterial, because the town's lights failed. Sam, the owner, brought in candles with a weary good humour. This was a common occurrence.

A fellow walked in and stood awkwardly by our table. 'May I join you?' he asked Mick, in Spanish. In the dim light it took us a moment to realize that he was the man who had pointed out the way to the restaurant for us. Now he introduced himself.

His name was Saul. In his early thirties, shabbily dressed, painfully polite, he seemed desperate for company. He looked anxious, down-trodden.

Saul was a primary school teacher. He said he taught English, German and biology. One hoped he made up on the German and biology what he lacked on the English, for he could not speak English at all.

Like all the teachers in Peru, he had been on strike for more than two months. The union had run out of money to pay its striking members and he was penniless – and bereft, without his children to teach. He looked hungry.

We invited him to eat with us, and talked. An unusual story emerged. Saul was unmarried and had no family in the town. As a younger man he had tried to become a priest, but had failed his exams and given up.

He said he had lost his faith: but when he began to talk about the Catholic Church he seemed unable to stop. He talked blindly on, his eyes as white as his knuckles in the candlelight, while he gripped the side of his rickety chair: '... whereas I believe' (all this in rather formal Spanish) 'that only the soul can be free. The body has no freedom except as a creature of the will, or subjugated to it, or part of it. But, just as the body is only the agent of the will, so the will is only the agent of the mind. The mind, the brain, deliberates before taking a decision and activating the will ...' Sam the restaurateur came in with what appeared (in the candlelight) to be some leathery fried eggs on a heap of boiled rice, and a great pot of hot pepper sauce.

'... Can the mind, then – or brain – be free? No. It is determined by its own nature, its history, and the external influences upon it ...' John glanced wretchedly at the steaming mound of food, then hastily positioned a paper bag on the table so as to hide the eggs from his vision.

'... Only the spirit is free: only the soul.' Saul glanced up, miserably. 'The soul is not the same thing as the mind. They are separable. It is possible' – he stared, almost suicidally, into the candle – 'to have a mind, and body, without a soul.'

John lurched towards the door, looking panicky. Sam interrupted the conversation. He seemed to know the teacher and approached him with respect but also a certain sympathy. He had clearly decided it was time to rescue us, and he sat down, calling his children over: two little boys. 'Speak to our guests in English,' he told them, and stood back, waiting for us to be impressed.

The little boys knew no English. They stammered out a few garbled words, one of which sounded like 'window'. 'Ah – *window*,' said Ian, pointing at the grimy, cracked glass. The boys squealed enthusiastically and their proud father led them away. He was a gentle person: there was an almost academic air about him. A most unlikely restaurateur.

John returned. 'I just disturbed a soldier out there, crapping, with a machine-gun across his knees.'

Sam started to tell us about Chiquian's most famous living son, 'now a professor at a celebrated university in Europe. It is called Oxford. Do you know of him?'

But we were interrupted. In walked two drunks, one of them carrying a violin case. Uninvited, they made what would have been, if they had been capable of it, a straight line for our table and dragged up chairs to join us and introduce themselves. Their names were Oscar and Raoul.

Oscar ran a freight and shipping business – which turned out to mean that he was part-owner (with a brother) of a pick-up truck. Fat, pasty and dirty, he punctuated his boastful conversation by spitting on the floor. This he did every few sentences.

Raoul told us that he was blind, and that he was a Jewish violinist. How total was his blindness, we never did establish. As for his being Jewish, we were happy to take his word for it. He was certainly not a violinist. This became clear when he fumbled for the black case, pulled out a battered violin, staggered to his feet and – the whites of his eyes rolling heavenward – started to play 'El Condor Pasa'. It was awful.

We were determined not to let them corner us into buying them drinks (as was their aim, and as Sam's expression warned us), so we sat tight-lipped and unencouraging, until they moved away – Oscar spitting all the more furiously.

It was late. Saul had slipped dejectedly out. Sam now gave us the celebrated professor's name, and asked that we visit him. And we decided that it was time to go. Leaving Ian to finish his drink and teach Sam's two boys more English, the three of us started back to the Hostal San Miguel.

It took a while to find it; and just before we got there I missed my jacket. Leaving John and Ian, I headed back to Tio Sam's to recover it.

The power was still off and the streets were unlit and silent. In the distance, a dog was barking. I rounded a dark corner. There in front of me was a shadowy figure, waiting. I started – but it was Saul. He smiled, nervously.

'I wanted to ask something,' he said. 'Do you believe in the human soul? Do your friends believe in it?' I began to reply but he was not listening. 'Because I think I've lost mine.' He spoke quietly, matter-of-fact and without emotion – as one might report the loss of an umbrella or cat. 'And I *think* – but I'm not sure – that I know when it was taken.

'I slept with a woman when – you remember – when I was trying to become a priest. When I went to bed with her, I know I had it – my soul, you understand – with me at the time. In the morning after she left, I thought I noticed it was gone; and later I became certain of this.

'She must have taken it. But I never found her again. I am worrying about how I can get my soul back ...'

We had reached Uncle Sam's. Saul did not come in, but carried on walking down the alley, away from me. It was the last any of us saw of him.

I had hardly got through the door when I met Ian coming out, carrying my missing jacket. He looked angry and bewildered. 'You're too late! I went out the back for a piss and that bloody Raoul was there bloody pissing on your jacket. Bloody Oscar was holding the jacket out for him to aim for ...'

Oscar interrupted us, stumbling past, Raoul leaning on his arm, violin case in the other hand. Oscar spat. Before we could speak, they staggered off into the night. It seemed best to let them go. As he walked back, the town's lights came on. But our room was pitch dark and Mick and John were fumbling for the switch, which seemed to have failed.

A torchlight inspection revealed that there was in fact no switch mechanism beneath the plastic cover: just two bare wires, separated, and each kinked into a little hook at its end.

To switch on, you poked at the live wire with a piece of wood or plastic, manoeuvring it into conjunction with the neutral wire. Then the light came on. To switch off, you decoupled them by the same means.

Our beds were straw mattresses on sheets of pressed steel. When you bounced on them they rumbled like stage thunder in a village-hall pantomime.

We slept deeply.

Mick sat bold upright, just before dawn. 'God, what a dream! I was lying in bed between a man and a woman. I moved over towards the woman to make love to her without waking the man. Then I thought: better not. Best save my strength to climb the mountains. Suddenly I was at my grandmother's house for tea. We were all wearing cat-mask balaclavas in bright colours – orange and yellow ...'

'How do you feel, John?'

'Better.' John sat up with a loud rumbling from his sheet-metal bed, and threw open the wooden shutter that gave on to the street.

Clear strong light flooded in. At first it was so harsh that – as in an over-exposed photograph – the window was just an unbearable pale yellow glare. But eyes began to adjust to the brilliance of an Andean dawn.

Over the street opposite our room was a little family backyard, and in its centre a crackling fire. Two pigs lay grunting in the first rays of the sun. The kitchen door opened. An Indian woman, two chickens and three little girls walked out. From within a transistor radio played a haunting melody on the flute and guitar.

John opened the other shutter, giving inwards onto the veranda and over the courtyard. Bathed in the yellow dawn, the highest peaks of the Cordillera Huaywash rose behind the tin roof.

They soared above the painted corrugated iron roofs, the creeping bougainvillea and the blue balustrades of our sagging veranda. They soared above Maria-Carmen's garden, its lilies and daisies opening now into the morning sun. They soared above the little fountain she had constructed at its centre.

The veranda creaked as we made our way down to Maria's courtyard. She was already up, watering and pruning. Her fountain was made of concrete studded with sea shells a Belgian had given her, the Spanish for 'faith', 'hope' and 'love' etched, one word on to each of three of its sides. As it was a square fountain she had been obliged to supplement the Sermon on the Mount with an extra virtue, and had chosen 'chastity' to complete the square. Though the yard was tiny, she had criss-crossed it with radial paths, very geometrical, leading out from the fountain. They were edged with upturned Inca-Kola bottles, nose-down into the earth.

The fountain played, the flute and guitar sang, the pigs grunted and the chickens squawked. Today was the day of preparation for our journey.

There were still a few provisions we needed to find. This would give us a chance to see the town. And then – we thought – we might try some afternoon walking in the hills behind us.

Huaraz had seemed provincial after Lima. After Huaraz, Chiquian was hardly even a town. It can have changed little in eighty years. A handful of streets, narrow, cool and shabby without being squalid; a handful of motor vehicles (for there was nowhere to go); and a dozen shops, all selling candles, needles, bread, oranges, *Crema Nivea* and plastic baskets ... and that was about it.

Behind the town, the valley rose up towards the plateau from which we had descended. At the town's edge, the valley dropped on down a thousand feet or more to the river below: just a ribbon, flecked with white where the rapids and gorges were. Across the river rose the mountain range which was our destination.

It was to the town's edge that we walked as the noonday sun rose in the sky and shops began to close for the siesta. There was a little park with a statue of some long-forgotten admiral, dominated by Chiquian's military post. A modest building, continuously manned.

But there was really nothing for the soldiers to do. One lay flat out on the park bench, fast asleep, in full uniform. He had laid his sub-machine-gun neatly across his chest. Another, also in uniform, lay on the grass, entangled with one of the local girls. He had laid his sub-machine-gun to one side. It was a peaceful scene.

The peace and the soldier's passion was disturbed by the arrival of a party of French tourists, the first foreigners we had seen in the town. They were dressed in designer walking gear, all bright, primary, harlequin colours, skin-tight nylon track suits, and hair in expensive disarray. They looked like a conference of presenters of children's television programmes. Where did they find the means in this primitive place to dress so sharp? Why did they bother?

We walked back, ate a little more rice at Sam's, then set out to walk in the hills behind.

It was hot, here. Hummingbirds flew beside us, reviving John's spirits completely. They seemed to whisper to him of torrent ducks to come. Pink and yellow roses vied with clumps of arum lilies and banks of cactuses: a strange mixture of the Mexican scrub and the English country garden. On the biggest cactus leaves people had cut graffiti: 'Rosa – I love you – Eugenio 1983'; 'Abortion free and on demand'; and, extraordinarily 'Release Rudolf Hess'.

Rudolf Hess had died since the message was carved. Perhaps, incarcerated in some grim Eastern European prison with no prospect of release, his last hours might have been lightened had he known that his name was being carved on a cactus somewhere in the high Andes, and visited daily by hummingbirds. Who knows?

This walk had been a sort of test run. As such, it proved worrying, for Mick was in obvious difficulty.

Now Mick, who is in his early fifties, is physically strong. And, despite his morbid fascination with illness, he lacks neither strength nor guts when it comes to the crunch.

But for high-altitude walking you need something rather different: a sort of stringy stamina; an ability not so much to push very hard, as to keep up a plodding, head-down teamwork between heart, lungs and legs. You can really go as slow as you please, but you must *keep* going.

Mick couldn't, or wouldn't. That afternoon, as he fell further and further behind us, we had our first inkling of this. And tomorrow, we were to start for Llamac . . .

'Llamac'. It seemed to be pronounced *lyam-ak* and, so far, it was just a name on our map. But it was the first settlement (on our chosen path up into the mountains) which seemed to be more than a handful of huts; and it looked like about a day's walk. We had chosen Llamac as our goal for the first day, which now lay ahead.

That night, singers and flute-players came to Tio Sam's. Though they were hardly polished, the music was too moving to talk against. They sang a song called '*Ojos Azules*' – 'Blue Eyes'.

Blue eyes,
You swore to be tender for all our lives.
After two or three days, you deceived me.
I shall drink a little phial of poison, to forget.

Sam came over with a letter he had written to the professor at Oxford, and asked us to post it in England. On the envelope was simply the man's name, and 'Oxford, Europe'.

Sam's wife brought a little parcel of maize flour and cinnamon, for John's stomach. She had written out instructions for preparing the porridge. We said goodnight, and goodbye. As we left we were assailed, outside the door, by an old Indian gentleman carrying a placard with a picture of Christ. He was marching up and down the street with it, calling, 'Turn to Jesus' into the doorways. Other Indians ignored him, pretended he wasn't there, exactly as the English do.

It was early. Chiquian's diesel-engine electricity generator was still throbbing and the lights were on. We took a turn round the main square, assailed again by the old evangelist who now seemed to be picketing an establishment whose signboard read (in English): 'FAMILIA MINAYA – THE CHEAPEST, MOST CENTRAL, MOST WONDERFUL HOME IN CHIQUIAN. WHILE MY WIFE COOKS *DELICIOUS* MEALS, I, *RODOLFO*, WILL WEAVE YOUR OWN *PONCHO*!'

Townspeople were milling around, some gathered by a blackboard in the square itself announcing (in Spanish): 'Sportive and Social Club Santa Rosa of Chiquian: Band – THE BIG POMPATA BAND and a single dish of GUINEA PIG and 'EL AGUADITO' of chicken. Fizzy Beer.'

Less cheerily the church portico bore the message carved in stone: 'TIMES PASS, GENERATIONS DIE, ONLY GOD PERSISTS'.

We slept heavily. There were no dreams of cat-masks.

Chapter Seven

On Foot

Nine o'clock was disgracefully late to start, in a country where the world is up at dawn. Maria-Carmen shook hands with each of us except Ian. Ian she kissed impulsively. As we left she made the sign of the cross – an exaggerated gesture, as the day's walk to the village of Llamac, at the foot of the Cordillera Huaywash, was hardly the ascent of Everest. Mick blanched as she did so.

Maria, and everyone else we met, thought we were crazy to walk. Not because it was difficult, but because it was unnecessary. Llamac is reached only by footpath, there are no roads ... but we were rich, and heavily laden, and – as an old man on a mule exclaimed as he passed us – '*Rico es burrico*' (To be rich is to ride). Why were we taking on the job of beasts of burden when these beasts could be hired for next to nothing? Mick seemed dangerously attracted by this logic. The old man's parting shot (to Mick) was 'Beware of the cold, and the bandits. I'm a widower and I ought to know.'

Downhill was fine: an hour's wonderful descent to the river through flowering trees, singing birds and little children dancing in our path and asking (in Spanish) 'Where from? Where from?' It was a cry to which we were to become accustomed.

The land was lush and the people looked prosperous. From time to time, where the path passed a village, enterprising residents had set up refreshment stalls – selling beer, oranges, sweets and Coca-Cola – with shady places to sit, and troughs to water beasts of burden. These places were always busy with Indians exchanging news and information about the route ahead and discussing mules. They were the unmotorized equivalent of motorway service areas; and we quickly realized that a continuous stream of traffic passed along these narrow paths between the town and its surrounding villages. The animals that carried it were at the centre of people's lives. Riding was not a hobby.

When the path reached the river, we followed it, downstream, snaking up and down through the little hills and fields and settlements that clothed its banks. Gradually, the hillside grew sparser, the soil rockier and the sun hotter. Villages grew fewer and further between and then disappeared altogether.

Once we passed a convoy of men and horses travelling in the opposite direction, towards Chiquian. The first and the last were uniformed and heavily armed. The man on the middle horse, who was plump and well dressed, was handcuffed. He appeared to be being brought to justice in Chiquian. He nodded rather grandly to us as he passed.

Mick was beginning to feel the heat and altitude. Donkey trains passed in both directions and he looked tempted more than once. Around the middle of the day, a donkey train of American tourists passed us, on its way back to Chiquian. It consisted of eleven donkeys, with drivers. Our eyes grew wide with amazement (and Mick's, with envy) at what they carried: tents, trestle-tables, folding chairs, lamps ... One donkey was devoted entirely to carrying Coca-Cola.

In the dust left in their wake, Mick sat down in despair. We lightened his rucksack a little.

The sun grew more intense, and we stopped for lunch in the shade of a grove of strange cedar-like trees, through which the river rushed. We put down our packs and cooled our feet in the icy water, then lay on the grassy bank, talking.

After that our path left the river and doubled back and upwards along the course of one of the tributaries coming steeply down from the mountains.

It grew hotter and windier, and, as we climbed, the lack of oxygen began to tell. It is easy to forget altitude while you are walking along the flat. As soon as you run or climb, though, breathlessness comes suddenly. You are left weaker even after you have caught your breath again, and sometimes a headache or nausea sets in.

It is interesting to ask why this happens, and why it affects only those who are new to altitude. After all, the mechanism by which we breathe harder when we need more oxygen should be instinctive and normally is. What is there to learn?

An animal capable of putting oxygen 'in the bank' by noticing when extra supplies were shortly to be needed, and breathing harder *before* it became necessary, would certainly have a survival advantage over one that couldn't. Perhaps that is what we do, without being conscious of it? If so, an animal accustomed to the oxygen-rich air at sea level will be unconsciously under-reacting to physical tasks when it finds itself in thinner air.

The answer would be to make yourself pant harder, and earlier, than seems natural, when you are at what is (for you) an unnaturally high altitude. Try it. Breathe hard, self-consciously and exaggeratedly before you even reach a slope. It works.

'We're on the wrong side of this river,' said Mick. 'The map says we should be on the other side.'

John looked across at the sheer cliffs above the opposite bank. 'Well, there must have been an earthquake since this map was published. Look at it!' he said. 'It would be impossible.'

'It's pretty bloody impossible over here.'

John was on the mend. He had just enough strength to keep going, but not to argue. He looked away, resuming his search for torrent ducks – so far, fruitless.

A donkey train overtook us. 'Shit!' said Mick. 'That was an empty donkey. I could be on that.' Silence. We climbed onward and upward.

Mick broke the silence. 'They say that what goes up must come down.' He paused, to pant. 'But here in the bloody Andes, what goes up just goes further bloody up.' Another bout of panting. 'In this southern bloody hemisphere everything's bloody inverted. Except Matt's bloody optimism ... Howling fucking gale, temperature like a bloody oven ... What the hell am I doing in this vertical desert?'

Of course the valley was not, quite, vertical; or, quite, a desert. But it was hot, dry and getting steeper all the time. Our little mule-track clung to its side, now hugging the stream, now climbing above it. On the hillside the ground was more rock than soil and supported only spiny cactuses and thin scrub. By the side of the stream was a narrow ribbon of green, and occasional meadows which the peasants came down to work. It was in one of these meadows that we later found Mick.

Noticing that he had not caught up and could no longer be seen, Ian had retraced our steps, to search. Mick was asleep, with his head on a stone, in the green grass. Ian called us all back. It took an effort to wake Mick, and even more to persuade him to carry on. He seemed deaf to reason. At this point, each of us inwardly accepted that it was best to face the fact that Mick was not a great hill-walker. And it was Ian who came to terms with that first.

Ian had already made his name among the youth of Chiquian with a dazzling impromptu performance in a street football match: so dazzling that he forgot the altitude and was later sick. Now, on today's journey, he had fallen in with a lad on his way home with horse and mule to Llamac.

The boy was called Nazario and was travelling alone: a village youth of about eighteen, slightly built and diffident in manner, but eager to help.

Nazario let Ian try riding his horse, and Ian, who had never ridden before – let alone bareback along a precipitous mountain path –

pronounced it 'great'. Now Ian suggested that Mick try. In any other circumstances, Mick (who could not ride either) would not have dreamt of such an attempt. But these were desperate times.

Without that horse, and Nazario's help, it is hard to see how Mick could have continued. By the time the sun set, Nazario was our friend.

Night had fallen when we walked into Llamac. It was a strange experience for all of us. To arrive by night should be to come out of the dark. Arriving at Llamac was walking into the dark. Or so at first it seemed.

So much of the technology we take for granted serves to amplify. It broadcasts sound louder and wider; it intensifies and spreads illumination; it accelerates travel. Our senses adjust for this; they protect themselves from over-exposure by turning down some internal volume-control knob so that we are not deafened or dazed, but experience this supercharged world as though it were normal. In doing so, we reduce our ability to experience sensations offered on a lesser scale. We are, perhaps, numbed to those little sounds and feelings that a quieter, darker, stiller world would offer.

Llamac was a village of some size – perhaps 1,000 inhabitants. A traveller in England, reaching a place of similar importance at night, would be greeted by traffic, noise and light. He would have come out of silence into an atmosphere which would burst into his solitude. When you reach anywhere in Europe, you know immediately where you are: the place is bigger, noisier, stronger than you, the lights are brighter than yours. You plug in – so to speak – to a stronger current.

A remote Andean village is quite unlike that. It seems at first almost to be playing possum, hiding, hoping to be taken for dead. Llamac had no streets, only alleys, and no street lights. It had no electricity at all. And not only was it pitch dark outside, but so soft were the lights within that at first there seemed to be none. No light came spilling out of the little houses. Few windows had glass – only shutters, and they were shut.

Nor was the noise of our party – of horses' hoofs clattering over stones, and excited conversation – matched by any sound from the village. It was not answered at all. There were no cars there, no engines, no machines, no televisions and no loudspeakers beyond what a torch battery would operate. There was no night life and nobody, nobody at all, outside.

The first impression as we stumbled in was of a community in hiding – curfewed, muffled, blacked out. Where was everybody? One stood in silence. The dark was profound, the air very cold and the stars very bright. To each side of our valley loomed the massive flanks of the high Andes: great dark walls, almost overhanging, above us.

At first the silence seemed to grow. As we accustomed ourselves to it, we heard for the first time the noise of the river rushing below. Then other little nocturnal sounds began to impinge upon us.

Torches extinguished, our eyes began to see again. The huts were not in darkness after all. Soft lights became perceptible through cracks and holes in the shutters: lights of different kinds – guttering candles, the steady glow of an oil lamp and, here and there in richer households, the brighter yellow of a kerosene pressure-lamp, whose hiss and roar we now began to hear.

We could hear voices now, too – children's voices, parents' conversation, comrades laughing – inside the houses. The voices mingled with fireside and domestic sounds – of tin plates rattling and ashes being stoked. A tap was running in the alley outside, some distance away; and from far across the other side of the village, perhaps, drifted the sound of a flute and guitar.

Llamac was not dead at all, not hiding. It was alive, awake, full of activity: a patchwork of little pools of light and sound. Its quiet presence had grown on us now that we were silent and still: now that we could see and hear.

Nazario helped Mick off the horse. He had crinkly black hair, and the high cheekbones of all the Indians. But there was an openness in his face, an enthusiasm, a readiness in his smile, that marked him out from others. In any village there is usually a boy who should go far. He is waiting, all too often, to grow into a man who never did. Nazario was such a boy.

He and Ian had established a firm friendship on the basis of a shared interest in football and Ian's willingness to try Spanish, Quechua (the Indian language) and bareback horse-riding, all in the last three hours. There was now no question, Nazario told us, that we should stay anywhere but with his family. Besides, he added, when he saw us wavering, they ran a hotel: the best in Llamac. We were glad to accept, and Mick asked the tariff.

Nazario looked embarrassed. It was not exactly that sort of hotel, he explained. 'Pay anything you like . . . whatever you think.'

His family did not in fact run a hotel. They did not run a hostel. They did not even have a spare room. But they were genuinely delighted to receive us. We were offered a mud floor in the eating-room of a two-storey mud-brick house, roofed with corrugated iron and straw. And such was Nazario's friendliness – and our exhaustion – that it could have been the Ritz.

We sat down, some on the floor, some on chairs. Candles were lit, and the rest of Nazario's family came in.

Nazario introduced them proudly. His father was called Elias, his mother, Apolonia. His three sisters were Doris, Gladys and Iris. His little brother was Adolfo, and their aunt, Wilma, from Chiquian, was also staying. He himself, he explained, was actually called Amaure, but went by his surname, Nazario. His father, Elias, was the shopkeeper, and their shop was next door. So Coca-Cola was sent for.

It arrived – the bottles almost white around their sides where the glass had been ground away by a truck ride from Lima to Huaraz, another from Huaraz to Chiquian, and then a donkey-trek from Chiquian to Llamac. Surprisingly, this had added no more than 50 per cent to the price we had paid for Coke in Lima. But we were probably the beneficiaries – and Llamac the victim – of Peru's raging inflation. The up-to-the-minute price of those bottles could well have doubled since they left Lima on their long journey; Elias would have had no way of knowing. When he told us – for instance – the price of a small live pig, this turned out to be almost exactly equal to what he was charging for a large tin of peeled cling peaches.

In any case, the Coke fizzed violently out of the bottles, as well it might after a thousand lurches and pot-holes and a climb of 3,000 feet.

Nazario's mother, Apolonia, asked us what we would like to eat.

'What is there?' Mick enquired.

'Potatoes.'

'And?' We were ready for anything.

'Guinea-pigs.'

Well – not quite anything. We settled for potatoes. As Apolonia left to prepare them, a chorus of shrill little squeaks from her kitchen over the alley confirmed that news of our decision had been well received in the guinea-pig pen.

Nazario's older sister Doris shot a few shy glances at Ian, but cast her eyes down whenever he actually spoke to her. Her younger sister was more forward, and simply couldn't keep her eyes off him. He asked her name. Gladys, she replied, with an excitement she could barely contain, and shortly afterwards ran out of the room bursting with the news (which every child in the village was soon to learn) that he had enquired.

Was England like Llamac, Nazario asked Mick. Did it ever rain there? Did people use donkeys at all or did they all have Chevrolets? He had heard they had many cars in Europe: 'And there are many in Chiquian, also. Five – or perhaps six, if you include the truck which is waiting for a new gearbox from Lima. I have seen all of these vehicles, and met their owners.'

He had never been to Lima, although he had heard that Huaraz, which he had visited, was very similar. 'Is it a greater distance from Lima to London than from Huaraz to Lima? Or have you almost reached England when you get to Lima? It is not far to New York from there. Rich Lima people go all the time. Also to Miami, where they have money in American banks.'

Was Scotland in London? He had a picture of a man in a kilt. Were America and London the same country? Were there rivers and mountains? Had we seen the Queen?

The walls of our room, which were mud, were papered by pages from Lima newspapers and magazines, stuck side by side. These had been selected for their interest, and were mostly about football. Nazario pointed to an article with coloured photographs, describing a recent air crash in which Lima's entire football team had been killed. It had been a national tragedy. The whole family murmured in sympathy.

With Mick's help, Ian explained that a similar accident had once happened in Britain. A whole team had been involved ...

'Yes,' Nazario interrupted, 'of course. That was Manchester United, at Munich, on a flight home after playing Partisan Belgrade in 1958. The team captain, I think, was Roger Byrne. Such a loss – particularly Duncan Edward.'

When supper was ready, the whole family left us to eat alone. However friendly, Peruvian Indians very often did this when it came to a meal time. We had the impression not so much that they were unsociable about eating, but that joining someone for a meal was thought very familiar, and one was left alone out of respect. Before the potatoes, Apolonia brought bowls of what she called soup but was really just hot water with salt and noodles. Still, it was quite palatable and at least warming. So were the potatoes, though they were served dry, alongside a heap of crushed rock salt for flavouring, and some slices of a cheesy white substance which was not easy to enjoy – though we tried, as it was served with evident pride.

There was only water to drink. All our resolutions about boiling water, or putting Mick's little chlorine tablets into it, crumbled. After all, had we not already eaten the potatoes, drunk the soup out of chipped metal bowls, and used knives which must have been washed under the alley stand-pipe?

Besides, it *felt* healthy here (well, it felt cold, anyway). Ian, still untroubled by diarrhoea, gulped his water thirstily. The others followed suit.

We exchanged glances, though. And this was the last time that any of us seriously considered the possibility of insulating ourselves from Peruvian bacteria. Like many decisions, it did not seem very important at the time: only later. But, really, we had no choice.

After supper the whole family rejoined us. It was very late – about 9.00 p.m. You soon got used to the fact that without electricity, let alone television, nightfall is soon followed by bed. You awake and are up with the dawn.

But, late though it was, this was a special occasion. Would we sing for them, please?

Mick turned out to have a meek but romantic tenor voice. He sang a Latin love-song, '*Cielito Lindo*' to general admiration:

> A bird which leaves its nest,
> If it finds, on returning, that the nest is occupied –
> Then surely that is well-deserved ...
> Ay, ay, ay-ay ...

Apolonia's eyes misted with tears as he sang. She left to prepare our beds. Then the girls in the family performed an Indian song: lively and repetitive.

We were asked for a second contribution. 'Greensleeves'? Nobody knew the words. Mick struck up 'Onward Christian Soldiers', which at least we all knew.

At first John did not join in. 'I sang my last hymn at school. I vowed never to sing another,' he muttered.

Noticing that he was sitting this one out, two of the smaller children started giggling at him. Shamed, he sidled into the next verse along with the rest of us:

> ... Brothers, we are treading
> Where the Saints have trod!

He sang, with a broken look: a lifelong resolution smashed, as three comrades smirked.

After this, John's second resolution, never to sing the British national anthem, was quick to crumble when our hosts asked us for a rendering. Would they give us the Peruvian anthem, Mick asked, wondering whether this was what we had heard the schoolchildren in the poor quarter of Lima singing.

The whole family burst into song. They sang with both enthusiasm and tenderness:

> We are free: let us always be!
> You would deny the light of the sun, before denying that ...

There followed a mellow silence, broken, eventually, by Apolonia, who had not been part of the singing. She came in, now.

'Your bed is ready.'

Bed? Surely she meant 'beds'?

No. On the mud floor were laid out two layers of cowhide, to form a base about six foot square. Over it had been placed an assortment of blankets, clothes, hides, ponchos, rugs ... everything, it seemed, that the family had been able to lay their hands on. Into this mound of cloth we were expected to climb as a group, together for warmth.

At one end was a row of rock-hard bolsters on which to lay our heads. It would not be necessary to use our sleeping-bags, Nazario told us. He was proud that, by much effort, the family were able to provide for our comfort entirely out of their own resources.

Ian braved it. The rest of us sneaked into our sleeping bags once the family had left. Come dawn, each of us was to find himself bitten by some mysterious insect – except Ian.

We lay in the dark, talking. Nazario's father had offered us donkeys to take both us and our belongings on the steep climb which lay ahead. Our plan had been to walk up from Llamac, using a mountain path which zigzagged to the top of the ridge above us; and then across (at an altitude of about 14,000 feet) to a high glacial lake called Laguna Jahuacocha. This lay at the foot of the highest peaks of all, the ice-covered summits of the Cordillera Huaywash: the great Jirishanca and Yerupaja, soaring 20,000 feet into the sky, permanently in snow. It would be a tough journey, harder than the one we had just accomplished, taking another full day.

Looking back, it is now hard to understand why we felt any resistance to the idea of using donkeys. Perhaps it was because an unspoken ideal of self-sufficiency had been built into our original plans: ourselves versus the mountains. We seemed to have given so little thought to the existence of a race to whom these mountains were home; to the comradeship or hospitality they could provide; to their way of doing things; or to the pleasure and interest to be found in learning about it and joining in with it.

So it was not because we wanted to, but because it seemed unlikely that there was any other way Mick could carry on, that we had agreed with Nazario that we would accept his offer, in part. We would take one donkey, to carry the heaviest of our possessions. But we ourselves would walk. Nazario and his father would accompany us.

Sleep came upon us, one by one. Now, there was only the sound of the guinea-pigs squeaking: 'Cwee, cwee' – exactly the pronunciation of the South American word for the animal, *cuy*. Beneath their cries was the muffled roar of the river below.

In our different ways, we all slept fitfully.

I lay for some time with the words of the Peruvian anthem running through my head. 'We are free ... You would deny the light of the sun, before denying that.' In my half-waking, half-sleeping state, the guinea-pigs seemed to be chanting it, squeaking in unison.

Unable to relax, I walked out into the alley to fill my lungs with cold night air. The moon had risen, lighting one vast flank of mountainside opposite in ghostly white. Low in the sky, the Southern Cross shimmered. It recalled a poem read in childhood, now all forgotten except one phrase which sank – as curious oddments do – into a boy's consciousness, and stayed. The poem was (I think) about a British soldier killed in the Boer War and buried in the southern hemisphere. Above his grave, the poem ran, 'strange constellations' wheeled, at night. Strange constellations ... There was a thin white frost on all the leaves.

A donkey sighed in a nearby field. Perhaps it was the beast chosen to help with our climb in the day ahead.

'We are free. Deny the light of the sun before denying that ...' The guinea-pigs' squeaks grew in a crescendo as I stumbled past their door, back inside.

I dreamed of searching for a *colectivo* van in Lima, to take me up some daunting hill, where I was expected at the summit. Angela Rippon had commandeered the van and was on her way to the summit without me ...

Ian sat bolt upright, shouting in terror. He had been dreaming that a devil was biting his neck. John mumbled incoherently but with a contented sound. Perhaps he was diving among torrent ducks. Mick was silent. If he was at another cat-masked tea party, then it was a very sedate one this time.

At some point, further into that night, came a low, tuneless murmur. It was John singing in his sleep: 'Onward Christian Soldiers ... (mumble, mumble) ... With the Cross of Jesus, going on before ...'

Chapter Eight

Up

Dawn brought the whinnying and clip-clop of a wholly mule-and-horse-borne society. Everyone rode, and there were animals tethered by every second shack. Carts would have been useless on the footpaths, and there were none. Men clattered up and down the cobbled alleyways, some finely dressed, with ornamented saddlework, rich ponchos and stirrups which were pyramid-shaped boxes to protect the rider's feet from thorns and rocks, made of intricately carved hard leather. There was manure everywhere, and the smell of horse piss hung sweet and rank in the air.

It was a teeming little place, busy with agriculture and commerce.

At the end of yesterday's weary climb, Llamac had felt like a high outpost, the end of the line. Now it appeared for what it was, the beginning of the line: the first and most important of a string of little villages hugging the valleys and gorges upriver. In its way, Llamac was a base camp to a fertile hinterland above. To and from this self-contained world upstream, passed most of Llamac's trade. The world below – the world downstream – Chiquian, Huaraz, Lima: well, Chiquian was the big city, Huaraz was a distant metropolis visited by just a few, and Lima was another planet.

Llamac had its own football pitch: a grand affair, rivalling only the main square where a thatched church was confronted by a moth-eaten bush which – in a brave attempt at topiary – the villagers had clipped into the shape of a pig. Ian, already famous among Llamac's youth, became involved in a dawn football match, making further friends. Afterwards, he queued at one of the village stand-pipes to shave and wash his hair.

'I took my styling gel,' he said, 'but it didn't seem appropriate. First time I've managed without it. How do I look? The water was freezing.'

'Our water is the best,' Nazario had boasted, 'better than Lima's!'

'You haven't been to Lima,' said his sister, Doris, who had worked there but was now back with the family. 'But he's right. It *is* the best.'

*

Our route was to take us away from this river artery. We were striking straight up the mountainside, to the higher plateau, to the snow and sky.

Negotiating for donkeys raised the same problem as paying for our shelter. How much? '*Voluntario*,' said Elias, Nazario's father.

Between us, we four could draw on wide financial and trading experience: seven years in Parliament, analysing the Chancellor's annual budgets; sole control of a youth hostel's profit and loss account; twenty-five years running the church bazaar ...

But what is the going rate per day, per donkey in the Peruvian Andes? Mick plucked a figure from thin air: 'Ten dollars for everything,' he volunteered. We watched Elias's face for anything that might betray his feelings, suspecting that he would probably hide his disappointment and agree the figure, even if it were too low. Elias looked pleased, but not delirious. Nazario smiled. Mick had got it about right.

It was soon obvious that not one but two donkeys would be needed, just to take the rucksacks. A second beast, smaller than the first, with softer hair and rather dewy eyes, was brought forward. 'A young burro,' Nazario confided to Ian, whose Spanish was improving fast. 'First journey to the mountains. Training. Experiment. Test. Learn. Practice. Try.' This did not inspire confidence on our part, and must have depressed the burro – if she could understand. She looked mournfully at us all, her big eyes filled with moist dismay as the whole family wrenched and tugged the rucksacks tight.

Loading burros was a laborious business: important, as the day's experience would prove, to get right. And we had far too much weight. All the way from Lima, we had carried a week's supply of food, as John was permanently convinced that there might be no food in the next settlement. The argument was never concluded; for, when each successive destination turned out to offer food, John simply transferred his doubts on to the following place.

Huaraz had been doubted. Chiquian had been unlikely to provide meals – beset, perhaps, by siege or famine. Llamac was certain to see us starve rather than offer food. Now Jahuacocha, smaller than anywhere we had so far been, would be inhabited by tribes who either didn't eat at all, or subsisted on sheep's droppings, or had all died since the last traveller had reported their existence.

True, one book said a handful of Indians lived by the lake, and Nazario confirmed it. We put it to John that where there were people there would be chickens, and where there were chickens there would be chicken soup. But for John, only the comfortable clunk of weighty tins in his rucksack would reassure. So in went the tins.

We walked away to let the experts get on with the loading, and visited the guinea-pigs. They were organized in a most businesslike way: not thrown together in one enclosure, but sorted into three separate pens, in order of guinea-pig size. The little ones were in the first pen, medium-sized in the next. Closest to the kitchen fire was the pen for the fully-fattened *cuys*. Some of these peered anxiously out at John.

By the kitchen fire, a woman knelt in the gloom. Bent double, blowing the coals, she looked as old as time. She had so little strength in her lungs, so shallow a breath, that she needed to put her face almost into the fire to make the embers glow. She was just a withered human bellows, still – at least – of some small use to someone. When we left she had not moved from her position on the floor, wheezing patiently into the ashes.

As we walked out of the kitchen, a hen walked in, all unawares. A lurking cock leapt straight on to her back. It was over in seconds, and the two fowls walked out together. 'Chickens are not very big on foreplay,' Mick said.

By now the donkeys seemed ready. And here followed a small but revealing episode.

Apolonia, Nazario's mother, had seemed to play a pretty subservient rôle. In this she was no different from most Peruvian Indian mothers. Seen, but not heard – and only seen when their presence was useful, such as to bring in the food – the older women appeared to yield, in almost everything, to the men. But, now that the men and donkeys were ready to depart on a journey which was a little more difficult than the routine, her husband called for her.

Apolonia knew her authority. She came out of the kitchen without speaking, and walked up to the larger donkey, fully and intricately loaded. She gave its side-load a terrific push, almost toppling the animal. The load shifted a little.

Then a foot emerged from a sea of grubby ankle-length skirts. She planted it on to the burro's side, grabbed the same load with both hands, shook it violently, and then wrenched it towards her. She was very strong and all but pulled the burro on top of her. It stumbled among the stones to keep its balance. The load shifted again.

Apolonia said something very sharp, in Quechua, to her husband, turned and walked back into the kitchen. Elias made no reply, but bowed his head and muttered to Nazario. Resignedly, they both began the complete unloading of the donkey, so that they could start again.

Later we saw Apolonia catch a sheep that was straying off. Picking up all her many skirts, she sprinted about three hundred yards up the hillside, jumping from rock to rock – caught it, picked it up and carried it down under one arm. You realized that she could not be more than about thirty-five: yet she had the leathery complexion of a fifty year old, and the authority of a grandmother. She, as much as her husband, was really in charge of our despatch.

We were cheered out of Llamac by a small but enthusiastic knot of Ian's juvenile admirers. It was a heartening send-off.

The first few hundred yards of the journey further buoyed our spirits. Brightly coloured birds hummed around us, the sun – still pale and low in a clear blue sky – warmed our backs, and women labouring in the little walled fields that patchworked the valley, sang out to us as we passed. 'This,' we thought, 'is easy!'

It was; until the path reached the edge of fields, and began to climb. Up it went, like Jacob's ladder, breathtakingly zigzagging into the sky. The flanks of the mountains were not far off the vertical – too steep for any vegetation except prickly sisal plants (a vicious sword-leafed cactus-like thing, with serrations of tiny spikes down each side of each leaf). Tiny streams tumbling down from above were clad in greenery and hung about with birds and butterflies; but, except where we crossed them, our trudge was through stone and cactus, in the glare of the sun, and always uphill.

Slowly, Llamac dwindled below our feet into a toytown, a small splodge, and by noon a dot. The path was precipitous and the burros showed skill, teetering always on the brink, hugging the stony outside rim of the path, never actually stumbling.

It was unrelenting. We had a little over 3,000 feet to climb that day – the height of Snowdon – and the first 2,000 came in one unyielding slog which *commenced* at an altitude of some 11,000 feet.

From time to time one of us would stop to let Mick catch up. His trudge became ever slower, dogged by diarrhoea as well as exhaustion, and no better, it seemed, for having no pack to carry. We climbed ahead of him, but not so far ahead as to make him despair, nor so close as to let him think for a moment that he could afford to slacken his pace further. In this way the whole group kept moving. But it was very, very slow.

We passed two ancient Indian women, shuffling down the descent to Llamac. These creatures seemed to be indestructible. One of them looked witheringly but not without tenderness at Mick.

'*Pobrecito!*' (Poor little thing!) she said. 'He's broken.' Mick claims she said, 'He's tired' (for which the Spanish is similar). But the rest of us were sure we'd heard right.

By the afternoon we had reached a flat grassland plateau the Indians called *pampa*. Our altitude was some 14,000 feet but from here the climb would be gentler, undulating along the side of a ridge which ran up to the foot of the mountain peaks. We could see these clearly now, brilliant white with high streaks of ice-cloud being blown in a sunlit slow-motion gale from their summits.

We stopped to rest and eat. Nazario and Elias shared our oranges (a great delicacy with Andean people, but well known to them, and found in unlikely places – at a price). They explained that the donkeys you could see grazing on lonely slopes were not wild, but left to fatten up. The ownership of each was well established and known to all, and each would eventually be fetched down. Little boys would be sent up from the valley to do it: an exciting task for a youngster.

Our two burros were released to find their own lunch and they wandered off at complete liberty, still loaded up with all our belongings. It was odd to see your rucksack grazing contentedly in a grove of bushes a few hundred feet above you.

But it was time to move on. Our path took us through narrow rocks, and clambering between the roots of dark, magical trees – Tolkienesque gnarled conifers of some primitive genus, clad in orange-flowering climbers, orchid-like.

Quite often we needed hands as well as feet to negotiate the path. Yet the burros always made it through. They would hesitate, falter and bridle as Elias goaded them forward. Sometimes they would sway alarmingly like overloaded lorries on a narrow wheelbase as they tottered down narrow rock-steps, whacking our side-loaded rucksacks against the granite walls. But they always made it. It was probably on one of these clambers that the kerosene can in Ian's rucksack began to leak into the biscuits.

Late in the afternoon, we passed the first habitation since Llamac: a couple of poor stone huts with straw roofs, and, outside them in a little stone-walled field, two women winnowing corn in the late sunshine. Thin smoke scudded across from a fire in one corner of the field. The women ran over to us, friendly and curious, but politely declined to be photographed. They offered us food, though: hot cooked root vegetables, something between a potato and a carrot, yellow and sweet. They were good; and John had to concede that, if the natives were starving, they were putting on a brave imitation of hospitality.

Now we were within sight of the glaciers at whose skirts Jahuacocha lay. Mountains towered all around us, some snowy, others – lower – made from raw red rock, like mountains from another planet. Granite cliffs, and groves of the strange, dark conifers clawing fingers up impossibly steep and remote places, combined to give the scene a science-fiction quality.

And Jahuacocha, when we reached it, was blue: the most intense, opaque, turquoise blue. It was a lovely lake, about half a mile long and 200 yards wide, surrounded by yellow-brown beds of reed, caught now in the evening light. At its head rose a great grassy mound of moraine, a hundred feet high. Torrents of ice-water poured in a gorge through this into Jahuacocha from a smaller lake above, flecked with ice floes; and to that lake a huge glacier reached down from the mountain, crumbling into its edge.

From each side of Jahuacocha the valley rose steeply (at about forty-five degrees) to the spines of two high ridges, themselves reaching down from the mountain. These valley sides were brown with tufty grass and purplish blue with hundreds of thousands of flowering lupin-like bushes. One side was lit by the evening sun, and some cattle grazed far up on its sides. The other side was in shadow.

At Jahuacocha's foot was another barrage of moraine, behind whose wall the lake had formed, breaking through in a second gorge to the next valley: a wide green pasture, marshy and flat. Here the stream meandered and horses grazed.

It was along the edge of this meadow that we were now passing – tired, jubilant, aware of only part of this scene. We were to see it all in the days ahead.

As we reached Jahuacocha we passed a small settlement of huts. Vicious-looking mongrel dogs charged wildly at us, barking deliriously (Mick said 'rabidly'). But if you stood your ground and made as if to pick up a stone they soon stopped in their tracks. Elias and Nazario were more afraid than we were.

In this valley we had decided to camp. We had already identified a likely site half way along one side of the lake. Ian went ahead with our two friends, their donkeys and the luggage. They wanted to unload fast, and make a start back towards Llamac before nightfall. Mick had caught up now: walking along the flat he regained strength fast. So the three of us left Ian to forge on, and ambled along more gently.

From the huts a man came forward. He introduced himself as Armando. He could supply trout, he said, and eggs, fresh or hard-boiled. Also donkeys, if we needed them to proceed onward from here – which, he insisted, we most assuredly did. Armando was in his fifties, perhaps: weather-beaten. There was something, not evil, but a little sly about him. He was certainly a better salesman, more hard-bitten, than Elias and Nazario. We thanked him and walked on.

As we approached the site we had chosen, we met our two friends with their donkeys, heading home at a cracking pace. We paid them and said goodbye. Nazario seemed moved at the parting. Repeatedly he said that we must come back and stay. 'Llamac is your home, now, and we are your family.'

Nazario kept turning back to wave as we moved on. Soon Elias and his son, and their two intrepid burros, were small dots on the hillside.

The shadows were lengthening, and it was growing cold.

Chapter Nine

El Condor
Pasa

John was convinced that he had got fleas.

His stomach had never recovered, but he had got used to that and did not complain. He found the fleas more interesting. Bites had first been noticed after our night on the cowskins at Nazario's house; and since then every spot, every itch, every blade of grass which brushed against him, caused such a peering and scratching and grooming that he looked like a demented baboon.

Mick, never a straggler in the race to be sicker than the next man, began to imagine that he had fleas too, but could not identify any new bites since Llamac. In his case these worries took second place to those concerning his diarrhoea (which was not imagined) and his altitude sickness.

As we sat by the fire we had built and stared at the mist rising from the lake into the clear night, John's flea search moved into top gear. The sound of fish jumping in the lake punctuated a distant groan and the rustle of toilet paper, marking Mick's position behind some rocks a stone's throw away. It was a bizarre way to greet such a peaceful scene.

We were right by the edge of the lake. On a little mound behind us, sheep grazed. The family who owned them – an Indian and his wife, mother-in-law, two sons and two daughters – lived in two huts just over the mound. He had welcomed us to his shore of the lake and asked us what we would like to eat? Trout? Potatoes? Chicken soup?

'What food do you have?' asked Mick.

'Chicken soup, potatoes and trout,' replied Fortunato, 'and boiled eggs.' His old wife nodded. She looked and smelt like a dusty kipper.

We said that would be fine, and were dismayed to see him hurry his eldest son off towards the lake with a fishing rod and net. But the boy was soon back with four smallish fish and we fell to pitching camp, confident that food would follow.

Wood from the gnarled old conifers – the only trees we had seen on these slopes – was easy to find, and one wondered how they survived at all, being so available a source of fuel. When we tried to light the wood, we discovered why. You couldn't get more than a smouldering heap.

John had broken off from his flea search for a moment to insist that the tents be pitched thirty yards from the fire, in case the leaping flames set fire to them. The tents were fireproofed.

'Those tents are our life-blood,' he explained, offering an unusual metaphor, 'especially as it looks like rain.' The sky was so clear that there seemed to be more stars than spaces. Only a wisp of smoke from our flameless fire smudged the clarity.

'Well, at least the rain will extinguish the burning tents,' Ian volunteered.

John did laugh. Mick didn't. Fleas and dysentery were forgotten now as he faced a new disease: pulmonary oedema.

Mick had learned the symptoms of pulmonary oedema by heart on the flight over. This sudden illness, caused by oxygen starvation, is frequently fatal; it starts with a head cold and sore throat, and breathlessness.

Of course we were all breathless – everyone is, at 14,000 feet. But in his own case Mick was now sure that there was more to it than that. Besides, his nose was running.

Those ignorant of medical science might have put this down to a massive overdose of mentholyptus pastilles – or to the extreme cold, for, as the sun sank, the temperature had plunged to well below freezing. But the running nose was for Mick ominous and near-final proof of the onset of this mortal fever. Declining food, he lay on his back, consumed with terror – very real terror – and sucking mentholyptus sweets with manic energy.

We left Mick, to join Fortunato's family for supper. Everyone sat outside the hut, by the fire, eating sweet potatoes and spitting out fish bones. Family, sheep, pigs, dogs and chickens all mingled together.

These people loved animals and paid great attention to them. This is not to say that treatment of the animals was not at times – to our eyes – cruel. But supper with Fortunato was accompanied by much talk about (and to) the dogs and sheep, much patting, teasing, goading, slapping and stroking.

And, like other Indians we met, Fortunato had a very present sense of the beauty of the place where he lived. He told us the names of all the mountains; which were higher, which more dangerous, which most beautiful. He told us, too, that a handful of European climbers were killed in this range every few years. Smiling, he said he believed that the gods of the place required a few bodies every now and then, so he would not dissuade tourists from climbing there. 'Let them take gringos,' Fortunato chuckled, 'instead of our people.'

His children sang us a song about Yerupaja, the most striking and dangerous peak above the lake.

They were a poor family, but not desperately or degradingly poor. Their old mother-in-law was ill, but they had enough food and adequate shelter. They all slept in the same room, 'for warmth,' Fortunato explained. Would we like to sleep in their other room, the store-hut? I said I would, and would return. The others preferred to stick to their tents.

As we walked back down to the lake, the night was filled with a distant rumbling, which slowly swelled in a crescendo, then began to fade. 'Look up!' said Ian. 'Look at Jirishanca, at the bottom, where the glacier is.'

We looked. There was no moon, but the starlight alone shone white on the snows of Jirishanca. Part of the glacier had detached itself and was streaming down into the lake below in a cascade of ice. Sound, travelling more slowly, lagged a few seconds behind vision, so that the roar continued, even when the cascade had dwindled to nothing. It was a chilling sound. One thought of all the force, all the energy, being blown in those few seconds: and how few there were to witness it. How many such avalanches went completely unwitnessed?

Mick had crawled into his tent to sleep and the others did likewise, leaving me to walk back to Fortunato's with a sleeping bag.

Fortunato ushered me through a low door and closed it behind me. There was no light at all. Never before have I slept somewhere which I had never seen and was completely unable to see. Fumbling round on hands and knees, there seemed to be bottles and baskets everywhere, boxes stacked up, and things hanging from the ceiling. I made a clearing on the bare earth, scattering dozens of little round, hard, dry objects, laid out the sleeping-bag, and slept.

Through dreams of avalanches and sweet potatoes, an insistent 'cwee-cwee' noise intruded. I woke up. It was still pitch black. Something warm and furry was wriggling behind my shoulder, inside my sleeping-bag. Thank God I heard the 'cwee' and thought 'guinea-pig' before I felt its presence; the idea of ferret or rat would have shot me out of the sleeping-bag and through the straw roof. Removing the guinea-pig was easy. Removing the droppings (in the dark) took a little longer. But no *cuy* returned and, drawing the strings of the sleeping-bag tight round my neck, I tried to sleep.

But, awake now, I needed a pee. Reluctantly I felt for the door and found it. Fortunato had barred it – no doubt to keep the dogs out, as they had snapped at my legs as I went in. The door would open a few inches, until a chain which could not be reached from inside drew tight.

There was no way out. The more this sank in, the more I believed I had to relieve myself. There was only one answer. I undid my trousers and thrust my loins as far as possible through the crack in the door. At that point, with a terrific snarling, a dog lunged out of the darkness and threw itself at the other side of the door, making a most ferocious sound with its teeth. I withdrew in the nick of time and retreated, shaking to my sleeping-bag, which, in the dark, I could not now find. In fumbling for it, my hands encountered an empty bottle, then the sleeping-bag itself.

Both problems solved, sleep came quickly.

Not long, perhaps, before dawn, the sound of another avalanche pouring down from the glacier reverberated around the mountains. The gentle splish-splash of fish jumping in the lake, which had continued all night long, ceased for a few moments after the roar had died away, and then – tentatively at first – began again as I dozed off.

The crash of the glacier must have woken Fortunato. Through the mud and stick wall that separated me from the family dormitory, came some muffled grunting and stirring sounds: then, a few seconds later, the unmistakable noises of Fortunato making love. As with the chickens, there did not seem to be much foreplay.

A wonderful day followed.

With dawn came the courage to brazen out the dogs, get my arm out of the door and loosen the chain fastening it. Outside, Fortunato's family were breakfasting on seared guinea-pig. Inside, the daylight revealed my bedroom to be the family store. Heaps of carrots and potatoes were barricaded off from the guinea-pigs by bottles, saddles, cowhides and baskets. Chickens had access to one corner through a hole in the mud wall. In the other were piles of magazines full of pictures of football teams. From the ceiling hung whips, bridles and corn.

Down by the lake shore, the others were still asleep, but the risen sun had cut across our valley, diamond sharp. The water was turquoise, the grass white with frost. Mountain sheep nibbled among the tents, pieces of coloured wool tied in their ears. Fish were jumping frenziedly in the lake. I looked around at the encircling green mountains, with snowy peaks behind. The sky was the deepest blue. Lupins bloomed purple all across the hillside. This was one of the most beautiful places I had ever seen.

Outside his tent, Ian had hung his damp socks. Now they were frozen solid, swinging – stiff zigzags – in the morning breeze. The temperature at that point (after dawn) was eight degrees below freezing.

Ian was soon out, up and into them, with many cries of pain. Then he helped make tea – a quick task as water boils at a lower temperature at these altitudes; and you can taste the difference.

Squatting on his haunches watching the kettle, Ian absent-mindedly scrabbled among the leftover plates and biscuits from the night before. The biscuits had not been a success as they were steeped in kerosene, but Ian was hungry now, and raised a frozen brown fragment to his lips.

'Ugh! This tastes like shit!' He chewed reluctantly, then spat. He had spoken truer than he knew. The fragment was a piece of frozen donkey dropping. The incident brought everyone out of the tents, laughing.

But Mick soon returned to his sleeping-bag. He felt no better.

Ian wanted to see the glacier at close hand, and set off alone. John and I went to investigate a waterfall tumbling into the other side of the lake.

But we were soon beyond it, scrambling up the mountainside, hopelessly short of breath, through fields of glorious lupin bushes, and butterflies. Little rock-rabbits scuttled under the boulders as we passed. Snake-holes in the bare earth set the heart beating, but we saw only lizards. Once, by a stream, we disturbed a flock of partridge-like birds, grazing on the green moss; and as they scattered and we climbed, two black and white eagles escorted us upwards, wheeling above our heads.

It was another world at the top. This was the highest we had been and the highest we were to go: nearly 16,000 feet. Breathing was difficult, the sun seared our bare arms, and our heads hurt. But what a landscape! Short of the great rock and ice peaks themselves needling their way into a deep blue sky, this was the top.

Above a Martian terrain of viciously serrated red ridges, yellow scree and crumbling lava-fields, those peaks stood like sentinels. At their feet, basins of bare earth and frozen ponds had been scooped out in some primeval shock. The wind blew all the time, shaking tiny clumps of flowering yellow gorse that clung to what shelter they could find.

We stood, braced against the wind, taking it in.

'Look!' shouted John into the wind, face to the sky. The excitement in his voice could only mean birds.

Monster birds! Two huge condors were wheeling out of the blue towards us. Even at this distance they looked bigger than men, and were.

'It's a male and his mate. They're hunting,' John said with great and sudden authority. 'Keep dead still so as not to scare them.' They did not look easily scared. I did keep dead still. *They* scared *me*.

The two birds swooped directly above our heads, perhaps twenty or thirty feet away. They were enormous. Perhaps we are so used to seeing small birds fly that we suspend the natural assumption that a creature with weight would drop to the earth and could not long remain airborne. But when you see creatures of this size the disbelief comes rushing back. How could they stay in the air? They looked so big, so heavy!

As they passed over, you could see every detail. The male was larger. Both were riding the wind, their wings and bodies motionless like a freeze-frame photograph, still, against the empty sky. Movement was betrayed only in the feathers at the tips of their wings, which trembled violently like leaves in a gale, and in the birds' heads. Each was sweeping its head from side to side in small, methodical jerks, searching for prey. Each interrupted this routine to fix us with a long stare, the neck craning round as it passed over, the eyes still, trained on a single point.

Their passage seemed to last for ever, branded into memory, though it can only have taken seconds. Then they were wheeling away across the lake 2,000 feet below, towards the other side of the valley.

'Drop!' said John. 'You're the smaller of the two of us. Pretend to be a young animal in difficulty. I'll be your anxious mother. That may bring them back for a second look.'

I was reluctant to play this role too convincingly, and dropped half-heartedly to my knees, ready at any moment to end the pretence should either bird get too interested in the performance. It worked. The larger bird marked time across the valley, wheeling in tight circles, while his mate swept back across to us, circling me twice.

'Writhe on the ground as if you're dying!' hissed John. 'I'll move away from you as if I've given up trying to protect you. Perhaps she'll come right down to land, to see for herself.'

I declined to develop my rôle in this direction. 'What if she decides to go for me, John? She might get carried away.'

'No condor has ever attacked a grown, healthy man. She'll soon back off if you jump up.'

'How can you know that? Maybe nobody's ever tried this trick on them. Once they get excited, they may be slow to revise their judgement . . .'

I stood up and waved my arms at the bird. She soared disdainfully off. John shook his head in sorrow.

The same eagles escorted us down again as we scrambled headlong through a drop of thousands of feet. Hands and arms scratched by the cactuses, we lost count of how often we fell. The lake beneath – Fortunato's hut and our campsite beside it – grew as we descended. It felt like parachuting.

By the time we reached the shore, our valley was in shadow, the sun was sinking and it was cold. High above, the peaks still shone. Lapwings (John said) flapped across the lake, while a flock of jet-black water birds waded out, away from us, and stood staring back from the middle of the lake. They looked like evil spirits.

Our route this time took us round by the head of the lake, where we had seen another encampment.

They were South Africans, come to climb Yerupaja. Most of them were Afrikaans-speaking and their English was very thick. They had flown direct from South Africa, across the South Atlantic to South America. Some of them had never been to Europe, and you could sense a defensiveness towards Englishmen.

'Of course you people probably think we're all monsters. We've heard what your newspapers and television say about South Africa. Totally biased, man. They make us feel like shit wherever we go ... You know Peru is one of the few Third World countries that let us in; and when you see how they treat the poor, the Indians, in this place, Soweto looks like paradise, man ...'

We were talking to a hearty-looking, bearded bloke who seemed to be their self-appointed spokesman, though he had broken a bone in his foot on some practice climbs and would not be climbing this time ...

'I mean you tell me *we've* got a race problem ...' He was warming to his theme, although in fact neither of us had expressed any point of view at all. 'But I tell you that they've got a race problem *here*, in Peru. Have you noticed what colour the rich people are? I tell you, man, they're white: all white. The government? White. The businessmen? White. The generals and officers? White. So why don't they call it apartheid, hey? Why don't your newspapers start talking about Peru for a change instead of always clobbering us ...'

His wife, a doctor, spoke to him in Afrikaans. You could pick up enough to guess that she was reminding him that they had only just met us and it was foolish to start an argument on so slight a basis with people you didn't know, in the middle of Peru.

He relaxed, and changed the subject.

They told us about Yerupaja. It was apparently a fearsome mountain, attempted only once or twice every year, with many casualties. There was a rumour (which they were trying to check) that a New Zealander had just died on his way down from the summit.

The South Africans were using this place, by the lake, as their base camp, waiting for the weather to stabilize (as it now seemed to have done) so that they could establish a second camp on the lower slopes. Though they were a party of some fifteen or so, which included wives and girlfriends, only four planned to make the final assault. They were nervous. That, added our bearded friend apologetically, was why they were a bit jumpy.

Everyone gathered curiously around to meet us. Except for an orange light on the tips of the summits above us, the sun had gone.

*

It did not take long to get back to our camp, but it was almost dark when we did. As we approached the site, we were startled by a party of men in combat jackets – some walking, some riding – who met us with torches, going the other way. We talked briefly. They were in a hurry: Peruvian soldiers, going for the body of the New Zealand climber. They confirmed that he had been killed after reaching the summit, solo, and trying to descend by a new route. A sudden avalanche had swept him off the side. His girlfriend (who had flown from New Zealand) and the consulate were waiting for the body in Lima.

Ever eager for gloomy auguries, Mick took this news with a sort of doleful glee. He had had a bad day. He was coughing, now, and, though the symptoms were still no more than those of a common cold, they were enough to convince him of what he already suspected. 'Death,' said his medical notes, 'can ensue rapidly, unless the victim makes a rapid descent to a lower altitude. Even a thousand feet or so may be sufficient.'

Mick had decided that he must return in the morning to Llamac. Ian offered to accompany him, but Mick said that Armando had called by, and offered a burro and two boys to accompany him. This would be enough, and we were to trouble ourselves no further on his account.

It may be that there are acts of heroism, scarcely noticed, whose courage surpasses even the acts of the saints, yet whose sole ambition is not to hold other people up or cause a fuss. Considering that Mick believed he might be dying, his decision was braver than anything the rest of us were capable of.

For our part, we would continue up through the mountains ahead. But where our planned route crossed a higher stretch of the river we had left at Llamac, we would turn and follow it back downstream to Llamac, to rejoin Mick.

Rather than take the upstream route which would have led eventually to other villages, and another way back to Lima, we would then go down from Llamac to Chiquian, returning to Lima the way we had come. As it might take us two or three days to reach Llamac by our highland route, Mick would wait for us there, recuperating.

This gave us much of the walk we had planned, including the most beautiful parts, but was a small defeat – or, as John put it, 'an adjustment to reality'. Another adjustment was that the three of us who were to go on agreed to take Armando and his other donkey as far as the 16,000-foot ridge over which our forward route took us, to carry the equipment. After that, going mostly downhill towards the river, we would make it alone.

We dined on trout again that night, with Fortunato and relations. Fortunato had seen the army posse too. 'They should leave the body on the mountain,' he complained. 'The gods will be cheated if the body is removed, and require another one. Does his family not have a photograph?'

Fortunato retired early, as usual. We regathered by the tents for some kerosene-flavoured cocoa. Mick busied himself preparing for bed. It was important, after all, to survive just this one last night at altitude.

One of the guide books said that an early sign of oxygen starvation was that parts of the body where the skin is semi-transparent – like lips or fingernails – show a much bluer tinge than usual. From time to time we would examine our fingernails, to check: but hands and nails got so dirty that this evening it was impossible to get any clear reading.

John speculated that (for men) there was another place to check. So we got out our torches and, amidst much unseemly chuckling (but modestly, from different tents) examined shades of blue. The colour was certainly very intense, but the problem was that nobody could quite remember what the *usual* colour was. We resolved to review this in Lima.

Hilarity was interrupted by a feeble cry for help, from Mick. Ian went over. Wild shrieks of amusement followed. 'Hey, Matt, John, come and look at Mick!' We zipped up our trousers and trooped over.

Torchlight revealed a sort of Egyptian mummy, or figure in a medieval brass-rubbing, face up, heavenward; arms stiffly down by its sides, as though standing to attention flat on its back.

Mick had put on all his underwear, including long-johns; both his pairs of trousers, three vests and two shirts; two pullovers and an anorak; and a matching waterproof top and over-trousers. On his head was a full balaclava, pulled up to below the nostrils and down over the eyes. Two bulges under the wool, on each side of his head, were rolls of toilet paper stuffed into his ears for protection. Up each nostril was a carefully rolled wedge of tissue, to prevent dripping. He had then tried to get into a binliner.

His immediate problem was that the whole outfit rendered him almost completely immobile, and he was unable to roll himself up in the rug that he had laid out, let alone insert the whole thing into the two sleeping-bags (one inside the other) that were waiting by his side.

We all helped. Mick, of course, could not speak properly through the balaclava; nor could he hear, through the toilet paper. He had forgotten to take one of his pills, and had lost the mobility to unscrew the bottle or get the pill under the balaclava and into his mouth. We helped. It was possibly the most elaborate do-it-yourself intensive care outfit that has ever been devised.

We left him, by now entirely strait-jacketed, the only sign of movement or life being his cheeks fluttering desperately in and out as he sucked his mentholyptus pastille. It was pitiful.

As I crept away in the dark towards my hut-bedroom, a plaintive cry – and much laughter – signalled that Mick's diarrhoea was playing up again, and he needed to undress.

Standing on the hillock outside Fortunato's hut for ten minutes, until the noises died away, I saw the moon, still hidden from us, strike the mountaintops. Its cold light caught the whole of one great icy face of Yerupaja, 21,000 feet high. It shone, a sort of luminous grey against the black sky, lighting our valley, too, with a pale secondary glow.

Where on that silver mountainside was the body of the man they were looking for? Strange constellations wheeled above him, too.

From far away, towards the base of the mountain, the roar of another avalanche swelled; and, suddenly, while the sound was still rising, I saw it: a thin white veil, hovering against a dark cliff on Yerupaja. It glittered for a moment in the moonlight, faded and was gone just as the roar reached its climax.

The cliff stood, black and unclothed, while the sound, unaccompanied by vision, roared on, and dimmed, and died too.

Chapter Ten

The Moon-
Invaders

With the dawn came Armando, on his way to trade with the South Africans who, he said, were New Zealanders. He informed us gravely of the dead climber – a South African, he said, whose wife and children were waiting for the body in Huaraz. According to Armando, an Israeli corpse was also being sought. And all this, he concluded, was one more reason why we must not proceed forward without him. Had we considered his offer?

Pleased to discover that we needed no convincing, he hurried on, promising to return in an hour with burro and boys for Mick and another burro for himself and us. A third donkey, a young female, would accompany our party, unladen. This beast was apparently coming along for the experience: she was a *novicia*, he said, and our climb – which was a difficult one and very high – would test her.

We agreed. Mick had recovered somewhat and told Armando that we charged for burro-training. It was a relief to leave Mick in good heart, joking with the two youngsters, the older of whom, Carlos, was barefoot. The younger looked no more than seven or eight.

'At what age does a boy start making this journey?' Mick asked Armando.

'As soon as he can walk.'

Fortunato had been good to us, and it was sad to say goodbye. Although poor, he did not haggle about money. '*Voluntario.*' Our last glimpse of his yard included Mamai (mother) whose bad back had taken a turn for the worse. The old kipper was lying in the sun on a heap of carrots, with chickens crawling over her, chewing a few of Mick's aspirins. The dogs barked and snapped at our heels.

At the head of the lake we passed the South Africans. One of the women had lost a gym shoe in the stream, and the entire party had fanned out along its length to search. A reward had been offered to the Indians, who were searching with great enthusiasm.

Another group of Indians was preparing food for the party, which

71

had purchased (from Armando) an entire sheep to eat. There was a clear master-servant relationship between the South Africans and their peasant staff which both seemed quite used to. You saw the townspeople from Lima and the coast treating the Indians in that way too, and – yes – the South Africans were right, those people were a different race from the peasants.

It is just that, to us, there were so many people of mixed race that the one shaded into the other and you fell into the lazy mental habit of seeing them all as Peruvians – some more Latin, perhaps, and some more Indian: but on a sliding scale with no division of a kind capable of causing pain. Besides, Peru was a left-of-centre democracy with no race laws on the statute book: and everybody knows that racial oppression is in Africa, not Latin America . . .

We left with a packet of pills for Mick's altitude sickness, and some diarrhoea tablets to supplement our own fast-disappearing stocks. According to the label, in Afrikaans, the drugs came from a government dispensary in Pretoria.

'*Totsiens!*' (Cheerio!) shouted the South Africans as we left, their guard now lowered.

'Cheerio – and thanks for the pills!' shouted John, who had spent a lifetime boycotting their oranges.

It had been a strange encounter in an isolated place. Neither side felt secure enough, here, to enter the hostilities that might have tempted them in more familiar surroundings. Both had a greater need for companionship. The mountaineers were excited and scared by the assault ahead. The others, some of them wives, knew there was a real chance they might not see the climbers again. Perhaps the atmosphere would be familiar to someone who knew the feeling of a military encampment before battle.

'Agh, these Indians!' came the fading sounds of conversation between two of the Afrikaans girls, as we walked away. 'They don't bother to skin the sheep properly – just like the blacks . . .' As we climbed above them we could see Mick's group – ant-like figures, now – heading down the short way to Llamac. They should be there by nightfall.

Armando irritated John all the way to the top by choosing him for a relentless interrogation about his family life, which we had to translate for him.

'Is he married?'
'He says are you married, John?'
'*Si.*'
'How old is his wife?'
'He wants to know how old Anne is, John.'
'*Veinte-y-nueve*' – John had learned the numbers – twenty-nine.

'Is she beautiful?'

'He wants to know whether Anne is beautiful, John.'

'*Si. Mucho.*'

'Blonde or dark?'

'How would you describe her hair?'

John replied that it was dark.

'Dark.'

'Never mind. You can't have everything in life.'

'What's he saying?' growled John.

'He says never mind.'

John looked puzzled. 'I like dark women.'

'Our friend likes dark women.'

Armando grinned. 'There are plenty in Chiquian.'

'He says there are plenty in Chiquian, John.'

'No thanks.'

Armando tried a new tack. 'How many children does he have?'

'He doesn't have any,' we replied.

'What are you saying about me now?'

'Nothing, John, just that you don't have any children.'

'Why, did he ask?'

'Yes – hold on, he's asking something else. *Qué*, Armando?'

'*Why* docs your friend have no children?'

'He's wondering why you and Anne don't have any children, John . . .'

'Tell him to mind his own business.'

'Our friend doesn't know why. They have tried.'

'What are you telling him?'

'To mind his own business.'

'Ah!' Armando grinned again. 'This happens also in Peru. Has he tried smearing eucalyptus oil on . . .'

'Are you sure you told him to mind his own business? Doesn't sound like that to me.'

'Yes, John. He's just getting a bit carried away. Why don't you drop behind a little? That should stop the questions.'

John did so, leaving us to absorb Armando's lecture on fertility alone.

At the top of the pass we shared some soup and rice with Armando, whose donkey (the novice donkey) unfortunately shat on John, while he was eating – possibly out of nervousness. Then we paid Armando off and bade him farewell.

'Remind your friend about the eucalyptus oil,' was Armando's parting shot. 'Tell him also that the women in Chiquian are very fruitful.'

The journey back to Llamac took two days. From where we left Armando, we descended very steeply, choosing our own path.

At first the country was unbelievably lonely. For a day we saw nobody, only glaciers and eagles. But as we came down by a swift-flowing stream, sheep and cattle began to appear. Eventually, some neat (but very primitive) round stone huts with straw roofs came into view.

These people saw far less of strangers than others we had encountered. Some ran back into their houses. None of the adults hailed us, but, round one bend of the stream, we came upon some children playing. A little girl, bolder than most, called, '*De qué pais?* (What country are you from?). This was the cry with which we had been greeted so many times by children that it was beginning to grate. It seemed to be their only question – apart from '*Caramelos?*' (Sweets?). And we were tired of saying '*Inglaterra*'. So, for a change, Ian called, '*La luna!*'

The little girl's face crumpled in an expression of absolute horror. She believed him. It was terrifying to her.

She and all the children ran headlong away from us, panic-stricken, towards the huts. In her flight, the little girl fell over and lay for an instant petrified in the grass, momentarily too frightened even to move.

For that instant, before she recovered herself and ran on, she almost certainly believed that she was about to be eaten by three men from the moon. We walked on.

When we reached the big river, the one that flowed down towards Llamac, we encountered many villages. Here they were more cosmopolitan and would run out asking for aspirins or skin cream (the two most sought-after medical items, it seemed) while their dogs did their best to take off our shins.

There was little point in dispensing aspirins, but one woman brought John her baby to show him a horribly dry skin rash on its cheeks. Did he have any skin cream? One of us had a small bottle, labelled 'Embassy Row Hotel, Washington DC'. We gave her that.

As the river flowed down, the valley became more fertile. Once, it broadened out into what was almost a mile-wide garden of brilliantly flowering bushes and trees, blue, orange, red, and acid-yellow. There was such abundance here, so many blossoms, birds and butterflies, combined with such wildness – savage mountains for a backdrop and the valley itself a thorny and untamed profusion – and such perfume in the air, that you wondered whether the Garden of Eden could have been more lovely, or more wild.

As it grew dark on the second day, we became convinced from our map that we were almost in Llamac. The valley had narrowed to a spectacular limestone gorge (as the map said it would) and our estimate of distance squared with the thought that we would emerge from it into Llamac.

We had asked some children how far to Llamac, but they had only replied, '*tarde*' (late). They thought in terms of time, not distance; and it seemed as though it were still a long way off. We ignored them, and hurried on, anxious to reach Nazario's before nightfall.

The gorge seemed to go on for ever, and the darkening sky and enclosing walls gave an urgency to our step. But the path was rocky and our rucksacks heavy. It was nearly dark when we saw the hurricane lamps of a settlement ahead, at the mouth of the gorge. Llamac at last!

It was not Llamac. It was a village called Pocpa five miles upstream. Another gorge lay between us and our destination. We stopped in the main square, dispirited, and contemplated staying here.

But there was something unpleasant about this place: an evil atmosphere. The huts seemed to breathe it, and the people looked at us askance. Time and again in South America, people would say to you, 'Don't go there. It's a bad place. Full of thieves.' And one thought, 'Oh come! A *place* cannot be good or bad. Perhaps in some places there are a few more thieves, in others a few less, than the average; but surely the mixture of good and bad stays pretty constant; most villages and towns are a balance between the two.'

But experience in Peru suggested otherwise. Villages and towns had very strong atmospheres. Some of them seemed to exude menace; and fellow travellers kept bringing back tales from personal experience which reinforced the fables one heard. There was something rotten about Pocpa and we decided to move on.

Our moonlight rush through the last gorge was positively headlong. Tripping over rocks and stones where the moon was in shadow, starting at every dark bush or donkey coming at us out of the moonlight, we felt unaccountably scared. It seemed an ideal place for highwaymen; and in this horse-borne society, childhood recollections of bandit stories came sneaking back.

The black walls of the gorge towered above us, and we stumbled forward, tired, jumpy and longing to see the lights of Llamac.

There were no lights, of course. We were almost among the houses before we realized that we had arrived; we were, in fact, on the main football field. We tottered with weary gratitude to Nazario's door.

A fully recovered Mick bounded out to greet us.

Chapter Eleven

A Night Out
in Llamac

Seeing Nazario and his relatives was like coming home. They brought us a drink of hot water with sugar in it, and Nazario confided that they had doubted even whether we would get beyond the lake. They had not expected Mick to return on his feet.

Had we heard about the New Zealanders? Apparently a New Zealander and his Israeli girlfriend had been killed on Yerupaja. His mother, who was South African, was waiting in Chiquian for the body.

It was a lively homecoming, with much exclaiming, many questions and a few tall stories. Rested and refreshed, we asked Nazario whether there was a bar in Llamac, and whether he would have a drink with us there.

'Yes,' he replied, rather hesitantly. 'There is a bar called La Venta. But are you sure? Are you sure I should come?' Obviously the high life was not something he was used to.

We had seen this village, first, as a high outpost – smaller and more remote than anywhere we had been before. Now it was different. Llamac was the big city, the king of all the little settlements and villages we had been passing through during our days in the mountains beyond. There, people spoke of Llamac as one might of Babylon or Kansas City. The timid and the infirm had never been here. There was even a bar.

So now it looked different – busy, prosperous, boasting the two-storey houses and tin roofs that were the envy of lesser villages. Here there was a water-borne sewage system – water coursing down gulleys in the centre of the main alleys. Here there were not just burros and mules, but horses tethered outside. Here there were transistor radios – though, unfortunately, a shortage of batteries – children singing, and pigs and ducks in the road.

It was late, for Llamac, by the time we reached the La Venta. It seemed to be shut. Nazario had come with us after much urging on our part, and much doubting, on his, whether he should. We guessed that he did not normally drink.

He knocked hesitantly at the wooden door, then rattled it violently when there was no response. The proprietor opened up, in a nightshirt. We would have apologized and left, but he was insistent, so in we went.

It was pitch dark. Our host lit two candles and fetched beer. Nazario did not know how to pour his, and spluttered violently after his first mouthful. We sat, talking, the candles guttering, and the proprietor gazing benignly on, delighted not so much by Ian's taking of a photograph as by the flash, which he had never seen before.

Mick told us about his journey down, with Carlos and his younger brother, Flavio – how Carlos had shinned up a tree to rob a dove's nest but come down empty-handed. 'Only one hatched. I left them. I will return in a few days when the young chicks are ready to eat. *Palomitas tiernas* (tender little chicks)!' – and how Carlos and his brother had quizzed him continuously about life over the seas, but in particular about how long people lived in Europe and America. This question seemed to fascinate them.

Nazario was becoming quite animated. A glass of beer was going rather to his head, and he kept shaking hands with each of us in turn.

'Do they have bandits in Europe?' he asked, apropos of nothing much.

'Not as many as Peru,' I replied.

'You have met them here?'

'Not this time, but three years ago.'

The others groaned. They knew what was coming.

'Tell me! Tell me!'

'Go on then, Matt. Tell him. I'll translate. *Again*. It's beyond your Spanish. The others can talk among themselves.' So, with Mick translating, I began.

We were three friends: Luisa (an Italian interpreter from Luxembourg), Francis and I.

A Social Democrat candidate for the European Parliament, Francis was taking a holiday before hitting the campaign trail in Hampshire. Once his inevitable defeat had taken place, he planned to write a book about European political parties. It was my first time in Peru, Luisa's first time camping, and Francis's first time high-altitude trekking.

The story begins as we came to the end of a long day's march in the mountains somewhere between Puno and Cuzco. Following the little Rio Tigre towards its source, high in the Andes, we had steadily gained altitude all day. We were hopelessly overloaded: tents, stoves, sleeping-bags ... perhaps it was because Francis wanted to make sure that Luisa (whom he rather liked) did not have to rough it too much.

Mobbed by swarms of Indian children, we had passed through a whole string of little riverside villages. It had been hot, and heavy going: but now as the air grew cool and thin, and the villages more scarce, cares lifted from our shoulders, and a pleasant weariness began to descend. Where should we camp that night?

Just before dusk we reached a rather poor Indian settlement, called (as I remember) Jajachaca. Its atmosphere was as strange as its name. Nobody came out from the mean huts to greet us, save three hideous old men, more than usually far gone on coca leaves, green remnants hanging from their teeth. They blocked our path and begged for money.

There was something threatening in the air, but we made nothing of it. 'The llamas look in better condition than their owners,' Francis chuckled. 'Probably llama-rustlers.' We gave them a few small coins, and hurried on.

Night was falling fast so, with the village now behind us and our path clinging to the edge of a high, steep gorge, we clambered down to the banks of the river, a hundred feet below. Here there was a little patch of grass. It felt safe, enclosed. The tents were soon pitched, and supper on the boil.

In the fading light Francis thought he saw a man halt for a while on the path above us, as though looking at us, and then move off. But we were not much disconcerted.

Luisa was tired by now, but quite thrilled with camping. Francis had offered to help her with her bedroll, in that 'Happy, darling?' way they do in the movies. We had pitched her tent for her, and she retired, full of relief that this was not the ordeal she had feared.

Francis and I stayed up a little, talking. After a lively argument on the financing of London Transport, he began a story about his last trip to Haiti, when one of the legion of prostitutes in Port au Prince discovered his name from his mischievous companions. Back behind the high walls of their hotel garden he had been entertaining a French girl he had just met to cocktails on the terrace, when over the parapet of the perimeter wall appeared dozens of bony hands, then dozens of soulful black faces. 'François! François!' called half the prostitutes of Hispaniola . . .

We laughed together, taken out of ourselves and, for a moment, miles from this strange gorge; then we lapsed into silence. The sound of the river seemed to grow.

Suddenly, there was a man's voice, shouting. It seemed to come from the dark path above us – high and hysterical and in no language we could understand.

I shouted back in Spanish: 'What do you want?' The response was immediate – and enraged. A scream of what sounded like abuse poured down from above.

'Come down,' Francis called, 'and talk to us.' Like all centre politicians, his instinctive preference was for dialogue.

For myself, I asked (as one always does): 'What would Mrs Thatcher do?' The answer was clear. 'Let's go for them with our penknives,' I said to Francis.

His response, again, was in character. 'No. Better find out how many of them there are, and whether they're armed. Keep them talking.' He peered up into the night. 'We're friends!' he shouted.

A great rock whistled past my ear, narrowly missing me, and thudded into Luisa's tent. She scrambled out, terrified. There was singing now, but a strange, wild sort of singing, and we were thoroughly unnerved. 'Better sing back,' said Francis. 'Sound confident.' And he launched into a tuneless rendering of 'John Brown's Body'. We had forgotten that in the Americas this is better known as 'The Battle Hymn of the Republic'. Whether or not the melody was recognizable, it provoked a hail of rocks and stones. Luisa began to cry.

There was something nightmarish about being trapped at the bottom of a gorge, your enemy above you and invisible in the dark. We crouched behind boulders and bushes, missiles raining down from the black mountain-face in front of us. But they were haphazardly aimed, for we were as invisible to the enemy as he was to us.

All my life I have been a little afraid of the dark. But now I saw that the moon was about to rise above the rock-shoulder in whose shadow we hid.

And the darkness was our friend. To find security in darkness must be an experience as old as mankind; but for me it was new, unfamiliar – and strangely exciting. Obviously we must keep away from the moonlight.

'Quickly,' I said. 'Let's get out. Let's fan out separately so we don't make an easy target. Take off your white anorak, Luisa, and follow me. Let's dodge them, get above them – meet again up there ...'

Luisa and I crept from bush to bush, zigzagging out of the light, up towards a stretch of path away from the shouting. Francis took a different course. We could not see him and dared not call. Reaching the path, I handed Luisa the penknife and our only torch. 'Run back to the village. Stay there or bring help. We'll try to stay within sight of the tents.' She hesitated, then ran.

All our money, travellers' cheques and passports were in those tents, now bathed in moonlight. It was silly, I thought, to run off at the first scent of danger, leaving our belongings to be ransacked. We still did not know what sort of a threat we faced. I must find out.

I was free now from worrying about Luisa. And we had the advantage of being able to size up our enemy from a position unknown to him. I began to enjoy myself. This was like a boys' adventure story! I scrambled a little above the path, then slid along the mountainside in the direction of the shouting until I reached a cockpit of huge boulders, perched just above the source of the shouting. I peered out from behind the boulders.

It was only one man! He was very short and wearing a light-coloured poncho. Standing with his back to me he was yelling and loosing off rocks in the general direction of the tents. From time to time he would sway weirdly in a sort of stationary dance, holding a stone in each hand and smashing them violently together, before hurling them at what he thought was us. He seemed to be in some sort of trance.

I could have surprised him by leaping on him from behind and above, but I was not that confident of my prowess: and Luisa had the knife. I contemplated the possibilities, chuckling: I had left unfinished in London a correspondence with Sir Edward Du Cann about my hopes of assembling an all-party civil liberties group. Now I felt rather careless of this man's civil liberties.

Abruptly, the man stopped his noise. To my dismay he loped off down the path in the direction of the village. That was where Luisa had gone. Should I follow him, or find Francis?

Francis called softly from behind a nearby bush, and we rediscovered each other. I told him what had happened; but before we could decide what to do next, Luisa returned.

She was sobbing. Even in the darkness we could see that she had been in some kind of a struggle. There was earth all over her face and clothes. She told us what had happened.

She had been locked out of every hut. The village had barred its doors, all the lights within had been extinguished and when she called, nobody answered. So she had set out on the path back to us. There she had met our enemy, coming the other way, though she had not recognized him until he was almost on her. He had grabbed her, knocked her down and dragged her along the path – for no obvious reason: she had the impression that he was drugged.

It was Luisa's religion which had saved her from whatever fate was otherwise in store. Instinctively, she remembered, she had started shouting intercessions to Jesus and the Virgin Mary. It was the cries of 'Maria' which had shaken the man and he had momentarily let go. Luisa escaped and he did not follow.

We returned to our tents. But we could not contemplate staying there now. What if he came back with reinforcements? Besides, the place just felt unsafe. So we chose the boulder-lookout I had used earlier, and started to install ourselves there. From here we would have the advantage of height over anyone who came along the path.

We had ferried Francis's and Luisa's belongings up to our new hideout, and I had returned alone to fetch my own, when I heard a whistle, and looked up at the path, now bathed in brilliant white moonlight. Six men were approaching from the direction of the village. So – he had done as we feared.

I left everything behind except money and passport and ran for cover into the undergrowth, snaking my way back up to the boulders before the men reached that section of the path. This they did, stopping directly above our campsite.

I had dived into a convenient bush, below the boulders. The men were now fifty odd yards along the path. I could see everything and hissed a commentary to Louisa and Francis, crouching behind the biggest rock with our belongings.

'There are six of them. They've spread out along the path . . .' There was an anxious pause. 'One of them's started throwing rocks . . . they're all throwing rocks . . .'

The men started shouting and whistling towards the tents.

'They think we're still there. They've stopped. They seem to be talking. They're . . . one of them is . . .'

It was at this point that the situation turned. Up until then, it had been frightening, nasty. We had been afraid – perhaps – of being beaten up, and we were certainly fearful of being robbed. But that had been about the extent of it.

But, as I watched the men set alight to the undergrowth along the path, systematically, in a wide sweep around our tents, it was suddenly clear that we might be murdered.

For people (like us) not accustomed to facing situations which encompass the possibility of death, the dawning of that thought is an odd sensation. Flat: not frightening, not sad: depressing, not scary at all. Even at the time, you feel conscious that you are not rising, emotionally, to the occasion.

Or are you? Perhaps the art of storytelling has led us to expect the wrong thing.

Storytellers must frame events like paintings. Nothing just 'happens' out of the blue. Key figures must be introduced beforehand: clues and pointers must be laid, the stage props identified. Your audience, in short, must be looking in the right direction before anything happens. Properly framed and hung, the canvas is now ready for viewing. That is what you are to look at – not the wall or the light switch.

Cast your mind back to a television film in which the cameraman himself has not been aware of the significance of what he was photographing. A crowd scene, for instance – filmed for 'background colour' – when a sudden crush, a balustrade giving way, has made the footage 'historic'. The components of the disaster are all there, but the incident, as it is has since come to be called, feels flat. Why is the action in the bottom right-hand corner of the frame? What has the ice-cream vendor in centre-frame got to do with it?

Witnesses to such evidence often use the word 'disbelief' to explain why they are not feeling what they suppose the situation requires. But it is not belief that we lack. We lack the time to sort out what it means and arrange our reactions in accordance with what we believe is proper. A good narrator can make these arrangements for us, in advance of the event; but life takes us by surprise, leaves us focussing on the wrong things and unprepared to rise emotionally to the occasion. That is why art is so much more satisfactory than life.

Compare those unwitting records with the subsequent – so triumphantly subsequent – 'documentaries', in which all that was later judged irrelevant has been conveniently removed, and the reactions which were later judged appropriate conveniently inserted.

Life is so shapeless. Stories well-told make the real thing seem a continuous disappointment and saddle each of us with a secret feeling of inadequacy. Reality never coheres. Its narrative is either incoherent or it is a lie.

Instinctively we ran, clambering under cover up the mountainside. Then we stopped, out of the moonlight, to regroup, panting for lack of oxygen. In the panic, Luisa had left her rucksack back at the boulders. 'Hide and wait,' I said, rashly. 'I'll get it.'

I clambered down, and reached our old hideout fast. The view from there was terrifying. Flames were leaping from the campsite, fires crackling up the hillside towards me. In their light I could see men running back and forth. There was whistling and shouting and a dog barking. What when they realized we had got out? Surely they would come for us?

I grabbed Luisa's things and scrambled back up the mountain, towards the others.

But where were they? All the bushes looked the same and I dared not shout … hissed whispers brought a response from underneath a large cactus bush, and the three of us huddled down together.

What were we to do?

It was no good going back to the path. One way led to the hostile village, the other led further up the blind valley – to who knows what? We did not even know from which side our attackers came, though they had approached from the village below. And there was certainly no returning to the camp itself.

So the only way was up the mountainside. Our maps were in my rucksack – burned, perhaps, by now. But I seemed to remember that high above us there was a ridge, and behind it a valley which led back down to the railway.

What I did not remember was that the ridge was 17,000 feet high. Somehow the top only looked another few hundred feet. So we just kept climbing.

By now the altitude was affecting us badly. In places the slope could only be tackled on all fours, and, sometimes, on our stomachs. Our handholds were sharp rocks and vicious cactuses with saw-like serrations down each side of every sword-shaped leaf. Our hands were soon badly cut.

We grew shorter and shorter of breath. I was exceptionally fit at the time, being in training for the London marathon, while Luisa was the weakest. Francis was basically strong, but no athlete. So, having no rucksack to carry myself, I took both his and Luisa's. This left him with the full-time job of helping Luisa, hauling her up slopes and steadying her in the more precipitous climbs.

We were spurred on by the sound of thin, distant whistles and shouts coming up from the valley below. Once we looked back and saw the opposite side of the valley lit by a great, red, flickering glow. With horror we realized that it was the reflection of our campsite – now hidden from us in the gorge. When she saw this and heard the whistling, Luisa started to cry again: this time with an edge of hysteria.

Francis was better at comforting her. I tried, too, but was alarmed to find that my real feeling was a desire to hit her. What a stupid response! As useless, in its way, as hers. I suppressed it. Soon Luisa recovered her nerve.

Up and up we scrambled, breathless to the point of nausea. We could not know it, but we had climbed nearly 3000 feet; and it was by now some hours since we had left our campsite.

But what was worse, there was no sign that we were nearing the top. The rocks were becoming steeper. Yet, if the shouts and whistles from the valley were more distant, it did not seem so. We were overwhelmed by the feeling – hard, now, to explain or understand – that our enemies were in hot pursuit. Every night bird's shriek sounded like a whistle close at hand. Every rock we dislodged became the clatter of assailants, scrambling up behind us.

Then, to our dismay, what appeared to be a cliff-face rose sheer before us. To left and right it was impossibly steep. Yet behind and beneath us lay the valley of bandits. Upwards was still the only way.

We caught our breath as Luisa screamed. She had momentarily lost her footing. Quickly she regained control, but the mindless rhythm of climbing was snapped, and we sank to our knees, cliffs towering above us. Nobody spoke.

Through the silence came a spine-tingling sound. Far, far below us, in the dark valley, someone was playing the Indian flute. It was a thin, clear, high song: the same strange melody, repeating and repeating. 'We know where you are,' it seemed to call. 'You cannot leave. We can wait.' Luisa started to cry again. She and Francis were exhausted.

'Stay here,' I said, 'with our stuff. Rest. I'll look for a way past this cliff.'

I was soon alone, out of sight, and climbing. With nothing to carry and no companions to depend on me, all my fear dropped away from me again – as it had while I shadowed the man in the poncho. Exhilarated and free, I climbed quickly, gaining height through the broken rocks, dogged only by the thought that it would be hard for the others to follow.

The worry grew: until I came face up to a rock wall which seemed simply impossible. I stared at it for a while, and sized up the precipices to each side. Then I tried a couple of footholds.

There was a way up. I reckoned on a good chance of doing it without falling, though a fall might have been fatal. But I knew that Luisa and Francis could never make it.

I looked at the problem from all sides, and followed each possible choice through to its range of possible outcomes. It was the last of these which proved decisive.

'Whatever should I say to Francis's mother?' I thought. That clinched it. That, in the end was the reason I went back.

Francis and Luisa were huddled together under a rock. 'We're pretty much trapped,' I said.

There seemed to be little choice. We would try to sleep until first light, then spy out the land and consider whether and how to return.

A bitter wind had got up. We were too tired, and the mountainside was too steep, for us to search for anywhere sheltered or level. But now that we had stopped moving, the cold bit deep: so I wedged myself against a cactus, wrapped in a llama-wool blanket decorated with pictures of llamas (a souvenir) and slept. The others couldn't. As I drifted away, the distant song of that flute pierced the night again: Francis and Louisa lay there waiting for the dawn, listening for an attack. None came.

Just before dawn, they woke me. In the pale light it was clear that the next outcrop beneath us afforded the best lookout, so we clambered down the mountain. What had taken hours to climb tumbled away in a fraction of the time. It was more of a controlled fall than a descent. Once, I led the other two over the edge of a small cliff, and the three of us landed, arms and legs flailing, in some thorn-scrub at its feet. Seconds later our luggage landed on top of us, but nobody was hurt – though Francis had ripped the back of his trousers in a rather final way. Perched more than a thousand feet above our campsite, we awaited the sunrise.

Agonizingly slowly, the light crept over the white ridge of the mountains. The sky was clear, the sun orange. In its light we could see right

ABOVE *Kiosk in Huaraz.*

LEFT *Ian with Lis and grandmother.*

BELOW *Restaurant in Huaraz.*

TOP 'Rico es burrico'.
ABOVE *Climbing to Jahuacocha*.
RIGHT *Apolonia's youngest daughter*.

TOP *Fortunato's house.*

ABOVE *Nazario's shop and family, with Ian.*

RIGHT *'La Venta' Bar.*

Captain Gloria.

Christian.

A man of Cuzco.

TOP *Second class.* ABOVE *The Train to Cuzco.*

Peruvian beds are too short for Mick.

ABOVE *Tio*.
RIGHT '*The Executive*'.
BELOW *Caesar Augustus*.
BELOW RIGHT *After the hemlock.*

TOP *Down into the Amazon basin.*

ABOVE *The lower horizontal on the right-hand vertical nearly killed Luceo.*

LEFT *Unloading beer before towing.*

ABOVE *Marcelo approaching the middle distance, and Brazil.*

RIGHT *Gold-washing barge on the Madre de Dios river.*

BELOW *Puerto Maldonado – journey's end. From left to right: Ian, Mick and John. Fanny was not at home.*

down to the river we had left so many hours before. Our campsite was still smouldering, and all around it the hillsides were blackened. But the tents themselves did not seem to have been burned. All was still. There was no sign of the bandits: not from this distance, at any rate.

Had they fled with the dawn? Or were they hiding, waiting for us?

It is remarkable how confidence returns with daylight. Many arguments, all leading to the conclusion that we were in no real danger – arguments which were as true in the dark as they were in the light – now gathered persuasive force.

Higher up the valley we could see smoke curling from the chimneys of huts. A small boy, with a little dog running beside him, was scampering from one settlement to another, his mother calling him back. Cocks were crowing, and there was music – that same flute perhaps? – coming from somewhere. This was not a world, surely, in which people were set upon?

I agreed to go down alone to the tents for a reconnaissance. The others would follow me as far as the last descent, then wait, watching me from cover. I took the penknife!

It was difficult descending into that gorge. When I reached the campsite, ashes still fresh, I had to stop for a moment to summon the courage to search it. What if they were concealed inside one of the tents? The rushing of the river nearby made it worse for it deprived me of one of the senses by which I might be alerted to movement. And if Francis were to shout a warning, would I even hear?

I tried to keep watch in all directions while searching. But throwing back the tentflaps and entering each was heart-stopping.

There was nobody there.

I had not realized that the tents were fireproofed, but they must have been, for though cinders had burned holes in the fabric they were otherwise intact. But all our belongings had gone – all, that is, that we had not taken in our flight. So we still had our money and documents and two rucksacks: but my rucksack was gone, with all it contained. I smiled at the irony of losing my heaviest possession, a textbook I was studying: *Cases on Civil Liberties*. I hope the bandits found it useful. At that moment I would gladly have razed their little huts to the ground without due process of law.

I looked up to the skyline to gesture the others down. As I did so, I caught sight of the silhouetted figure of an old woman, skirts gathered, hobbling away over the hill. The others saw her too.

Anxiously, we packed the tents. There was nothing for it but to return the way we had come. We could not avoid passing the village which had so unnerved us, and shut Luisa out. I would go through the village first, unladen, ready to spring. The others would keep some way behind me, observing.

People withdrew into their houses as I passed, but nobody challenged me, nobody acknowledged me, nobody spoke. Eyes were averted. Two snowy-white llamas, shampooed and back-combed with scarlet tassels in their ears, raised their heads and stared at me with an ill grace as I passed. I signalled to the others that all was well but they could see that and had already started to catch me up.

Before they did, an old woman, looking like one of the witches in *Macbeth*, stepped out of the shadows and hailed Francis in broken Spanish.

'How are you today?' she cackled. Francis and Luisa answered that they were tired and hungry and that the night had not been good. They thought it best to confine themselves to generalities.

'Oh dear,' she smiled. 'What a pity! Tell me, which side of the mountain did you go up? People were wondering ...' They made no reply, and quickened their step. She did not follow, but called out after them: 'The night is over. Now you are safe. Goodbye!'

When we reached the railway I slept, very, very heavily.

Nazario was wide-eyed at this story. The characters and events were as far from his own experience as they had been, then, from mine. The place – down in the south of Peru – might as well have been the South Pole for all that he knew of it. The people there were not his people. He shook hands with me – and then again with all the others, for good measure. We drank another beer.

Out of the blue, Nazario asked Mick: 'How old was your grandfather?'

'Ninety, when he died.'

'*Ninety*? Do people live so long?'

'Often longer, in England.'

'How long?'

'A hundred, even, some of them'

There was an incredulous pause. 'Here, many people die young, but old people when they are about sixty, usually. That is old for us.' Another pause. 'Do you think *I* would live to be ninety, if I came with you to England?'

As we were preparing to leave there was a whinnying, a barking of dogs, and a clatter of hoofs outside. A horse must be approaching at speed.

Very great speed, in fact, for the next thing that happened was the appearance of the front end of the horse through the open door of our bar. It had been going too fast to stop. The animal looked – startled – at us, and reversed out, saving its rider from certain decapitation.

We could see him, now, outside. He was trying to get off the horse. When he had accomplished this, and tried to walk into the bar, it became apparent that he was too drunk to stand. The barman went out and helped him in. Nazario looked embarrassed as the newcomer ordered four bottles of beer, ignoring our presence completely. He hardly seemed aware we were there.

This was an Indian of about thirty-five, dressed not unlike a cowboy, with a wide leather hat. It seemed from what he told the others that he had just ridden up from Chiquian – in four hours! He had been drinking in Chiquian and had stopped for more alcohol in one of the villages. The last part of the journey – the precipitous part, up along the sides of the valley – had been completed almost entirely in the dark. But his horse knew the way.

He was a swashbuckling customer and cut quite a dash, even in this condition. Nazario and the barman were impressed by his achievement; but it seemed to us that his horse was the real hero. She waited, untethered, outside for him. No doubt she knew the way home well enough: the only question was whether her master would be able to get back up into the saddle.

We did not stay to find out. The long walk back to Chiquian awaited us next morning.

Passing the village school ('Our Lady of Guadalupe') in the dark on the way home, I stopped, looking back towards the hills from which we had come down. There was no moon, this time, only the Southern Cross sparkling at the horizon, and the sound of the barman trying to persuade the drunken cavalier to leave.

. . . Free. Rather deny the light of the sun, than deny that . . .

Going down was an easier business than coming up. Nazario had some business to do in Chiquian (or so he said) and was to accompany us with a donkey. Carlos had wanted to come too but was sent back to his father in Jahuacocha.

'They like to go,' Apolonia told us, 'to see the cars.'

We left a present for her: an empty plastic bottle which had once contained mineral water in Spain. It was of simple design, but fluted down the sides, and all the family had admired it ever since we arrived. It had been noticed approvingly by every Indian who had spotted it. There must have been something in the design which struck a chord with Indian taste. The family were delighted, and carried it off, rejoicing.

We too were a cheerful party. Mick was by now pretty much recovered and John had simply got used to having diarrhoea all the time. Ian's stomach was bad, but he did not talk much about it, and nothing seemed to dent his spirits.

Led by Ian, our party was escorted out of Llamac by most of the village children. He had become the Pied Piper of Llamac. He had taught the children to blow on blades of grass in cupped hands and this had become the latest craze among them. A squealing like that of a hundred bagpipes piped us out of town.

People from the village had given Nazario letters and messages crudely written on scraps of paper to take to Chiquian, some of them for onward transmission to Huaraz by the same informal method – simply handing on to an intending passenger. One girl who could not write gave him the message verbally: it was to be passed on to someone else who would in turn pass it on, verbally, to someone going to Lima.

As we left, a little girl (her mother holding her back) strained to join the throng. She had been one of Ian's tiny followers and he had taught her a word or two: but her l's and r's were muddled.

'Glingo!' she shouted as we passed: 'Glingo, Glingo.' Then, as this seemed to have no effect on us: *'Engrish* Glingo!'

Chapter Twelve

The Plymouth
Fury

'For fuck's sake, John. Forget the fucking bananas. *Quick! Get on!* We're *going!*'

Our lorry, *El Aguila* (Eagle), had paused at a roadside stop, but, even as we shouted, was being eased into gear. John was at a fruit stall, having a misunderstanding with a peasant about the price of bananas. Just in time he clambered up the side: 'I'm *sure* she said fifteen *intis* for the whole bunch, not each banana. I mean compare the price with those ones we had in Lima ...' but his voice was lost in the wind as we gathered speed.

And the Eagle would not have waited. For this was no ordinary truck. Passengers meant nothing to its madcap driver and his mate.

We had made it easily back from Llamac to Chiquian on foot. At Uncle Sam's in Chiquian, Nazario had got slightly maudlin on two glasses of wine with us, and said an almost tearful goodbye, begging us – and all our friends and relations – to come to Llamac again. We wrote him out a letter, recommending him to other tourists. Nazario asked us to read it translated into Spanish for him, which Mick did – tactfully rendering 'basic' as 'homely'.

A truck going back to Huaraz had taken us as far as the Lima road. There we had joined a crowd of Indians heading, like us, down to the coast.

We were hard-bitten travellers by now – quicker and more ruth-less even than some of the locals. So when a huge petrol tanker pulled in briefly, Ian had shinned up the side and the rest of us had tossed our bags up to him before the driver's mate could tell us what we already knew – that this truck did not take passengers. Seeing that we were firmly installed, he shrugged his shoulders and let it rest.

He didn't much care. Barranca was the name of the place he said they were going to. That was a straight run down from the mountains to the Pacific: half a day from here. At Barranca the road meets the coastal highway, and it would be easy to find transport from there to Lima – perhaps on the following day.

Petrol tankers are not equipped for carrying humans on top. That was why the driver was trying to stop passengers boarding. But only half-heartedly – and it did not prevent his collecting money from us later. After all, we were a *fait accompli*. We found ourselves in the company of other *faits accomplis* – people who had boarded while backs were turned: most of them boys, nimble enough to do it.

Atop the massive cylindrical fuel-storage tank itself was a small, flat metal platform, surrounded by a shallow guard rail. If you held on you were reasonably secure. Or so we thought for the first five minutes of our journey, which was across the flat plateau.

Then the Eagle reached the rim of the mountains. We were running down, empty, to the coast; the driver knew the road; and he was in a hurry.

None of us had realized that a petrol tanker could go so fast. That it could weave and dive and corner and brake like a Formula Four racing car.

Looking back on it, we know that the road from Conococha to Barranca drops more than 12,000 feet, snaking in an uninterrupted series of hairpin bends down a great valley from the high Andes to the sea. Indeed, we had done the same trip, coming up – but in the dark, and much, much more slowly. We know that this time the journey was accomplished at an average speed of forty miles per hour, which left even impassive Indian peasants gasping. And we know that the road was littered with the burned-out hulks of trucks whose drivers had misjudged the corners.

So perhaps we should have been scared. But looking back, the feeling was simply of exhilaration. The driver knew what he was doing and the truck was new. Our job was just to hold on – manning our metal turret – amazed, as three geographical regions and four distinct climatic zones flashed by in the space of an afternoon.

So much movement, yet it comes back – freeze-frame again – in still pictures: breezy, scary moments, each complete. A biting wind at first; then later a hot wind, as the altitude dropped. Vicious bends, tyres squealing. Blaring horns as we rounded blind corners. Two string bags of live chickens, broken free from their moorings, skidding crazily from one side of the platform to the other – chickens staring from their string prison, stiff with fear – until a violent roll had one basket over the side of the tanker and tumbling in the wind . . .

An old woman standing by the roadside, motionless, gazing impassively into thin air and holding two sheep on a piece of twine. An eagle hovering on a hot current above, immobilized like a butterfly on a pin. A slowly passing backdrop of crags and ridges so desolate that even the cactuses were dying. A foreground hurtling by in a blur of roadside rock and dust, punctuated by sudden flashes of human colour: acid-bright. Racks of oranges and limes in straw stalls, tumbledown huts of painted tin, squashed dogs and wrecked cars ...

It all happened so fast. Before we knew it, the valley had flattened out. Irrigated plantations of sugar cane waved, livid green in the hot desert wind, and we could smell the sea.

Like those toy aeroplanes whose propellers are wound up with pains-taking care on a rubber band, we had climbed painfully into and through those mountains over many days: one move, one stage, at a time. Like the toy plane's short flight – a sudden whirr, a rush of movement, and it is over – the mountains were unravelling before our eyes, all in a heady rush down to the Pacific.

As passengers prepared to disembark, one clumsy youth stood slam on the middle of the second string bag of chickens – the one that had not gone overboard.

Barranca was vile: a concrete mayhem. Pimps and prostitutes mingled in the filthy streets; unpainted cement-block houses of haphazard con-struction jostled with shacks and shanties and fiercely painted bars. A forest of television aerials and rusted reinforcing rods poked from unfinished walls into the sky. A thin grey mist and an all-pervading smell of fishmeal hung in the air, shrouding the town.

And there were so many motors! Nazario's youngest brother, little Adolfo, had told us that he loved to go to Chiquian, 'to see the *carros*'. There were half a dozen *carros* in Chiquian. Here Adolfo would have been in paradise. Sometimes you saw a donkey, broken down and gasping in the traffic fumes, whipped on by its master. Our burros up at Jahuacocha would have wept to see the state to which their cousins on the coast were reduced: the last remnants of a donkey-borne society.

Adjusting gradually to life in the Andes, you do not realize how attuned and sensitive you have become to the understated sights and sounds of rural life. Soft noises, dim lights and the very gentle indications of human activity are stimuli to which eyes and ears become keenly sensitized in the mountains. To hit the streets of Barranca, now, was like tearing an adhesive plaster from the skin. It hurt. Such noise! Such movement! Such smells!

And hit the streets we literally did, for the tanker was in no mood to wait. The driver's mate had yelled instructions to us to flatten ourselves along the top of the tank just before we reached the town (perhaps because he was not supposed to carry passengers), so we had entered like infantry in an occupation force, hidden atop our tank, waiting to spring down. All we could see was roofs.

'Get off! Get off! Go!' shouted the driver, as his truck paused, throbbing, by the roadside: and everyone dived for the road.

The first thing to be seen was a chicken in the remaining two of its original three dimensions, spread-eagled on the tarmac. Almost the next thing was a pimp who had scented foreigners and hustled in for the kill.

Big girls? No? *Very* big girls, then? No? *Little* girls, perhaps? No? A confiding smile crept over his face. Of course: little *boys* – yes, he had those too. '*Palomitas tiernas*,' he said lovingly – 'tender little chicks'.

When the pimp found us uninterested even in this delicacy, he feigned astonishment. What in heaven's name was it that we did want?

'A bus to Lima,' replied Mick. Like all of us, he had silently decided that, though late in the afternoon, it was worth trying to get out of this place.

The pimp looked only momentarily perplexed. He switched mental directories, from 'Sex' to 'Transport'. It did not take long.

'Follow please.' So we followed – weaving through a crowded market and dodging cars. Still deafened by the noise and dazzled by the commerce, we had no idea where he was taking us.

He stopped, breathless, beside a decrepit American limousine: a black and white Plymouth Fury of some twenty-five years' vintage, with smooth tyres and rotting side panels.

'Bus,' he said. 'To Lima.'

The car's driver emerged: a short, squat, bald, black man in dark glasses. Something changed hands between the pimp and the driver.

'No, not a taxi. We want a *bus*,' Mick said.

'This is a bus.'

'No. This is a taxi. This is a car.'

'No doubt. It is also a bus. Cheap like a bus.'

'How much?'

'Four hundred *intis*.'

Four hundred *intis* was incredibly cheap. For something like a ninety-mile journey, this was only a few dollars more than the bus would have cost. We accepted and made to climb in. But there were already three passengers on board. With us, that would make seven. Mick protested to the driver, who looked like Papa Doc Duvalier.

'What do you expect, for four hundred *intis*?' he chuckled. 'Anyway,' he added – eyeing our unwashed faces and dusty clothes – 'my other passengers forgive.'

Within minutes, the squalor of Barranca was receding into the fishy fog behind us, and we were speeding down the Pacific coast.

By early evening we had reached Lima. It was probably the fastest time ever recorded from Barranca to the capital. For much of the journey John just blocked his eyes, while Mick struggled not to be sick. Recollection is only of a blood-red sun, setting on a desert shore which more resembled a hundred-mile municipal refuse tip. Dunes, burned-out cars and dead dogs. This was a magnificently wrecked environment.

The road hugged the cliffs which crumble into the Pacific – rising even higher and more breathtaking as you go south. At their feet, where huge breakers eat at the coastline, the carcasses of buses, trucks and many, many taxis could be discerned. Along the highway an assortment of still-mobile wrecks – some with doors and windows, some without, some with lights, some with none – raced each other to perdition. By the roadside were little shrines: bunches of flowers – memorials to the victims of road accidents – scattered by the wind of passing traffic. It was a scene of grotesque desolation.

Along this nightmarish racetrack plunged our Plymouth Fury, shock-absorbers shot to pieces, lunging and heaving from pot-hole to pot-hole, slaloming around stationary vehicles, donkeys, peasants and other avoidables, overtaking on blind corners high above the ocean, and honking wildly at everything that moved. Only the Virgin of Carmen, whose doll-like image in red and gold was strapped to the Fury's dashboard, remained unperturbed.

Perhaps it was she who saved us from the ancient bus, stuffed to bursting with passengers, which loomed suddenly out of the night on the wrong side of the road, entirely without headlights, foglights, sidelights – or anything, except the interior reading lights inside the wagon itself, which were on and dimly working. Papa Doc avoided it at the very last moment. He cursed at the bus, crossed himself to the Virgin of Carmen, and opened his second packet of cigarettes. Turning to look behind, Ian noticed that the bus had no tail-lights either.

Does it need to be said that through gathering night, swirling dust, and nicotine-smeared windscreen, Papa Doc never once removed his sunglasses?

As we hit the traffic streaming out of Lima, an old man walked straight out into the road in front of us. All seven passengers saw him at once and screamed. An instant later, Papa Doc saw him. He threw the Fury sideways. The old man dived headlong for the kerb, striking it flat on his face. We missed him. This time, we all crossed ourselves to Maria Carmen.

Who could forget such a ride? They ought to call it 'The Devil's Corniche'.

Lima was in the grip of one of its transport strikes and everyone was looking for a taxi. This gave an unusual edge to our passage through the city centre as, every time we stopped to yield to other traffic, pedestrian taxi-seekers would charge at us from the kerb and try to get our doors open, to board. With seven of us (plus driver) already within, this was quite a challenge, and Papa Doc was visibly impressed at the initiative shown by the Limans. He cursed them good-humouredly and warned us to lock the doors and wind up the windows – though we were not far from our hotel.

Before we reached it, an enterprising nun managed to wrench a door open and throw herself on to John's lap. 'Where are you going?' she asked our driver.

'Barranca, little mother,' he chuckled, pulling away. 'And you?' She seized the chance offered by the next red traffic light, and leaped out again.

The next set of traffic-lights was broken, replaced by a policeman in an antiquated uniform. He did not appear to be moving, waving or directing with any discernible gesture. Yet Papa Doc waited patiently, then moved forward again, in concert with the other traffic – without any prompting that we could see.

'How did you know to move, maestro?' asked Mick.

'The policeman's eyes. He looked at us. That is the sign.'

How far away Llamac seemed, now; and how far Chiquian, which we had only left this morning. Nazario – his friendly, open smile – Elias and Apolonia, little Adolfo … Another world.

As we stood on the kerb outside our hotel, waving off Papa Doc and his remaining three passengers and dreaming of hot showers, four silent thank-you's for our deliverance were offered up to the Virgin of Carmen.

And what, says Dr Johnson, is gratitude but the secret hope of future favours? We were to need them, soon.

Chapter Thirteen

... It Isn't
Working

Outside the darkened plate-glass windows of Aero-Peru's head office in central Lima crouched an old mad woman offering for sale in her outstretched palm a piece of her own excrement. She must have been turned out of a mental home.

Inside at the ticket desk was a señorita with all the well-groomed authority of a female newscaster, and all the poise of a princess.

How could such grace and composure pick its way through such squalor every morning without seeming to be touched by it? You never saw such delicacy in an English girl: yet this place, so different from England – a fractured, violent place – could contain something quite flawless and inviolate.

'It is best for you to buy your tickets to Cochabamba immediately,' she said. 'Tomorrow, all ticket prices will rise by 40 per cent.'

We had gone in simply to enquire. So far, covering ground had taken longer than we had planned. Now, we felt like finding a plane to take us further afield than we could reach on another bus from Lima. We could discover more of South America returning overland from wherever we reached by air. It was like throwing a stick for an energetic dog to fetch – as far as time and resources would allow.

Cochabamba, in Bolivia, was the furthest place to which we felt confident of flinging ourselves. That would leave us time to meander by bus and train back to Lima before our flight home. And if what the señorita said was true – well, that made up our minds for us. Best to get the tickets right away. We bought them and walked out.

The mad woman had gone, to be replaced (one block further down) by a retarded boy trying to sell an empty plastic bag. Later, a grand-mother with her tiny grand-daughter in tow tried to sell Ian a single piece of unwrapped chewing gum: 'Special price. Damaged. No paper.'

Mick bought a new cap from a hat stall. His first one had flown off, with the string bag of chickens, on the petrol tanker ride. The woman in charge of the stall had gained his attention by tugging feebly at his sleeve as he passed. She whined: 'Buy something from me, señor, buy something.' When he showed interest, the whines intensified: 'Very good cloth, señor, very pretty colour. The señora will like it.' She was spiritless, irritating, utterly unpersuasive. There was nothing cheerful in her manner: no confidence, no aggression, no sign that she took pleasure or interest in commerce. Just a whine, a pity-me tug-of-the-sleeve.

Mick had no stomach to haggle. He hated Lima, and his diarrhoea was no better for leaving the mountains. So he paid her the asking price for her cap. This must have been at least twice what she expected to receive, and probably doubled her takings for the afternoon. Yet she took his nodded assent with not so much as a smile. Without emotion of any sort, she accepted the money and handed him the cap.

If he had turned her down, spat at her wares and walked off, she would have accepted this with the same flat equanimity: with no more expressed sorrow than she could express pleasure at his purchase. As to what she was experiencing within – who knows? Her breed peoples the street markets in Peru. Full-time, lifetime traders, with – to all outward appearance – no scintilla of interest in trading.

Next to her stand was a magazine barrow, selling what seemed to be stock selected variously from a pornography stall and an English dentist's waiting room. Prominently displayed among American farming journals, old issues of the *Reader's Digest*, and Spanish girlie magazines adorned with pictures of women's bottoms, was an almost new publication: *Cat-Facts. The Magazine for Responsible Cat Owners. Issue No. 17.*

We took a taxi back to our old Miraflores hotel. It was a veteran VW beetle with no bonnet and no mudguards at the front. The wheels stuck out, unsheathed, like the wheels on a Grand Prix racing car. It lacked, too, the one thing that had always seemed to work on other Peruvian cars: the hooter. For this, the driver compensated by slamming his fist violently against the battered outside of the driver's door, producing a terrible metallic clank that achieved – by its novelty – an effect on pedestrians equal to what any ordinary hooter could do.

The VW's speedometer was afflicted in a way none of us had ever seen before. Usually, speedos carry on working until they begin to waver erratically and finally stop altogether. But the needle on this one started to revolve, like the second hand of a clock, as the car began to roll forward. Gaining speed, the speedo-needle, too, revolved ever more wildly. At 50 k.p.h. it was spinning as fast as an aircraft's propeller – just a blur.

The taxi left us at a smart restaurant, close to the hotel. Appetites returned with a vengeance, and half-a-dozen avocados stuffed with egg and potato, some garishly coloured pork sausages and a number of chickens were consumed: for a price which John calculated would have bought an entire donkey, or three pigs, in Llamac.

Alone among us, Ian still had enough appetite for a sweet course. He chose a sort of violet jelly-like substance, garnished with strawberries, heavily involved with a mango, and penetrated by a whole banana. It was called *Una Fantasia de Mango*. We watched him eat it with prophecies ranging from stomach cramps to dysentery. There was much hilarity.

The people at the table next to us had left their copy of the daily newspaper. Mick flicked idly through its pages. A full-page advertisement caught his eye. It had been placed there by the Peruvian equivalent of the Confederation of British Industry. Vested interests are inclined to overstate their case but this was a cry from the heart. It is reproduced here, loosely translated.

MR PRESIDENT:
'*It isn't working*,' you said in Paita (29.6.88). And you had every right to say so.
It isn't working, with this big a public-sector deficit.
It isn't working, when nationalized industries record losses with monotonous regularity: adding to the deficit.
It isn't working with inflation bordering on 400 per cent.
It isn't working when prices are controlled but raw materials and dollars keep getting dearer and scarcer.
It isn't working when credit is denied and diverted to the public sector.
It isn't working without liquidity.
It isn't working with inflation which makes balance sheets and profits ever more unreal.
It isn't working when you lose more of your birthright every day, to pay taxes on profits which are meaningless except to accountants.
It isn't working with myriad obstacles to investment.
It isn't working with dollars which cost 33 *intis* for some, 125 for others, and 176 for every other Peruvian.
It isn't working with constant uncertainty and new shocks around every corner.
It isn't working, with no guarantee of private ownership.
It isn't working, with no guarantee of life itself.
As you said yourself in Paita: '*Where are we going, with a country like this?*'

Later that night, as if to rub in the Confederation's message, there was a minor earthquake. No serious damage was reported.

But, by then, Ian was too sick to notice. It was at first funny (considering his extravagances with the Mango Fantasy) when, back at the hotel, he began to experience a combination of every ill which can affect the human digestion. His groans punctuated the night.

He was rather worse by dawn, and amusement changed to concern – even sympathy. But it seemed best to carry on with our plans to fly that afternoon. There was no reason to think he would recover faster in Lima than anywhere else; and we cajoled him into our taxi to the airport, though by now he was having difficulty in walking.

Mick – who one might have guessed would react with bad grace to a comrade's success in being iller than him – proved, in fact, to be sympathetic and practical: a sort of male nurse, full of concern and only *slightly* too interested in the medical details. We helped Ian from the taxi to the airport check-in desk.

Progress was delayed by scores of soldiers with sub-machine-guns, poking at baggage and passengers and anything else which had managed to run the gauntlet of the concourse entrance procedure. A large bomb had been defused near a check-in desk the previous day. It was thought to have been placed there by the Shining Path terrorists, and followed a recent success with an exploding child in a hotel foyer.

Ian could only sigh when a soldier asked him what was wrong. By now he was barely conscious of what was going on. Perhaps they thought he too was stuffed with dynamite, but official hearts softened when it became clear that was about to be sick. John got him into a lavatory just before it was too late. At that stage, being sick in public still bothered us.

We joined the flight queue. It was becoming a race against time. We had the feeling that if only we could get Ian into the air, then at La Paz, where we had to change planes, or in Cochabamba, we could get him comfortably into a hotel bed. There was an irrational urge to get him, and us, out of Lima.

But he was visibly weakening. He could not now walk without support, and appeared to be delirious. Even in this state he remained irresistible to Latin women who were drawn to what (in a more cheerful state) he would have called his Viking good looks. A number cooed sympathetically as we dragged him past, and one came over to see if she could help the fallen warrior. Poor Ian. He was quite unable to respond.

Then came another set-back. Twenty minutes of confusion as to which queue we should join for the flight we wanted caused a series of forced marches from one end of the concourse to the other. This further weakened Ian, who no longer had the least idea what was happening. And when at last we found the right queue, a two-hour delay to our flight was announced. Ian was sick again. 'That was the banana,' said Mick. John thought it was the jelly.

Then Ian collapsed.

The word 'collapse' is used so loosely these days that to be confined to bed with flu can be called a collapse; and to feel so weak that one has to lie down is certainly to collapse. But Ian *really* collapsed.

He had long lost the ability to walk unaided. More recently, he had lost the ability to walk at all. Now we had sat him on the floor with his back supported by a wall.

Suddenly – surprisingly suddenly – all the tension left his muscles, and he crumpled like a string-puppet whose string has been sheared. His back wouldn't stay straight, his head lolled, and his eyes began to roll. It was frightening. One had the odd and pointless instinct to make him sit up: to arrange him vertically against the wall and stop his head from flopping, and then to sit there patting him, as though that would make him all right.

Whatever would his mother think? What if he died? All the jokes about the jelly suddenly seemed in horribly bad taste. Mick ran to find a nurse.

It took a long time, but eventually professional help arrived. In fact if you have to collapse in Lima, the airport is probably the best place to do it. A wheelchair was brought, and three nurses fought among themselves as to which should hold and tend him on his journey to the nearby Anglo-American hospital.

It was clear that we could not get Ian on to a plane in this condition. We all, simultaneously, volunteered to stay. Mick sounded the most genuine. He pointed out that he could get a new passport at the same time. He and Ian would rejoin us in Cochabamba, or La Paz, depending on how long it took for him to recover. We would ring Mick at the hotel, every night.

John and I waved goodbye to a bizarre medical procession: Mick, in his climbing boots and new blue cap which, in all the tension, he had forgotten to take off; Ian, dramatically slumped in a wheelchair, now unconscious; and three nurses, flapping and wheeling round him like white-coated vulturettes.

One remembered Ian's goofy smile, and his susceptibility to pretty girls, and thought how he would laugh at the opportunities he was missing – and thought of the violet jelly, and all our jokes on the previous night. We were scared.

Chapter Fourteen

Eating Out
in Bolivia

'It's acute stomach-poisoning. They've cleaned him out and kept him in overnight. He's still pumped so full of drugs he doesn't know where he is. He's going to be OK. A few days, I think – oh – I had to bribe the ambulance-driver ...' Click – brrr ...

'Sod it! Cut off!'

Still, it was good news. An airport-stop had given us the chance to ring through.

We flew on to Cochabamba, Bolivia, with lighter hearts.

Depositing ourselves, as we now did, on the other side of the Andes gave us the chance to see something of Bolivia.

Here in Cochabamba was where our return journey started. We had half of Bolivia to cross now to reach our half-way staging post: Cuzco, the ancient Inca capital, in Peru.

If there was time, we planned one subsidiary hop, by plane, to Arequipa (also in Peru) and back. And if there was *still* time we thought we might fly from Cuzco down into the jungle (and back).

Our goal was to reach Cuzco. And the road to Cuzco led us first to the highest capital city in the world – the capital of Bolivia, La Paz.

Cochabamba railway station stands drawing up her skirts from a sea of wet cardboard known as the Indian market. Around her steps peasant women jostle for space among piles of blankets, flowers and fly-blown meat. Her colonnades – souvenirs of another age – confront this mayhem with a weary dignity.

A brass plaque proclaims, 'THE PACIFIC IS OURS AND WHAT WAS OURS WILL BE OURS AGAIN' – recalling the sea coast Bolivia lost in wars with Chile whose wounds were still fresh when the station was built. The country's fate seems to have been to contract over time on all sides, as successive disastrous territorial wars with almost all its neighbours have been lost. Perhaps the station's architect dreamed of a day when trains might run from Cochabamba to a Bolivian sea-shore.

But now the navy has been withdrawn temporarily to Lake Titicaca; and you are lucky if trains run at all.

We were not lucky. Though the booking office opened promptly as we arrived, before dawn; though there were clerks and inspectors and wheel-tappers; and though a roomful of smartly-dressed young men was already alive with the clatter of typewriters and the rustle of paper-work in quadruplicate – though, in short, the railway was creating the employment for official persons that railways always do – there were no trains.

'Not for some days; weeks perhaps.'

'Repairs to the track.'

'Please return on Tuesday.'

Another way to La Paz had to be found. It was back down the steps in search of information. John enquired at the bookstall, but its proprietor knew nothing and instead tried to interest him in a series of booklets entitled (in Spanish) *The World's Great Leaders.*

He only had King Arthur, Mrs Thatcher and the Ayatollah Khomeini in stock, and seemed to be doing a roaring trade in all three with the Indians. Whether the world's other great leaders had already sold out, or whether these three were the only leaders for whom there was any local demand, was unclear. John moved on, despondent.

We had made this early start, determined not to fail. So we ploughed forward through the market, asking advice wherever we could. Nobody knew much, so we selected next a little tea shack. Tea was being served and it seemed polite to order a mug first, and pursue our enquiries after that.

The sun was only just rising and it was bitterly cold, but the market was coming to life. In a dark corner nearby, a heap of damp sackcloth re-formed itself into an old man, and rose from a bed of damp metal to greet the dawn. A tiny bundle of coloured woollen rags screamed, and its mother pulled a withered breast from among her other belongings and turned modestly to feed it. The crying stopped. The sound was replaced by the wail of a transistor radio playing the latest popular song. Singing along with it, a woman brought us our mugs of tea.

Peering past the painted tin flap which served as her kitchen door, a pretty girl aged about fourteen could be seen preparing breakfast.

Holding a partially skinned, detached goat's foreleg in one hand, she trained the roaring flame of a kerosene blowtorch up and down the raw shin. She did so rhythmically, beating time with the song. She knew the words:

No quiero vivir llorando	(I don't want to live weeping,
Prefiero vivir durmiendo:	I'd rather live sleeping:
Hasta que tu vuelvas, diciendo	Until you return, saying
Que me quieres ...'	That you love me ...)

The sounds of the flute and guitar rose into the morning air, mingling with the smells of charred flesh and singeing goat's hair.

With the first rays of dawn, an Andean peak high above the town burst into flame.

The girl grilling the goat's leg knew all about buses to La Paz. Waving the smoking hoof in the direction of the bus station, she advised that St Francis (San Francisco) was a reliable company running that route: 'Or El Dorado, or Andean Cat or Condor of the East.'

St Francis was not our first choice. The ornithologist in John went immediately for Condor of the East and he left me at the café with my second mug of tea, to try his luck buying tickets. An hour later he returned, crestfallen.

'The queue,' passers-by had told him, 'is over there, on the next block.' So it was, and John joined it, and waited in line with fifty or more Peruvians. He noticed that they were exceptionally smartly dressed.

For half an hour the queue did not move. Then, suddenly, it surged forward – John with it – into a large hall where everyone sat down at rows of waiting desks and an invigilator handed out examination papers. In what subject, John's Spanish was inadequate to determine, but he thinks it was Public Hygiene. He beat a hasty retreat.

El Condor had sold out when he found it. So, together again, we tried San Francisco.

This time we were lucky. A few tickets remained. We bought ours and wandered across to inspect our bus.

It was magnificent. Across the windscreen hung a silk-tasseled fringe, embroidered in gold-threaded images of the Virgin Mary alternating with silver-threaded three-spoked emblems of the Mercedes-Benz company. It was the invariable sign that the owner took pride in his vehicle, this fringe across the windscreen or dashboard. Did the Aero-Peru Boeing 727s, one wondered, have the same decorations in their cockpits?

Across the top of our bus's boot, the gothic script (in Spanish) read, 'GOD IS LIGHT AND IN HIM IS NO DARKNESS AT ALL'. This, together with the lavishly robed Madonna in her own shrine strapped to the dashboard, and the painting of the bleeding head of Christ partly obscuring the driver's vision, led us to hope that the bus might enjoy some kind of divine protection. We could hardly investigate the mechanical state of the vehicle, but no expense had been spared on the religious trimmings. They were – as the fashionable phrase goes – 'top of the range'. With St Francis to lead, one thought, how can we stumble?

*

Nor did we. The new road up from Cochabamba to La Paz is a daring construction, sweeping majestically into the clouds. Doze off for ten minutes and you awake, suddenly breathless – whether from the altitude or from the escarpment dropping away almost at your wheels, it is hard to say. Yet without accident and with only one minor incident, St Francis guided us safely on and upwards.

As you climb, the people grow poorer: grindingly poor, harsher than anything I had seen. Temporarily, of course, calamities can bring worse than this. Drought, flood, epidemic and war send us pictures of suffering more dramatic and intense than anything you see here. But in its quieter way, this was worse, for this was a permanent, stable state of suffering. Here the rural poor had made their contract with their environment. Earthquakes apart, there were no surprises: just survival. But survival of a harsh and meagre kind.

In Santa Cruz, down on the plains, where there is oil and timber and crops really grow, life seems more confident. Black-market money-changers (a breed who, elsewhere on the continent, hiss furtively from dark corners) cruise the streets in their own cars, cheerfully hanging placards from their windows advertising today's rate for the dollar.

In Cochabamba, where we had just been, life had looked harder but not without frills. There was drug money to be had there. The shops offered luxuries like looking-glasses engraved with pictures of well-known personalities: Jesus, Mary, Simon Bolivar and Charlie Chaplin. On the pavements, notaries with gas-lamps and typewriters sat ready to compose whatever the customer required: threatening letters, love letters, job applications or writs. It was a lively town.

But here on the Altiplano – the 'high plain' – poverty was not gay. There is a lamp post in the old square in La Paz – we saw it later – from which the radical President Villaroel was hanged in 1946. Villaroel was a champion of the oppressed; and beneath his lamp post some of his last words have been engraved: 'I am not an enemy of the rich but I am a friend of the poor ... This is my banner, my flag, my standard. And if for this banner I must be broken ... then I am disposed to die.' When you have seen the condition of the Indian poor in Bolivia, you cannot fail to be moved by that.

Our bus stopped for lunch by a line of broken-down huts where the poverty looked typical. John tried to photograph an old Indian woman, and met a hail of stones. Rebuffed, we hurried behind the other passengers into the shack where our set meal was waiting. There was no menu, no choice: just thin, watery soup.

Suddenly hungry, we both spooned the liquid eagerly down. The level in John's bowl sank fast and, as it did, the solid components of the soup began to surface and take visible shape.

John shuddered at the solitary chicken claw sticking heavenward like the spires on those churches submerged in reservoirs. But he slurped on. When some stomach-lining floated up he hesitated, but, 'It's only tripe; they eat that in Sheffield,' he muttered, and kept drinking.

Then something rare and strange appeared. Struggling against the growing conviction that it was a cow's nose, John persisted until no other interpretation could be placed upon the glistening black lump in the middle of his bowl. The nostrils were unmistakable. He lurched out wordless into the grey light and a renewed assault from the old women.

And yet it was so beautiful. The shacks were of mud and tin, wretchedly poor; a family of raven-haired piglets rootled around St Francis's wheels; and everywhere was the smell of urine. But in a corner by the wall someone had planted a flowering bush. Rubbish lay all around, yet its scarlet blooms would have been the glory of any English garden. It was a red which made reds you have seen before look like early attempts at the final colour.

And our persecutors, the old women, seated on the bare earth in the way of peasant women everywhere – head and shoulders rising mysteriously from a great heap of dusty skirts, the location of hips, thighs and legs (if they are built like other women at all) a matter of pure guesswork: these leathery old women were wrapped about the shoulders with crimson and gold mantles so fine, so intricately worked, that no Englishwoman would dare to soil them with use. These women were trailing them in the dirt.

And as with the yard, so with the people in it: filthy, threadbare, broken down, but tinged always and at some point with an extravagant beauty. The scarlet bush, the crimson mantles, seemed to burn like small flames, hovering above the ashes which sustained them. Tiny points of intense colour, their vitality sucked upwards from the parched earth and withered bodies to which they clung.

And then that song again, this time from our driver's tape recorder, '*No quiero vivir llorando* ...' (I don't want to live weeping ...), rising in curious harmony with the throttled squawks of some distant chicken destined, no doubt, for the next soup sitting, the next bus.

St Francis was ready to go and hooting impatiently. We set off in a cloud of dust, the crippled dog barking and lunging at our wheels with a recklessness which explained the loss of his first leg and cast doubt on the future of the remaining three. The old woman threw one last defiant rock at John, who had at last managed to photograph her before she had time to duck.

She had her revenge, though she will never know it. As the bus rattled on into the afternoon and upward into the cold, meagre air, John began to feel the altitude. We were now at 14,000 feet. Nausea set in. It was not, for him, the first time, but he had always shown self-control and

and hoped to be able to master the pangs this time, too. John has an iron will, very English. But he also has an English fastidiousness. And when a huge and exceptionally smelly old woman collapsed herself into the seat beside him, her many skirts and petticoats flowing and settling around his whitening kneecaps, it was obvious John was in for the hardest test of all.

She was a new arrival to our bus. St Francis's engine had overheated and we had stopped for water from a stream near this woman's roadside village. This gave her the opportunity she needed to board. It was an amazing stroke of luck for her, as she had been waiting for transport to La Paz.

With her pig. We realized about the pig when we heard it screaming as she dragged it down the road towards the bus, on its back, by its hind legs.

Sweating and with enormous effort she reached the bus.

And now began the real struggle. Her aim was to truss her pig up with pieces of old rope: but the pig, sensing that from the road ahead there was no return, put up a magnificent struggle.

It was a large pig and fought with all its might, screaming continuously at ear-splitting pitch. Yet the old woman was deceptively well matched both in stamina and in sheer muscle power. And while the contest was not quite as important for her as it was for the pig, it was important: for this unscheduled stop, right outside her hut, was a heaven-sent chance to get her pig to market. It was unlikely to be repeated.

Moreover, the bus would not wait for ever. The driver was losing patience, while the passengers, who were becoming restive, had divided into four groups. The largest group simply wanted to get going again. The second group, also numerous, supported the old woman and cheered her on loudly.

A third group, comprising some of the rowdier elements in the bus, had taken sides with the pig – more (sadly) out of devilment than out of sympathy – and noisily applauded its best endeavours.

We English were simply trying not to look.

In the end, the pig was defeated after a heroic contest. Tied up, finally, and threshing like a cat in a string bag, it was heaved squealing into the boot – over which we in the back row were seated. We could feel its disconsolate thumping beneath us.

The Indian lady pig-tamer, flushed with triumph and soaked with sweat, plonked herself down next to John. The bus pulled away.

But the woman had still to pay her fare, and started reaching for the banknotes. You may guess where an Andean peasant woman keeps her money. Suffice it to record that there was a flurry of violent rummaging in which *all* her skirts and all her petticoats, too, came up. The smell was truly unspeakable. John was very, very sick. The sun set.

Through the bus windows and through the high, thin, freezing air outside ... across the dry hills, drained of colour in the fading light, you could see the face of an Andean peak, miles distant and miles above us, still catching the sun. It shone as if ablaze. Its foothills glowed against the cold sky as if drawing light not from above, but from the leached plains below.

That song, yet again, on a passenger's radio:

> I don't want to live weeping:
> I'd rather live sleeping ...

In a gentle soprano, the Indian woman joined in the refrain. John had stopped being sick, now. There was a tapping, as of trotters, from beneath us.

I fancy it was the pig, tapping along with the rhythm, too: tranquil now in the thought that this bus was San Francisco, and St Francis is often pictured with a little pig by his side. Or perhaps our pig had read the inscription as it entered the pitch-dark boot: 'GOD IS LIGHT AND IN HIM IS NO DARKNESS AT ALL.'

Outside the boot was the most glorious sunset, the pig's last.

> ... Until you return, saying
> That you love me ...

Chapter Fifteen

A Sort
of Exile

'These Peruvians have tiny feet. I combed Lima. Dancing shoes only –
yes, *dancing*-shoes – shade called 'aubergine' – *aubergine* – exactly:
puce ... No, that was all they had in size 46. They still pinch a bit ...

'Ian? He's much better – yes, we're back at the hotel now. I had to
bribe the ambulance driver again ... And I'm getting a new passport on
Tuesday ... What? No, it's Thursday today – don't they have days of
the week in Bolivia?

'Had to bribe the policeman. He said it would take two weeks to
prepare a statement certifying that the passport was stolen. But there
was an *express* service, he said – and he pointed to a cracked photograph
of the last Pope on his wall and he said it would cost two hundred *intis*
to reframe it. "Then he could show his face again." I suppose he meant
the Pope. So I gave him the two hundred ... It worked. Did the statement
on the spot.

'Yes, I'll wait for the passport, but we should be able to join you in
a few days, in Puno ...' Click – brrrr ...

'Sod it. Cut off again.'

La Paz looks and feels like the capital of a mountain kingdom. It is a
compact, cobbled city, full of steep streets, swirly wrought-iron street
lamps and grand public buildings with stone façades in baroque style.
Ceremonial guards in nineteenth-century toytown uniforms goose step
up and down outside the palaces. On all three sides the walls of the
Andes sweep upwards, enclosing the whole town and adding to an
atmosphere of siege, of suppressed hysteria, which hangs in the thin air.

To these impossibly steep slopes cling shanty-town slums, ready at
any moment to slip down into the city's mad traffic. And, standing like
a sentinel on the skyline, towers the classic outline of one of South
America's highest peaks: the magnificent Illimani, some 22,000 feet high.

The rich from La Paz can ski on a mountain-side above the city at
the highest ski-station in the world, where it is hardly possible to

breathe. From these snows, clear streams flow into what is – less famously – the highest slum in the world: *El Alto*, whose poverty stunned even the Pope.

Dirtier, now, the same streams cascade down an eroded valley into the top of La Paz itself. The poorest houses are here – if you can call them houses. It is a wilderness of tin and mud, morticians' parlours specializing in coffins for babies, flower stalls and the carcasses of dogs.

Now our stream – more polluted by the yard – enters the old city itself. In canyons and gullies it passes beneath one of the world's most vicious little traffic jams: a collective neurosis of mini-buses pointing randomly in different directions and hooting. European motorways may offer the connoisseur leisurely tailbacks which stretch for miles; New York's battalions of yellow cabs may be unrivalled for the raw power of immobilized traffic. But a La Paz snarl-up is a collector's item, small scale, but bursting with manic energy.

From beneath the old city, our filthy stream enters the lower suburbs: the rich quarter. Here dwell the diplomats, generals, police chiefs, drug dealers and politicians. The houses are modern, the gardens luxuriant, the flowering trees fragrant, and the dogs and security guards on each gate more ferocious than the last.

And out of this unlikely Eden pours – at last – a stream as foul as ever any river was, like pure urine, tumbling down into a moonscape of gullies, eroded pinnacles of bare earth, and municipal rubbish.

Bolivia is a mad, unlikely country. If prizes were awarded for the nation which had (over time) pursued the most unsuccessful imaginable military and foreign policy, Bolivia would be a leading contender. Most of the best parts of its territory have been lost.

As to the calibre of its domestic government, perhaps this is best illustrated by a remark made by the mother of one of the country's innumerable past presidents, after her son had attained power in a coup. 'If I'd known Enrique was going to be president,' she remarked, 'I'd have sent him to school.'

What is left, apart from the fertile forest basin and grasslands around Santa Cruz, is icy mountaintops and the thin soils of the windswept plains between them. Oil (near Santa Cruz) has brought the kind of artificial wealth that touches just a few. The despoliation of forest lands is bringing to a few more what is better described as plunder than as a living. Industry is rudimentary and crude; mining brings the fluctuating, unreliable fortunes, the ill will, the labour unrest and social poison that mining always brings; and, for the rest, the growing of coca provides a little income and a little solace to the peasantry and strikes its corrupt roots into the heart of the state, tainting business, law, politics and every arm of government.

From time to time regimes are installed which pledge themselves (with noisy backing from the United States) to tackle the drugs, the crime and the corruption. They never last. How could they? Poison is the life-blood of this country. Only from the total ruin of that semblance of order which stands between the masses and starvation, could the state be reconstructed. In that respect at least, Che Guevara, who was run to ground and killed here, was right.

The poorest in Bolivia are not so very far from freezing or starving. The middle class barely exists. The rich are outrageously rich. As a political economy, its room for manoeuvre is infinitely more limited than Peru's. Hardly a month passes without a general strike, hardly a year without a coup.

Yet there is a paradoxical feeling of permanence about Bolivia's turmoil. It is a durable sort of fragility, for, in a way, they have hit the bottom. You feel that it was ever thus, and life, now, will go on.

The feeling in Peru had been strangely different. It was a feeling that life might stop going on, for quite a large number of people, and quite soon. There is a bourgeoisie in Lima and Arequipa – a class which has done well enough to have something to lose yet not so well as to be able to take it with them on a jet to the United States and a Miami bank account. They are stuck. And they face a peasantry who are still able to hope and who still have a sense of justice to be affronted. These are fertile soils for the revolutionary left and the populist right. It could yet come to civil war between them.

In Bolivia the hateful gods of political and economic blight take their human sacrifices daily, predictably, according to some bleak and unspoken pact with history. Peru has made no such peace with its gods. There is a threat, in Peru, that the elements of conflict might turn finally and face each other. All that threatens Bolivia is a continuity of despair.

Ian had given us the address of a friend of a friend who was said to come from Sleaford in Lincolnshire, and to be headmaster of a girls' private school in La Paz. We decided to seek out this curiosity.

Peter lived in a smart suburb at the bottom of the town. It was an apartment in an elegant condominium, securely guarded. We had announced our visit by telephone.

'Ah, come in. Welcome! A beer?' There was only the hint of a Lincolnshire accent. Peter moved to switch off a video-recorder. There was some kind of opera on the screen.

'Prokoviev. Just arrived. So hard to explain to the customs people. Couldn't live without our cultural lifelines from Europe. Basilio's mad about Prokoviev – *no*, Basilio?'

'*Si*,' said a thin, timid-looking man with a wispy moustache.

'Basilio, this is John and Matthew,' Peter introduced us, then explained: 'Basilio does speak English, but he feels a bit intimidated when we all speak so fast.'

In fact Basilio spoke English excellently, as became clear when he relaxed a little. He worked as an accountant in the Bolivian ministry of agriculture.

'Do you like the apartment?' Peter showed us round. It was stylishly furnished – a sort of Bolivian art deco, bordering on, but not quite tipping over into, what Kenneth Williams would have called piss-elegant and others might call ersatz.

'This is my room. That's Basilio's. Do you like that screen? It's from Ceylon. They said our dry air might take the lacquer off, but it hasn't.'

We talked for some time. Peter asked us much about England. His questions had an edginess, a cageyness to them – as a man who had left his wife might cross-question people still in touch with her, to discover how she was getting on.

We talked with him about Bolivia and Peru; but it was that oddly unsatisfactory sort of exchange that one so often has with people who have been in a place too long to see it any more.

'The transport strike? Yes, there does seem to be one, doesn't there? I read something about it in the papers. Something to do with the price of fuel, I think. The government are going to do something about it, apparently. Can you remember what, Basilio? No? Nor can I.'

'Lima? Yes. Foul. Went there once. Saw a dog fucking a pig. Just about sums the place up. But you can't beat the shopping there. We're hoping to go soon. I need spares for my typewriter. I've looked *every-where* in La Paz. It's the bracket that holds the rubber roller thing in place, you know … Just hope we don't get blown up.

'… I don't know what these Sendero terrorists are all about. Nobody does, really. Do you, Basilio? Hard to get into the mind of the Indians. Things seem to be exploding left, right and centre in Peru. Nothing quite like that here – don't know why. It's worse here, really. Nobody knows their arse from their elbow.'

'Have you seen my driving licence?' He pulled out a tattered document and handed it to John.

'But this is a …' John squinted at the dog-eared card, 'a Lincolnshire County Library card!'

'Yes. I never got around to replacing my British driving licence after the last one was stolen. I just hand them this. It always works.'

Peter was tall and well built. For a man in his mid-forties he had kept himself in good trim. Talkative and in command, there was nevertheless something soft about his mouth: a wounded look. It was noticeable especially when his face was in repose.

Only when he talked about his school did this impression of defens-iveness melt. He told us about the families from which the schoolgirls came and how some of the girls enjoyed wealth rivalling anything to be found in Europe – yet were hardly loved by their parents; how he and his staff tried to build a family atmosphere at the school; and how difficult it was to impose discipline on rich kids.

'There are some unbelievably wealthy people in this place. God knows where it comes from.'

He told us about a small earth tremor that had shaken La Paz while his girls were singing the Bolivian national anthem (as they were required by law to do) at morning assembly, and how he had stood on the stage and told them to take no notice and go on singing; they had such trust in him and the school that they did.

As he spoke about the children his eyes burned with a cool flame. All his defensiveness, his hurt look, dropped away, and he spoke tenderly. This, not Lincolnshire, was now his whole life.

'None of my relatives has ever come to visit me, although I'm always inviting them. Except one cousin. She and I are going on a holiday to Rio next year.

'. . . Call in if you can, and see my people in Sleaford. Tell them about my flat here. I go every few years, but it's a while, now, since I was there and you lose touch. I should go again. I'd like Basilio to come too, but then again' – he looked away – 'maybe not. You see I've made myself . . . a sort of . . . separate life here. I'm cut off from all that now, in a way . . .' He looked away again.

'Strange,' John said, as we left. 'Basilio seemed so shy. Almost embarrassed. Funny about Peter, too. Funny to leave your home town in England, where all your family and all the people who know you, are . . . I mean why come here?' he said. 'This is about as far away from Lincolnshire as you can get!'

Choosing to walk back to our hotel, we jostled along the main avenue which sweeps down through the city. John's attention was caught by a section of the kerbside which seemed to be reserved for vehicles parked apparently semi-permanently – for they had cards inside their front windscreens, with printed messages.

'Perhaps,' he said, 'this is the quarter where people park cars they are trying to sell.' We walked closer to one van, to read the notice, translating it for each other's benefit. It said: 'THE DRIVER OF THIS VEHICLE MR PANCHO GUTIERREZ KNOCKED DOWN A SMALL GIRL, FATALLY INJURING HER. HE THEN ESCAPED WITH THE CORPSE AND TRIED TO DISPOSE OF THE CADAVER IN A CLANDESTINE CEMETERY, TO AVOID DETECTION.

'THIS NOTICE HAS BEEN ORDERED BY THE COURT TO STAND FOR SEVEN WEEKS.'

And each car told its separate story. It appears that part of a judicial sentence for dangerous driving in Bolivia may be to suffer a form of prolonged public humiliation, by being ordered to park your car with a notice displaying your own name, the nature of your offence, and details of whatever harm you may have done to your victims. This was a harsh country.

We stopped by the cathedral. It was a huge building, of warm yellow stone. Its great carved façade – in a style they call Indian Baroque – caught the evening sun. On the stone-slabbed forecourt as big as a football pitch, townspeople, peasants from the country and a few tourists warmed themselves in the sunlight. The noise of the city's homeward rush hour, the shouts, the hooting and the revving of engines, was insistent.

Inside it was so quiet and so dark that it took a minute for eyes and ears to adjust: and to see or hear anything at all. When they did, it was to the echo of dozens of little confessionals, all around the walls and alcoves, and the murmur of hundreds of peasants, praying at minor shrines. Jewelled light flooded down from stained-glass windows.

In one shrine was an image of the Virgin Mary, as gaudy in royal blue and gilt and fluorescent lighting as you can imagine. At her feet, held back by a wooden rail on which she had thrown herself, wept an old Indian peasant woman. She had cast herself completely at the feet of this gilt-and-plaster image, and wailed and sobbed as if there would be no end. Nobody took any notice.

Chapter Sixteen

Christian, Crystal and Walter

It is one of the few things that stay in the memory from childhood geography lessons: asking Mrs MacLeod what was the highest navigable lake in the world, so that we could giggle when she said 'titty'.

The frontier between Bolivia and Peru bisects Lake Titicaca. Puno stands by the lake shore, at the Peruvian end. La Paz lies some way off the Bolivian end. It was uphill from La Paz to the lake, and that was where we were going: back into Peru, around the lake to Puno. The best way to go was by bus – a full day's journey. The bus we chose was called Super Vikingo. It was on board that we met Christian.

Christian made the first approach. We had stopped for food at a lakeside resort called Copacabana – a place which stands in about the same relationship to its famous Brazilian namesake as Boston, Lincolnshire, does to Boston, Massachusetts. It is small beer.

But not too small for the Virgin Mary to have made one of her many South American appearances there. She survives in replica with real human hair (blonde) in a gaudy church visited by Bolivians on their way to the beach. Down by the blue lake, on a shingled waterfront, was a shack where 'trout' was announced on an Inca-Kola blackboard. We grabbed the only spare table. Christian asked if he could join us.

His impertinence was total. 'Mamamita!' (Little mother) he called to the young girl cooking and serving the food, and flashed her a grin that won us our fried fish before all the others. He seemed so confident. Only slowly did we realize that his Spanish was worse than ours.

Christian was good-looking in a sultry sort of way. About twenty-five, with big brown eyes, jet-black hair and the whitest teeth you ever saw, he told us that he was Swiss, 'Swiss-German.'

'German-Swiss, you mean,' said John.

'No. Swiss-German. I am Swiss *first*. German second.' There was never any point in arguing with Christian. 'How are the girls in Puno? They are – how do you say? – looking frontwards to my arrival, yes?' We replied that we did not know Puno, or the girls there.

'To know Puno is not necessary to know that there will be girls and they will be liking me,' he remarked, in a matter-of-fact tone. 'Always.'

Back on the bus, he persuaded two middle-aged German tourists called Walter and Crystal to move their seats so that we could sit with him on his side – the best side for views, or, as he put it, 'the – how do you say? – correct flank for the sideways aspect including the lake according to my guidebook.'

'But it is not fair to those two tourists you have moved,' John protested in slow, careful English, for Christian's benefit. 'When they realize that they cannot see anything from their side, they will think that you have cheated them.'

'They are Germans. They will accept that I have a superior guidebook and be respecting me. Even more when they try to purchase one similar in Puno, which will be impossible, because mine was purchased in Zurich.' Christian replied rapid-fire. 'Where are you learning your English? Mine is quicker. I am teach in Zurich.'

'I *am* English,' John protested. 'Anyway, surely you mean you *learn* in Zurich, Christian. "Teach" means instructing someone who is ignorant.'

'No. *I* teach because I am better than the instructor. And I am sleeping with her. Also I am her teacher in this respect, too.'

Walter and Crystal were craning over, from the dud side of the bus, trying to see the view of the lake.

It was very beautiful. Perhaps because of the thinness and clarity of the atmosphere, the blues of the water and the browns and yellows of the reed banks at its edge seemed to shine with an almost luminous quality, though they were soft, subtle colours. Sunlight sparkled on the waves as sunlight everywhere does, but with the filter taken away. No heaviness in the air dulled the sharpness. The light flashed and cut.

It brought to mind something I had forgotten – buried, perhaps: the time I experimented with the drug LSD at Yale in New England. Then, too, forms and colours, the edges of things, turned acid-bright. They were the same things – no shape or shade changed from the familiar – but so cruelly focused that the familiar hurt. It was (in the biblical language) as though the scales had fallen from my eyes. My eyes ached. I remembered seeing a deformed old tramp by the roadside, and wanting to destroy him, to erase, to wipe away an ugly stain on so clean a picture.

Here on this lake the sun's rays were thrown like knives from waves breaking on the shore, and beds of reeds as sharp as a forest of upright spears swayed dead parallel in the swell. Further into the deep, where a wind broke the sunlit surface, a scattering of diamond flashes burst like an exploding rocket into tiny, intense scatters of light. Only in one way was it beautiful, for it was painfully bright and very, very hard.

We still had a day's travelling to Puno, but Walter and Crystal were worrying about trains onward from there.

Walter was a tall, thin, bespectacled man with a permanently worried expression. Clad in broad-ribbed brown dungarees – anxious mole – he continually sought advice from fellow travellers. All such advice he then proceeded to ignore, forever in search of yet another authority against which to check his information. His English was mannered, but excellent.

'My good wife Crystal and I,' he announced, 'have an inferior guidebook. It is better to be honest, no? This book reports that railway tickets are available from the railway station between certain hours on the day prior to travelling. Other guidebooks, however – for instance that of our friend Christian – advise that tickets should be bought from travel agents in the town. Crystal and I are finding difficulty in reconciling these different accounts.' His brow furrowed.

'Walter and I,' said his wife, in English that was almost, but not quite, as good, 'prefer always to be prepared.' She turned to Walter: 'Ask them, please dear, what does their own guidebooks advises.'

'What does your own guidebook advise?' said Walter.

'Guidebook, not *books*,' she interrupted. 'Or you can say "advise" in place of "advises". This depends, my dear, upon whether you regard them as likely to possess more than one book.'

'My dear, my question followed precisely the phraseology which you recommended. But let us hear their answer.'

John checked our book, the indispensable *South American Handbook* which mentioned both the travel agents and the booking office and gave no advice as to which. To Crystal and Walter, perpetually in search of certainty in this most uncertain of continents, that was only depressing. It widened choice yet gave no guide to action.

Christian laughed. 'Travel agents must keep some money. So they add more expensive to tickets.'

'Ask him, my dear, why tourists do not therefore buy tickets at the railway station.'

'May I refer you to Crystal's question?' said Walter.

'Corruption,' Christian muttered, darkly. 'This is not Zurich.'

'Ask him, my dear ...'

But Christian was ahead now. 'Referring,' he said to Walter, 'to the question I anticipate your wife Crystal requires. I believe difficulties will be manufactured concerning the purchase of tickets at the railway station. About the nature of these difficulties, I expect to learn in Puno. All my life I am learning. When I am stop learning I am one point eight metres underground.'

We rattled on, in silence for a while, along a shore where poor little fields ran down to the side of the lake.

Much that is patronizing or naive is written about the superior wisdom of peasants. In Peru you see them all too plainly failing in the tasks they attempt. Their methods do not work. Their failure produces a life in which backbreaking labour – horrifyingly inefficient – alternates with mindless indolence. Often the indolence falls to the men, the labour to the women.

Here, by this lakeshore, the Indians lived just such a life. All afternoon, Super Vikingo followed the shores of Titicaca, heading north along a good road dotted with speckled auburn pigs, and passing many little settlements. The huts looked poor, the soil thin and life harsh. This was a bleak and exposed place, rimmed with low, black hills sloping gently into the shimmering lake. We passed an old woman with a leaking bucket, trying to water a field of moth-eaten potato plants. She looked so tired. She was wearing a bowler hat.

It was a bizarre environment. And this lake was a secret ocean, perched, almost ridiculously, on top of the world. Too wide for its furthest shores to be visible, you could nevertheless see a line of far-distant ice-peaks laced along the horizon. When the sun set, sheet-lightning flickered very low in the sky beyond them, reaching up (as it seemed) from behind and below. It was as though those peaks marked the very edge of our world, perched above the storms of some nether-world.

And so they did: for these peaks were sentinels at the limit of this highest of the Andean plateaus. Reach them, pass them, and you have dropped tens of thousands of feet down into the Amazon basin. At night, lightning was all we could see of the great rainstorms that rolled – soundless to us – across the jungle below. Here in the thin, brittle atmosphere of the mountains, it was hard to imagine the heat and heaviness of the world down there, just over the edge. We felt a thrill of excitement. We might visit such places, soon.

Some time before reaching Puno we passed the headquarters of the Peruvian navy on the lake.

It is hard to imagine how a naval engagement on Lake Titicaca could be a key element in some Bolivian offensive to blast her way through to the Pacific. Bolivia keeps a navy there because, having 'temporarily' lost her Pacific coastline, there is nowhere else to keep it. And presumably Peru keeps a navy there because Bolivia does. We found our Swiss friend a little sensitive about jokes on this score. His Zurich guidebook made no mention of the Bolivian navy.

Walter and Crystal's book did not mention the churches at Juli: so when the bus paused there at sundown, and someone suggested a short tour, loyalty to their book prevented them from joining in. They (and Christian, who was not interested in churches) agreed to stay with the Super Vikingo and have a room booked waiting for us at a hotel that all three books recommended. We would follow on after an hour or two, for there were frequent trucks and vans from Juli.

'When you are reaching Puno,' called the departing Christian 'the room will be reserved for you and the girls reserved for me. I am a very fast boy.' We wished him luck and sensed he wouldn't need it.

The drab village of Juli and its rather drab inhabitants seemed unaware of the jewels in their midst.

There are four great churches there, two decaying badly. The most ruinous, near the lake-shore, is the greatest. Built two centuries ago for a congregation of thousands, it is the size of a small cathedral. It is hard to imagine what need there can ever have been for such a place, no matter how numerous or fervent the Indians. Now it was locked up, and we had to force our way in past some tin sheeting which blocked a side door.

Bindweed sprouted up through the floor. Small trees had taken root inside the walls, and from the great stone pillars and arches above us flowering weeds cascaded down from their lodgement in the cracks between the stones. Part of the roof had caved in, and in the half-light, birds and bats shrieked and wheeled in from the open sky.

To a purist in classical architecture, for whom the grotesqueries of Indian carvings are an artistic corruption, this place was richly corrupt. There was a feeling of decadence about the florid carving. Christian arches, and symbols of Jesus's death and resurrection, were entwined with a profusion of Indian images, strange, swirling, magical stonework, organic in form: pillars, lintels and gargoyles that – though stone – seemed to be rooted and sprouting. There were carvings of cherubim, carvings of papayas and carvings of monkeys.

A cross dominated one nave, simple and unadorned. It looked out upon a debauched scene. For the greenery tumbling through the windows and down the walls, and the livid streaks of wet moss and fern advancing upon where the altar had been, combined with the Indian carving to suggest an austere faith under siege from something alien, something rich: throttled by it, crumbling as the roots of pagan magic prised and burrowed their way in, lasciviously tearing it apart. Nature had formed a conspiracy with art to choke the modern certainties the Jesuits had brought to this place; and all was returning to what it had been.

It had been worth pausing there.

Chapter Seventeen

Torrent
Pigs

The first thing we saw of Puno was the sign, 'PUNO ROTARY CLUB'. The second was the news banner, 'MAYOR OF PUNO ASSASSINATED BY SHINING PATH'. Apparently this was their first major success in the region.

Puno is a down-at-heel town, strewn between low earth hills and the muddy end of Lake Titicaca. A biting wind off the lake scuds litter up the dirty streets; and a couple of American drug addicts beg. The place has more than the normal Peruvian quota of robbers, but without the charm and bustle that often accompany a healthy level of street crime.

We checked into the Hotel Ferocarril (Railway). Christian, who had booked us a room, met us with a woman on his arm. 'This is Evelyn. She is making a holiday from Bolivia. In La Paz she is the English teacher, but here in Puno with me she has the happy chance of improving her English under my hand and also much enjoyment of masculine company offered by me. We share a room.'

'For economy,' added Evelyn, reddening. She was Austrian. Her English was grammatically perfect but delivered in a flat monotone. Over a beer, she began to recite all the things she knew about Puno.

'... And it is well known that railway tickets are impossible to buy at the railway station. They are sold only at a higher price by agents who buy all the tickets before they are on sale to the public. For this they pay a bribe to the railway booking clerks. People complain frequently to the railway authorities but the booking clerks pay a bribe to the authorities. It is said that the German consul in Lima had made a complaint to the mayor of Puno, but as you may know the latter has regrettably been shot by the Shining Path ...'

It was incredible that such technical command of our language should have been acquired without Evelyn's having acquired at the same time even the glimmerings of a feel for it.

'Some wonder has been caused by the observation, this evening, of a middle-aged German couple queuing with the peasants at the railway booking office. One man tried to explain to them that their mission was impossible and offered to indicate to them the offices of an agent but they suspected him of trying to rob them and refused to leave the queue. Apparently one of them is called Walter, and so far as we know they are still there . . .'

Christian caught our eye and grinned.

There was nothing to do at the hotel, so we decided on a night tour of Puno. It was a disappointment. Little seemed to be happening, except that in the main square two antique water cannon were being taken for a precautionary lumber round the sides. These battered green tank-like things seem to be the Peruvian authorities' response to any sign of insurrection: a way of showing the flag. A less appropriate response to a secretive, murderous organization combining Indian stealth with Maoist ideology, could hardly be imagined.

Drawing back from the cannon, John noticed a little group of towns-people gathered round something hunched back by the wall. We went closer.

At first it appeared to be some kind of animal. But when we reached the group, we saw that it was human. A little boy, on all fours, on the ground. He seemed to be cowering, but the spectators were not threatening: just curious. Beside him was a placard, neatly printed in Spanish. It read thus:

TO THE PUBLIC: The Overseer of Minors places at your disposition a boy of less than 13 years of age; certifying of the same, that he was abandoned by his family at the age of 4, lived in different households and places, and was taken away by the authorities and brought to this town. Thus he has nothing.

'Whoever might wish to adopt him would need to provide him with the means of life, food and study, and take responsibility for him. Any such person should present himself to the Overseer within 90 days at the Centre for Minors at Happy Forest.

'We would be grateful for any contributions towards his food, until somebody claims him. Thank you. The Overseer.'

The little boy, who seemed to be speechless, and perhaps mentally retarded, shrank away from the crowd, his eyes darting from left to right, like some kind of vermin at bay.

Back at the hotel it was late. But in the bar, drinking soda water, were Walter and Crystal. They were in despair. We greeted them sym-pathetically and explained that we had heard of their quest for tickets.

'Ask them, my dear,' said Crystal to Walter, 'what all the other tourists are doing. Why were we alone in attempting to make arrangements for our forward travel?'

Walter was too depressed to repeat the question, but nodded it in our direction.

'We plan to look for travel in the morning.'

'But' – in his dejected state Walter jettisoned the triangular method of communication and spoke to John direct, without reference to Crystal at all – 'you will be disappointed: for the booking office told us there were no tickets, although we were almost at the front of the queue. All the tickets have been sold already.'

'Yes. To the agents,' Christian chipped in. 'This is a primordial strike by the middlemen.'

'*Pre-emptive*.' Crystal's morale was pretty low – she believed that she and Walter might never leave Puno – but not so low as to prevent her putting a man right.

'Pre-emptive, primordial, I am careless of either, but I am not so stupid that I have not made the friendship of an agent. Or agent*ess* I should say. Tickets will be available in the morning. This is her promise. You shall join us.'

Christian and Evelyn retired to bed. John stayed behind to cheer Walter and Crystal. We left him trying to translate 'torrent duck' into German.

'And these ducks-in-the-cascades,' came the voice of Crystal, down the corridor from the room we had left, 'these torrent ducks: they are table-ducks, yes? You eat them?'

I dreamed that Russell Harty and I were spies together working for MI6.

Christian's lady agent turned out to be no agent, and not much of a lady. She was not (despite Christian's boasts) interested in his body: what she was angling for was a commission. She *knew* a travel agent, however, and for 10 per cent would introduce Christian, Walter and Crystal to him. This agent would procure railway tickets from Juliaca (the next town along the line) to Cuzco, which was where we were going. His commission was 50 per cent. It was good to see Walter and Crystal finally fixed up.

Over breakfast, Walter relaxed. In a moment of candour, he leaned away from Crystal and over towards our table. 'Perhaps you and your friends think we are just a couple of silly old German *fusspots* – that is your colloquialism, yes? But you must remember that my wife, Crystal, and I are retired people. We have never travelled outside Europe or the United States before.

'One day I said to Crystal: "Let us visit some of the exotic places, my dear, before we are too old." We agreed that we would not take an organized tour – as all the other German people do – but explore together, just the two of us. This is how we come to be in Peru.

'It is not easy here for Crystal. She is a very organized person. And we are uncomfortable and – how do you say? – bewildered, for much of the time. But still it is good for us to experience so many new things, and we will not give up our great tour until we have visited all those places which, back in Germany, we included on our plan ...

'No doubt everyone in this hotel is laughing a little at us. We understand why. But this journey has been the dream of Crystal and myself; and even the bad things ... are good.'

We invited Walter and his wife to take a boat trip on the lake with us, to an island called Takile about which we had read. They agreed, and John went down to the waterfront where, it was said, boatmen could be found.

He was back in half an hour. 'Filthy down there. Dead dogs and frozen puddles. Christian was no use: saw a pretty girl and tried to get us on her boat, but it wasn't going to Takile. Then I found a man who'll take us. Says he's going straight away ...'

So we got our bags together, bought some oranges and set off. Crystal picked her way distastefully over the dogs' corpses and round the puddles, and we all looked the other way as we passed the meat market.

Nearing the waterfront, a furtive-looking little half-caste man ran up to us and tagged along, tugging John's sleeve: 'My name ees Peter. That's cool, hey? You kids like a tomato?' And he brandished an old newspaper packed with tomatoes, as if they were drugs or pornographic photographs. Crystal gave a yelp of distaste.

Peter, it turned out, had come to pour poison in our ear concerning the boat we had hired. It was old, slow and leaky, he said; and the boatman was notoriously unreliable. Now it just so happened that he had a boat himself, sleek, modern, fast ... a Caribbean cruiser of a boat, the pride of Titicaca ...

It took some time to shake him off, and matters were not helped by Crystal's countermanding our own refusal to negotiate, and sending Walter in to start separate talks with him.

Eventually we got Walter back, keeping Crystal under surveillance to stop her launching another initiative. But now our own boatman, taken on by John, had disappeared, though his boat, *Eagle of the East*, was still there. Peter hovered by, smiling knowingly. His conniving air aroused suspicion. Sure enough, our boatman was spotted: he was trying to poach a party of French tourists off the boat they had already hired from someone else. We remonstrated with him. But, he protested, Peter had told him that we no longer required his services.

We rescued our boatman from the French, chattering among themselves with that collective insouciance which somehow detaches any Gallic group from the surroundings in which it finds itself; cocoons it in '*Ouis*' and '*Nons*', '*Merdes*', '*Ooh la-las*' and the last word in state-of-the-art suitcases and skiing trousers; lifts it several metres into the air; and wafts it around whatever continent chance has made its host, all but oblivious to its surroundings. Only in the very loosest sense of the term were these Frenchmen 'in' Puno, Peru or the southern hemisphere. The place was arbitrary: no more than a backdrop for displays of the latest in designer cycling-tights.

Joaquim (that was our boatman's name) gave Peter an 'I'll deal with you later' look, and returned to us. We boarded the *Eagle of the East*.

Nothing happened. Joaquim wandered off again. He appeared to be trying to drum up more custom and was importuning a Swedish couple.

Our boat was quite full enough. We elected Christian as our foreman, who marched over, established that the Swedes were not looking for a boat at all but seeking instructions on how to get railway tickets, and told Joaquim to get on with it.

Only then did we realize that Joaquim was not a boatman at all. He had nothing to do with the boat we had boarded, whose real owner was now summoned – by Joaquim. Joaquim had negotiated the deal involving us and this fellow's boat without consulting him. Now he expected to take a cut. The problem was that the owner did not want to go to Takile, or anywhere else, having business of his own to transact.

Peter (still there) made his decisive move. He darted away, and within thirty seconds darted back with a middle-aged woman and a little boy. 'This lady, Gloria,' he told us, 'is your *capitano*. She will drive the boat. You will pay her.' A hurried conversation followed between Peter, Joaquim, Gloria and the boat's owner. No doubt the bargain John had struck (a pretty modest sum) left generous margins for a whole raft of middlemen and these were now being apportioned. All the middlemen departed, friends again, leaving us with Gloria, her son, and the *Eagle of the East*. Gloria wore an orange deerstalker cap inscribed 'FERGUSON TRACTORS', and was perhaps as new to the boat as we were.

We struck off into the lake to the sight of a bus being driven – as it seemed – out to sea (but, in fact, into deep enough water for the driver to wash it) and the sound of Walter trying to explain to Crystal what the negotiations had been about.

'But why is there no booking office?' she kept wailing. She had applied so much barrier cream against the sun that her face was entirely white, as though in preparation for a tribal war-dance. Now a new fear gripped her and was rapidly communicated to Walter. What if Gloria refused to bring us back from the island, and demanded more money?

Crystal tried to persuade all the passengers to refuse to pay anything until we docked back in Puno. Most of us thought this rather untrusting and were loath to poison relationships with Gloria, in mid-Titicaca. As it turned out, Walter and Crystal alone saved their payment until the end. Crystal was convinced – and probably still is – that the rest of us would still be castaways on Takile were it not for her foresight. Who knows? She certainly made a fearsome sight in her white war-paint, haranguing Gloria, who remained entirely unmoved, being unable to understand a word Crystal was saying.

And while this was going on, we were drifting through a beautiful reedy world. The lake by Puno is very shallow for some miles out. Green and orange reeds, great, unending beds of them pierce the surface. The water is dark and clear, and the light very intense.

In places, families have made their homes on floating islands of reeds, their little huts built in wood and straw, with tin roofs covered in thatch. They seem to live by fishing and begging, and are apparently the descendants of a tribe which took to the lake to escape plunder. It was strange chugging past their little settlements, huts quivering slightly in our wake, corners of the island dipping as bands of children gathered to call out to us.

On one floating island, tiniest of the lot – no more than a few square yards – John spotted a family of ocean-going black pigs. 'Torrent pigs,' we laughed.

The sky was the fiercest blue now, and the lake turquoise. We left the reed-beds and were soon miles from land. White peaks, low and very distant, ringed the horizon. Contrary to all the geographical conventions, we were at sea on the top of the world. Even Crystal began to relax. Using us to translate, she asked Gloria to which tribe she belonged, and then disputed the answer. 'Tell her,' she said in perplexed tones, 'that if she lives by the lake here, she ought to be a Mare, not a Quechua.'

Christian showed everyone a photograph of a recent girlfriend. She was pretty. They had met in Lima. On the back she had written in an immature hand: 'To Christian – I am always remembering the happy moments we had together, and how I learned to love you in so short time.'

'Will you see her again?' John asked.

'My mission is to many women. This is not the only rock on the beach. And I am in – how do you say? – short supply ...' Then his mask dropped a little as he remembered this particular rock. 'But maybe ...' At first glance, Christian was a manly-looking man, but he had the soft, rather feminine eyes of a womanizer. 'Or maybe not.'

For all we knew, this was our last journey with Christian – and Walter and Crystal too – for the next morning John and I were to leave them, and interrupt our journey by taking the short flight to the city of Arequipa. Mick and Ian were not quite ready to join us, and we did not want to continue on the train to Cuzco until they had. We would do some sightseeing in Arequipa, then return to Puno. They could join us there, or back in Puno. Then we would be ready to board the Cuzco train.

We drew back alongside the dock in Puno that night badly sunburned, and happy. Tomorrow, Arequipa! All but a pale wash had drained from the sky. The reeds were black, the hills behind very dark, and the town lights sparkled.

Chapter Eighteen

Arequipa

'Oh Peru, Peru!' The Indian woman in the Entel office in Arequipa wailed in despair. Like us, she was trying to place a telephone call to Lima, and, like us, she was defeated by the bureaucracy surrounding the operation.

To make a call between towns it is necessary to queue at the head-quarters of the nationalized telephone company. Scores of Peruvians mill around in a grim waiting-hall.

From time to time an unintelligible voice crackles out over an antique public address system, calling someone by name to a numbered kiosk, where their call is supposed to be waiting. This causes panic as half-a-dozen Indians are seized with the conviction that it is they who have been named, and, unable to catch the number of the appointed kiosk, everyone rushes around, in and out of kiosks, begging the nearest person to tell them what it is the loudspeaker has just announced, and scrabbling at the doors of the kiosk they think might be theirs. If and when you do find the right kiosk, the call has often been disconnected.

We found ourselves advising Indians on how to proceed. One thing we learned was to make up a name for yourself which was easily caught and impossible to mispronounce. John plumped for 'Señor Bing' and this worked well.

We became experts through necessity: we needed to keep in touch with Mick and Ian in Lima.

The news now, from Lima, was good. Mick had his new travel documents, Ian was recovering fast, and Mick's aubergine dancing-shoes had been enormously admired by all the staff at the hotel.

We had flown to Arequipa from Puno hoping they might both meet us there. Now, it seemed, they would not be able to rejoin us for a couple of days. They would fly direct to a place called Juliaca, near Puno. We, too, would return there, by bus if we could find one, and all four of us would continue our journey by rail to Cuzco: back together again. John and I would explore Arequipa alone.

*

This city is the quality end of all Peru. It is a city-state on its own, surrounded by barren lands but itself prosperous, perched on a shelf high enough above the Pacific to guarantee a stable, dry climate, but not so high as to suffer the skin-blistering atmosphere of the bleaker cities.

Over the town towers a volcano – dormant, magnificent, bleakly geometrical. It is called El Misti.

Guarded by its private volcano, there is a feeling of civic pride about the place. They even check your passports at the airport, if you are arriving from Lima. The city has its own architecture, a unity of design helped by the use everywhere of a local white rock for building, a creamy volcanic stone, pitted with little eyes and air-holes, giving the impression of petrified nougat. Terraces of white marbled stone line the streets beneath a clear sky.

The narrow roads are arranged in a Spanish colonial grid surrounding a magnificent square, set about with elegantly arched colonial façades and planted with mauve-flowering jacaranda trees. An air of tranquil order reigns, and of money: here the shoe-cleaning stands are not only of polished mahogany, but consist of two, three and even four-seater emplacements, with canopies!

We walked into the Basilica San Francisco 'converted to the status of a minor basilica by our most Holy Pius XII, 1940'. Mass was being celebrated. A peasant woman was quietly breast-feeding her baby before a shrine of lavender and white. Someone was lighting candles, and, from somewhere, a choir was singing a song of breathtaking beauty. It seemed a world away from Puno, or the crackling of Mick's voice over the telephone lines from festering Lima.

Outside, darkness was falling. But this was still Peru. It being nightfall, they began the ritual of ploughing an ancient water-cannon twice round the main square just to let everyone know – precisely what, one was never quite sure. The Arequipans took no notice at all. Such was their disregard that one well-tailored fellow – a bit unsteady on his feet after a few sundowners at a pavement café – was almost mown down by the water-cannon as we watched.

The accompanying militia were armed only with truncheons. In Peru, where even traffic wardens seemed to be armed for guerrilla combat, this was nakedness. A smell of baking bread filled the air as we found our way to a little *hostal* – no more than stables round a courtyard of the traditional white stone, with the traditional rudimentary beds, and the traditional filthy lavatory and communal cold tap.

We ventured out once more, late, to change money. The *inti* was sinking fast. Our dollars bought more Peruvian currency than ever from the money-changers outside the bank. Another 'chino' clinched the deal for our travellers cheques, and, on discovering that we were British, recited the names of the entire British Royal Family – both major and minor members – while counting the notes. He seemed to regard this as a form of courtesy.

Travel agencies were still open. We booked a place on a bus to Juliaca for two days hence. This way, we would see the country in between, and have a day of sightseeing in Arequipa first. Especially, we wanted to see the Convent of Santa Catalina, the pride of this city, a city within a city: walled, self-contained, rigorous and tranquil.

This was among the greatest seats of religion for women in Peru. The nuns' cells were laid out along tiny streets each named after one of the principal cities of old Spain.

Around one courtyard were cloisters painted with fifty-five representations of Mary – 'Mother of Mercy, Mother of Peace, Mother of the Sea ...' and so on – all of which (and in the right order) the novices had to learn to recite. The paintings were brilliant, primitive, somewhat in the style of William Blake.

There was a grisly photograph of the corpse of a favourite Mother Superior, who had died in 1902. After her, the 'Blessed Anna de los Angeles Monteagudo' seemed to be the favourite figure from the convent's past. Her photograph was everywhere. Beside one such picture was a framed certificate signed by an (apparently) eminent doctor. He testified to the effect produced by the proximity to his patients of the Blessed Anna's relics. According to the doctor this had caused a miraculous recovery after an operation for seemingly terminal cancer.

And all this alongside oil paintings of the 'Cuzco School' dating back over three centuries: harsh, vivid, morbid. To our eyes the place was a bizarre mixture of the mystical, the kitsch, the absurdly mundane. But to those who had built this convent, there were no self-conscious categories for 'art', 'religion' and 'the real world'. This was the real world, for them. It was a strange reality.

On the altar was the most enormous beeswax candle imaginable. Where did they get the beeswax from? There were few flowers and fewer bees in this scrubland.

The thought of beeswax transported me, suddenly and despite myself, from this strange world to Cambridge University in 1972, where a threatened power strike first brought a young student friend called Rowland Johnson to public notice.

Hearing of the strike threat, Rowland went within minutes to both the ecclesiastical suppliers in the city and bought out their entire stock of altar candles – all beeswax. A few weeks later, with churches and chapels unlit all over Cambridge, Rowland's candles burning in students' rooms in his college, and Rowland a comparatively rich fellow, those who had paused to laugh stayed to admire.

That summer he bought an old car and criss-crossed northern England from the Irish Sea to the North Sea, selling shirts from Lancashire on the Lincolnshire coast, and lobsters from Lincolnshire on the Lancashire coast. When last heard of, some years ago, he was a scrap-metal dealer, operating out of Hong Kong ...

The memory faded. With a start, the orange trees in the courtyard of Santa Catalina swam back into vision.

It was before dawn when we left Arequipa. The pavement typewriter operators, who will compose and type a letter for you on the spot, were already clacking away in the streets, lying in wait for early morning manuscripts. We scanned the anxious face of one peasant woman standing before the typist on our street corner. 'Honoured Sir,' one imagined him typing for her, 'You will perhaps have heard by now of my husband's difficulties concerning the maintenance of his instalments on the fruit-pulping machine we purchased on 16 April last year ...'

The newspapersellers were out in force. 'DEPUTY MAYOR OF PUNO TARGET OF SHINING PATH ASSASSINS,' screamed the headlines, and a murmur of concern spread around our bus. 'Only the *Deputy* Mayor?' we thought.

But concern among the other passengers was not surprising. The bus had collected us from our *hostal*, confirming, as we had feared, that it was mostly for foreigners. Our coachload was dominated by a party of French tourists complaining to each other in French. Two of the young men were wearing what seemed to be skin-hugging turquoise cycling shorts, while another was in cerise rayon tights with yellow tennis shoes.

Mostly the French were looking at each other, but when one of them, forgetting himself for a moment, looked out of the window, a nun was spotted, tripping on her veils to rush across to the driver's door in search of a lift. There was a disapproving wave of francophone cluck-clucks, for our bus was nearly full. The driver let her climb up – nuns get away with much in Peru – but the French had moved quickly, rearranging their modish soft suitcases to prevent the nun sitting among them in the only remaining seat. A soldier stood up, yielding his.

We began up the road which ribbons its way past the shoulder of Misti.

This, you knew, would be a burning day, for it was the palest of dawns, clean-washed and cool silver. A pastel yellow disc of a sun hung low behind Misti. The volcano was a dark, geometric silhouette, standing sentinel along a skyline which might have been clean-scissored from black card: shape without substance.

Motionless from the very edge of the crater's rim streaked the slightest plume of smoke: just a feather, as delicate and still – and as harsh – as a Japanese print. The smoke formed a little question-mark in the sky, hint of mortality to a proud city at its feet: smoke from the end of a patient fuse.

How long a fuse? Across the horizon from Misti you could discern the footings of what had once been a volcano three times as high, blown utterly apart.

The French had acquired a newspaper. They were translating passages to each other about the explosion in Puno, with many little cries of froggy alarm, while our bus climbed onward on a deteriorating road. Scrubby brown vegetation, lit by points of intense orange and yellow blossom, stretched in all directions.

The bus shuddered to a halt. '*Vicuña!*' exclaimed the driver, and the French went crazy, scrabbling for their cameras and fighting to get out of the bus.

In appearance *vicuña* are to llamas what small wild hares are to the plump, tame rabbit. *Vicuña* are the free-range prototype from which the domestic beast has been bred. They are smaller, faster, more delicate, graceful and very shy. They are also rather rare, and a protected species in Peru. It was certainly a treat to see some.

But the problem was that they kept their distance, grazing hundreds of yards away and running further still as we tried to approach. Brown specks grazing among brown scrubland, the *vicuña* were in fact visually less exciting than the French tourists in turquoise tights.

So, while the French tourists photographed the brown bottoms of the distant *vicuña*, John photographed the multi-coloured bottoms of the French tourists, at close range. We still have the photograph. At the time it aroused suspicion among the subjects of our photography, but at least they did not gallop away like the *vicuña*. They returned, tame, to the bus.

And on we went, the driver's radio playing an Andean folk version of 'Come to the cookhouse door, boys, come to the cookhouse door,' until we shuddered again to a halt. This time it was a puncture which had stopped us – the first, it was to turn out, of four, on a twenty-hour journey driven without sleep or rest by one driver. He also mended the punctures, inflated the tyres and changed the wheels, single-handed.

While the French trooped off to look for some shade, their pink, green and yellow ski-tops bobbing down the road in merry procession, we purloined the newspaper they had bought in Arequipa.

The item about the assassination ('PRESIDENT GARCIA FLIES TO PUNO TO ATTEND FUNERAL') was on an inside page. The main story – on the front page, with pictures – was of a truck which had jack-knifed in Arequipa, though nobody had been hurt. The back page was filled with a photograph of a woman's bottom. There was no story at all about this bottom. There was not even a caption. Just the bottom.

We hit the road. Until our driver, mechanic and tour guide, too, stopped again, this time in a marsh.

'Flamingos!' he said, and John claimed he saw a flash of disappearing pink. 'And alpacas.'

'*Où sont les alpacas?*' The French peered around an empty landscape. There were no alpacas. The driver looked embarrassed.

'Elsewhere,' he said in Spanish. We resumed our journey; but John had spotted marsh (but not torrent) duck.

It was a long, hot, high, windy road, and lonely. The only settlement of any size we passed was the grim barrack-blocks and corrugated asbestos of the township sprawled around a copper mine. We stopped for *coca* tea, marie biscuits and jam. The people looked surly and the raw concrete walls were covered in trade-union graffiti. Someone had painted the crude image of a raised fist all about the township.

What is it about the mining industry which leads to just the same ugly settlements, and just the same ugly human relations, in places as different from each other as the Andes and Kent, or Zambia and West Virginia?

Apart from this strange place, the rolling, barren land supported no villages of more than a handful of huts. Yet every one – however mean – had its makeshift football pitch with crude goalposts and, as often as not, the boys of the village tearing around in the dust after some moth-eaten apology for a football. We thought of Ian and wished he were back with us.

Mick had said, over a faint phone line, that Ian was still weak but in good spirits. Their departure from the hospital had been as farcical as their arrival. The matron had insisted that he leave a urine sample and arranged for bottle and label to be provided. But Ian had no urine to give and, try as he might, could not produce even a drop to order. 'Hysterical retention. A common syndrome,' the orderly had diagnosed grandly, although it seemed more likely that poor Ian was not so much hysterical as drained dry.

It would not have mattered except that, at the check-out desk, the hospital clerk had billed them for this urine test. Plainly it could not now be carried out.

The wheelchair operator (for Ian was still weak) had had to be bribed to carry his patient, and relations had not got off to an easy start, for Mick had disputed both the principle and the amount of the payment. But now he came into his own. He became (Mick told us) Ian's self-appointed guardian, negotiator and advocate. Wading fiercely into the attack, he had waved the empty urine bottle and directed a volley of abuse at the clerk and (later, when she was called) the matron. How could you charge a poor, sick gringo for non-existent tests on urine he hadn't passed? Was there no limit to the rapacity of this establishment?

Did they charge for operations they hadn't performed? Would he, the wheelchair operator, charge for patients who had died in the operating theatre and been unable to take advantage of his wheelchair?

For Ian it had been a fierce start to his convalescence. But it did, finally, save them the cost of the urine test; and, when Mick spoke to us, Ian had been feeling much stronger. 'He walked as far as the ice-cream and soda café, had a milkshake to drink, and walked back. Tomorrow we're going to see *Three Men and a Baby* ...'

Again the bus juddered to a halt. This was a bleak place, more rock than soil; and the road's surface was dreadful. The sun had passed its zenith but it was a blistering afternoon. A hot wind was blowing. Why had we stopped? It was not at first clear.

Huddled in the half-shade of a huge boulder was a girl, with her baby. The girl was small, thin and seemed very young. The baby was tiny, just a wizened face peeking from a bundle of coloured cloth. Both were heavily wrapped against the dust and wind.

She had flagged the driver down. She spoke to him now, in an Indian language which he seemed hardly to understand. Her voice was high and childlike. It seemed she was asking for a lift to the next village.

The driver tried to speak to her in Spanish but she could not understand. She turned to the other passengers in the bus, appealing in her own language, but nobody could communicate much. The driver indicated to her to sit on the step of the bus, inside the door, which he closed; and we pulled away from the roadside, the bus resuming its lurching, hammering progress over washboard corrugations and rock. She fed the child a little, then the tiny infant closed its eyes and slept, and the girl began to sing, softly. It was only the doorstep of an old bus, but for her it was a magic carpet.

How old was she? An office girl from Arequipa who was among the passengers proved best at communicating. The Indian girl was thirteen. The baby was four months. They were travelling to her father's village, twenty kilometres away.

The bus has been a stroke of good luck. How, otherwise, had they planned to get there? She would just have walked, she said. At sundown they would have slept a little, then, perhaps, walked on by night. She had eaten before she left and would eat when she arrived. Meanwhile she had a little water with her, and the baby – well, the baby had her.

What was the baby's name? 'Tomasina.' The office girl's friend joined her and together they questioned Tomasina's mother. The two city girls seemed to be fascinated by this creature, enquiring closely into her language, village, parents, clothes ... as though some wild bird had flown in through an open window and perched awhile as we studied her.

For her part, Tomasina's mother stared blankly around at the interior of the bus – the strange white faces and outlandish clothes, the luggage racks overflowing with remarkable baggage, the sounds and gestures she couldn't comprehend – and returned to tending her child, rocking her gently, singing a little and fending off the questions from the office girls.

Into what alien world had she and Tomasina been temporarily pitched? Did it mean anything to her? What did she make of it? As the child slept, so, after a while, did her child-mother.

We left her, as she asked, outside the gates of the next village.

The worst of the day's heat was over now, and our driver suggested we take advantage of this pit stop (to deal with the latest slow puncture) to eat a little in the shack that passed as a restaurant there.

They served 'trout'. It was not very good, but we livened it up with hot pepper sauce. John was wary of this, but I took lashings of it, and fell upon the disintegrating fish with my fingers.

'Quick!' said John. 'Your camera!' He was pointing at the two nuns among the passengers. These were different nuns (so far as one can ever tell) from the nun who had hitched a short ride, and left us earlier in the day. They were sitting together at a cool table in the shade, by the wall. Their backs were to the wall and they were facing us. Penned to the wall directly above them was an enormous centre-page colour foldout of a naked woman with breasts the size of melons. The nuns stared impassively forward from this exotic backdrop, unaware (it seemed) of the reason for our smiles. We did locate the camera.

Months later, the picture – when sent to the developers – never came out. It was unclear whether God or the photo agency was our censor.

We recovered our composure, and soon the bus was tooting its horn and ready to depart. I rushed behind a wall for a necessary pee before the next leg of the journey.

The next thing I remember was the most agonizing burning sensation. With the utmost care I zipped up my jeans. I looked down. My fingers were still flecked with bits of hot pepper sauce.

'Don't touch it!' said John to his writhing companion back on the bus. It was many hours before the pain had really gone. As we pulled out of the little place, shadows lengthening, I regretted my irreverent thoughts about the nuns.

The village mechanic was busy as we left, welding with viciously effective equipment and only sunglasses for eye protection. The blue-white glare lit the street. Further on, we passed an old woman milking a scrawny cow into a ripped-apart kerosene tin. Further on still, a girl was harvesting with a scythe, as the sun set.

The bus climbed, slowly, until we were high over the village some half an hour later. It was nearly dark now, and the flickering glare of the village welder still shone from the gloom far beneath us. The driver turned on his headlights and we ploughed on.

A pot-hole – perhaps – caused us to lurch hard, and an orange dropped from the luggage rack directly on to John's head. One of the nuns crossed herself, and her companion murmured 'Jesus ... Maria.'

Shortly afterwards there was a terrific bang from underneath the chassis, somewhere near the back wheels. We jammed on the brakes and everyone woke up and piled out into the dark night air.

One of the four rear tyres has exploded – 'burst' would be too gentle a word. Wearily, our driver prepared to change his fourth wheel. This one, as it turned out, was to get us all the way to Juliaca. But we did not know that as once more we hit the road, and all except the driver slept.

'Ay-ay-*ay*!' An exclamation from the driver woke us. There on the road ahead, picked out in his headlights, was what looked like a huge black skunk blundering across our path. The driver steered towards it, trying to run it down. He missed. Both nuns crossed themselves. 'Jesus!' they cried in unison, 'Maria!'

Chapter Nineteen

Steaming
into Cuzco

'Hey there! Chico!' The voice was unmistakable.

So was the sleek head, jutting from the railway carriage as the train pulled in. It was Christian. Moving swiftly to mouse-trap the nimble fingers of an infant pickpocket, already well into my trousers, I helped bundle our belongings aboard.

We had met Mick and Ian at Juliaca airport. John put the violence of the plane's landing down to the altitude. 'Same with birds, you know. The higher the altitude, the greater the ground-speed necessary for take-off and landing. Some of them have quite a problem coordinating claws and wings ...'

Smoke coming from this Boeing's claws had interrupted the nature lesson. One of the tyres had burst on impact with the runway.

There was no danger, but we watched as passengers filed off, and three small men bowled one huge aeroplane wheel across the tarmac from a shed to the waiting jet. Behind them walked a man with a bucket of water and this was splashed on to the steaming metal housing of the crippled wheel.

A party of French tourists – most of them young men – dressed in tunics of what looked like white parachute silk and looking like orderlies in a mental asylum, were the first to disembark. Then had come Mick, in earnest conversation with a nun – and Ian, much thinner and paler than before. We had made our way happily to Juliaca, welcomed by a fading sign hanging from an old building on the road in from the airport – 'WELCOME TO THE GLORIOUS NATIONAL INSTITUTE OF COMMERCE'. This was a flat railway town some miles from Puno and the shores of lake Titicaca, of a certain bustling if shabby commercial spirit.

Everything centred on the railway station. It fronted on to a small square and gardens, buzzing with activity. Here you could find the Peruvian equivalent of job centres or labour exchanges – big blackboards on easels propped around the square. Employers chalked the vacancies they wished to advertise: 'Girl wanted, to help in shop, also to assist with small children. Experience with accountancy useful, also cooking. Room with bed. 2000 *intis*.'

On other boards, job-seekers could chalk up their own hopes. The service was free. Each board was surrounded by a little crowd of people, checking, taking notes or just curious.

Over the square was the Institute Charles Darwin. A billboard outside advertised the courses of instruction available:

PARAMEDICS
COSMETICS & BEAUTY
ENGLISH
SECRETARIAL
EXECUTIVE
RADIO ELECTRONICS
TAILORING

We had sipped warm sodas watching two trucks full of soldiers pass, heading for Puno, armed to the teeth.

An *hostal* had accommodated us for the night. Sitting late, talking and drinking, we had all slept well in the end – even Mick whom we had not told about the altitude.

And now, confident and excited, we started our first journey on a Peruvian train.

'What the hell are you doing on this train, Christian? We thought you had already gone to Cuzco with Evelyn.'

'I make a last-minute – is that how you say? – reschedule of my itinerario.'

'Why?'

'Woman trouble. Problems with Evelyn. She is boring. So I inform the others my ticket is no good. Forgery. Dud. Blank. Counterfeit. Therefore I am having to wait for a new train. Then Evelyn she offer to stay with me. "Take your opportunity, Evelyn." I advise her. "Maybe I am staying here for a month". Evelyn leave. Problem dissolved.'

'Oh, this is Mick and this is Ian, Christian: our two friends from Lima. But why did you want to leave Evelyn?'

'Too hot for me. I am trapped. Always I have this problem. You love a woman, of course, but ... the world ... is very extensive.'

All this passed between us as our train trundled slowly out of Juliaca, dozens of Indians leaping at the windows from the outside, trying to sell toy llamas with scarlet tassels, covered in real llama-fur, to last-minute impulse-buyers. Slowly, as the platform receded, the level of the ground outside sank too, and the Indian vendors – short people at the best of times – disappeared below window-level. Then only the llamas, held aloft on outstretched arms, were visible, bobbing, as it were, in space. Our parting vision was of a fluffy white toy llama pecking – bang, bang, bang – wildly at the carriage window, disembodied from its invisible bearer, its scarlet tassels flying in the breeze.

The train passed out of the station through great iron gates across the railway, opened for us now but otherwise locked. These provided a secure enclosure for the station and its sidings – though whether to keep the pickpockets in or out was a balanced question. At these gates was a shrine raised to the Virgin Mary, emblazoned with the arms of the railway company. Our Lady herself, in replica, had been placed sitting delicately astride a real, iron locomotive-wheel, surrounded by plastic flowers.

After that, the railway ran straight down the middle of the main street, vendors, carts, donkeys, chickens and children scattering in our path as the diesel engine whistled. It was odd to look out of a carriage window and see sidewalks, shop fronts and domestic porches to left and right.

We gathered speed to a dignified canter, and began to rattle across a flat, dusty plain, once (apparently) the bed of the original, larger Lake Titicaca. John stared out from the window, transfixed. He had seen eagles. Christian was trying out his girl-conquest stories on Ian, a new audience. But they were distracted by Mick, who was recounting a story about the Yorkshire sport of putting live ferrets down your trousers.

'Do you put ferrets down your trousers in Switzerland, Christian?'

A long slow smile . . . 'No room.'

The waiter – for so his soiled white tunic announced him – came round to take orders for luncheon. Something about the grubby uniform and the motion of the train touched another South American memory.

It was the same holiday that later brought the bandit attack, but a happier time. I had decided to try the train from Lima into the Andes. This undertakes the greatest railway climb in the world, from sea level to more than 15,000 feet: straight up the mountain. It is one of the wonders of nineteenth-century civil engineering, and vast human sacrifices were made to build it.

Unfortunately, the modern-day passengers, personnel and rolling-stock did not live up to the historical accomplishment. A few tourists were trying the journey, but mostly the old carriages were packed with peasants, livestock and soldiers going up into the mountains. The train was dirty and seedy.

But the greatest incongruity of all was the oxygen-vendor. We thought at first he was some kind of drug dealer, operating in a shockingly open way. He was a doleful fellow. Dressed in a filthy white housecoat – you might expect to see it on a Ministry of Agriculture veterinary inspector doing his rounds at the local slaughterhouse – he staggered from carriage to carriage with a battered black cylinder marked OXYGEN. From its top came a pink rubber pipe, terminating in a chewed rubber face-mask of the kind that air-hostesses wave in that ritual pre-flight ballet they call 'safety demonstration'.

As the train climbed, passengers (it was said) might feel faint from the altitude. If so, you could hail him; and for the equivalent of a few pence you were allowed to hold the mask over your mouth and nose and take a sniff while he twiddled a knob on the end of the cylinder.

The smarter sort of Peruvian passenger took advantage of this service – as if sensitivity to altitude betrayed a superior education or demonstrated class. Yet the dirty housecoat, black cylinder, pink rubber and steel tubes gave the whole performance the air of a macabre ritual. And ritual it surely was. Would it have made any difference if the cylinder had contained no oxygen? For all we knew, it didn't . . .

I chuckled at the memory.

And came back to earth. What, asked the waiter, did we want for lunch?
'What is there?'
'Chicken soup, followed by roast chicken. Then there is blancmange and coffee.'
'And the alternatives?'
'No. Only that.'
'We must have that then?'
'Yes.'
'Then that is what we will have.'
'What?'
'What you just said.'
'What?'
'Chicken soup, you said.'
'Yes, sir, chicken soup. What afterwards?'
'Well, roast chicken . . . You said there was no choice.'
'Wait – I am writing it . . . Chicken soup . . . then . . . .'
Laboriously he wrote down the list he had recited a moment ago. We didn't argue. After a few minutes, he had passed the blancmange and reached the coffee. He put down his pencil and turned to Mick.
'And what will you have?'
'The same.'
'You mean chicken soup . . .'
And so it continued. Another ritual, its origins lost in the mists of an age when there was a choice of menu on Peruvian trains.

There were many tourists in our carriage. The noisiest were a group of Germans. Ian had noticed them on the plane from Lima.

'They stood by the departure gate for half an hour so that they could get on to the plane first,' he told us, 'because there were no seat reservations. Then they sprinted across the tarmac and up the gangway, and staked out all the window seats on the side their guidebook said gave the best views of the Andes. They each had their own edition of the same book.

'At first their plan worked well. But it came unstuck when they got too ambitious. Having booked a window seat each, they tried to block Peruvian passengers from sitting next to them, by spreading their luggage over the adjacent seats. The first Peruvians to reach the plane put up with this, but soon there were so many looking for seats that people started demanding that the Germans move their baggage, and shouting at them.

'At this point the German discipline broke down, and they began arguing amongst themselves about what to do next.

'Then one emerged as their leader. He was that short, bull-necked man.' Ian pointed him out to us: a stocky character of about forty-five: he had a nervous cough, and khaki shorts. 'Mick and I call him Willi. Willi decided that being together was the most important thing, so the Germans abandoned their forward window positions and withdrew into a laager formation near the back of the plane. Willi organized a rota system for looking out of the window . . .'

Even as Ian spoke, Willi was already at work again, consolidating his leadership in the railway carriage. His troops all wore khaki: it seemed almost to be a uniform among them, their idea of 'safari' gear. A complicated dispute with a party of French tourists over luggage space ensued. The Germans won.

The French returned to their paperback novels. Alone in our carriage, and despite the heat, they kept their window closed. They appeared to be two couples, one older, one younger. All were well dressed, the elderly gentleman from a bygone era. He wore an English-style smoking jacket, which he never removed, flannel trousers, a silk cravat and sunglasses. The younger fellow had brogue shoes, corduroy trousers, a checked shirt and sunglasses.

Both women wore sunglasses too. They were just as smart, the younger one carrying a full-length calfskin coat in maroon. Their stylish suitcases, too, were leather. These, clearly, were Frenchmen of a different class and generation to the para-jumpsuited-and-hair-gel type we had seen elsewhere. They were in keeping with the gentility – however faded – of a first-class carriage in a South American railway train.

But they shared with the younger generation of French tourists at least this: it seemed to go without saying among them that one took only the slightest interest in the country through which one was travelling.

Obvious curiosity, or – worse – enthusiasm, was not acceptable. Their main point of contact with their surroundings took the form of complaining: finding the environment too hot, too cold, too dirty or dusty, and letting their companions know of their discomfort.

Like us, the French ordered the full meal. Unlike us, they did not eat it when it came. Each course was placed before them in succession: each course, in succession, was sent away untouched. They even ordered coffee and, when it arrived, pushed the cups away with small, affronted cries of disgust. They were thus confined to their own bottle of mineral water (which – utterly implausibly – appeared to be French), a small hamper of delicately cut sandwiches, and a game of mah-jongg. They kept themselves entirely to themselves.

The Australian ladies did not. These were the oldest tourists we encountered: a very elderly pair indeed, out for an adventure. Dressed rather noisily, game for anything – any souvenir, any toy llama which tapped at their window – they engaged us all in conversation, snapped away with their cameras continuously, and tried all the food. The Americans would call them 'golden girls'.

'How's Maggie' (she meant the British prime minister) 'doing in the old country?' one of them asked John.

'Oh, okay,' said John diplomatically. John is not a card-carrying Conservative. 'But she's rather a bully, you know.'

'She's got to be,' said her companion. 'We worship her, don't we, Sally?'

'Follow her to the end of the earth. The world needs a strong woman. We could do with someone like her in Australia.'

'Who's going to win Wimbledon this year? I don't like that German boy.' (She meant Boris Becker.)

'Do you girls play tennis?' Ian asked.

'Cheeky boy! Not at this altitude. Do you like Peru?'

Ian said he did.

'You haven't been to Australia then. Try the Blue Mountains. Lush! Not dried up like this.'

'Not that we're not enjoying it,' her companion chipped in.

Mick looked incredulous. 'Don't you get breathless at this height?'

'Breathless? We thought we'd breathed our last when we got off that plane. We were desperate. But a pill here, a sniff of oxygen there, and we keep going.' She patted the head of one of the brace of toy llamas they had just bought.

'You've got to take each place as it comes,' added her friend, patting Ian on the arm. 'No good worrying about flies here. Just get into the local atmosphere, let it surround you, soak you up . . . I suppose I'd say that I'm just a nature person . . .' She gave Ian another lingering pat.

The French party, who were not nature people, glanced across at us in distaste from their little envelope of cool indifference. If an all-round, wrap-around sunglass, of stylish appearance, could be devised to enclose their entire corner of the railway carriage, then they would have brought that too, along with their mineral water.

At first, our train had been rocking along an uneven track, at about thirty miles per hour, through dry flat country, raising clouds of dust as it went. In the fields, women and donkeys were treading corn underfoot. Whole families were winnowing it in the wind, by hand. But by lunch, mountains were rising to each side, funnelling us up a wide, then narrowing, valley. We were beginning to climb. Our pace slowed to a crawl. Within, Ian was arguing with the Australian ladies about the left-wing policies of the Manchester City Council. From without, you could hear the roar of the two great and elderly American diesel locomotives hauling the carriages, and see black smoke and occasional sparks flying from their exhaust stacks.

For half an hour the track was so steeply uphill that you could trot alongside the train – as some young chancers from the third-class carriages did. Snow started to appear on the peaks of the mountains outside, and we passed some fenced fields announcing themselves as 'HIGH ALTITUDE EXPERIMENTAL ANIMAL STATION'.

The Australian ladies consulted their guidebook. 'This is where they find out what makes llamas tick,' she said.

'How?'

'Don't ask me, dear. But they do.'

The train laboured on, the gradient so steep now that to walk up the carriage aisle was perceptibly uphill. Around the middle of the afternoon, it shuddered to a halt, whistle howling. A sign outside told us that this was the top of the pass. At more than 14 000 feet, it was one of the highest points on any railway in the world.

Outside our windows, scores of Peruvians had quit their carriages and were running across the brown turf. Why, one wondered? They seemed to be heading for a marsh full of steaming puddles. We decided to join them and investigate.

These were volcanic springs. Hot, sulphurous water was bubbling out of the ground in dozens of places, forming muddy water-holes and warm rivulets edged with yellow scum. As if in some religious ritual, the Peruvians all began to take off their shoes. Then they sat down by the mud-holes and dangled their feet in the hot liquid. Then they put their shoes back on and returned to the train.

Were these springs believed to have some health-giving property for feet? Or was the foot-dipping exercise just for fun? We never discovered. Mick asked one of the women why people were doing this, but, like so many of the basic questions that foreigners ask, the answer (whatever it was) must have seemed so obvious to the natives that they couldn't understand the question.

At any rate, people were given plenty of time as our train was waiting for the only other train of the day, coming the other way, from Cuzco. The line was single-track, and this, the top of the pass, was the only place where the two trains could pass. We were on the saddle. It was downhill, now, to Cuzco.

With much whistling and many cries of distress from travellers convinced that foot-washing companions were about to be left behind, our train pulled away. We watched the flashing red rear lantern of the Puno-bound train disappearing down the pass; and idly wondered why – with only one train a day in each direction – there was any need for a rear warning light.

We were on our way. Slowly, as the gradient steepened downhill, we gathered speed. Soon carriages were swaying wildly and sparks flying from the iron brakes as we rushed down the valley, engines whistling and hooting. Even the French looked slightly stimulated.

It was cooler now. With the top of the pass we had passed the top of the afternoon. Hills and valleys flew past, the land grew greener, the river deeper and stronger, and the villages more numerous. Evening approached.

Peruvian nightfall is a sudden affair. No lengthening afternoon and lingering dusk, as in England – no sun hovering reluctantly above the horizon – no long and indeterminate twilight. With admirable despatch the sun drops out of the sky like a golden bullet. Day yields to night without a struggle.

While we watched, the sky darkened from the east, its western horizon still edged in luminous yellow. The mountains blazed, then glowed, then turned black. The light died to a lavender wash, then purple, very dark. I saw a little Indian boy standing alone by the river's edge, fishing with a long pole. The train whistled and he wheeled round to stare as we passed, then resumed his fishing.

Tall eucalyptus trees crowded, black, over our passage. Birds shrieked and darted above. The night was purple, the stars shone sharp as diamonds, and we flew headlong down the valley into Cuzco.

Chapter Twenty

Not Cuzco

Cuzco deserves to feature as a centrepiece in every account of Peruvian travel, and usually does.

But one hardly needs to repeat what all the others say. Everyone has admired the colonial and religious splendours built upon an Inca foundation; everyone has wondered at the incredible Inca forts which surround the city; everyone has paid their *intis* to take their snapshot of the traditionally dressed Indian girl with the snow-white llama who appears as if by magic at historical sites whenever a tourist happens by; and everyone has been robbed, mugged, pickpocketed or cheated in the market.

Cuzco is one of the few places in Peru which is both worth seeing, and can be toured quickly and easily. The climate is good, the airport convenient, the hotels legion; and, within day-trips of the city, lie not only Machu-Picchu, but such a variety of excursions that this makes an obvious (perhaps the only obvious) venue in Peru for the international tourist.

But Cuzco has prostituted herself, and done so not with the friendly vulgarity (for instance) of the Niagara Falls, nor yet with the beguiling sinfulness of Rio; but with an ill grace.

Once the Inca capital of perhaps the greatest planned society mankind has ever known, the city was cheated and bludgeoned into submission by the Spaniards, and upon her Indian foundations their own capital was built. But the stone footings – all still visible – from which the Spanish buildings rise were not yielded willingly, and the Indian people were never happy under their European masters.

Now those masters have yielded, in their turn, to the collapse of their own mother-empire. In Cuzco now, Spain too is just history.

And the new masters, who are they? Not the old Inca order re-established; its people may have been 'liberated', but their culture is dead. The Indian peasantry have not raised themselves much – in spirit – from their old subjection. Nor is the new order – the Latin–Peruvian establishment, ruling from Lima – the new master: for Cuzco is a tourist town, owing as much to New York and Miami and the plane-loads of backpacking students from Europe, as to Lima.

So amidst all the beauty and curiosity which the city owes to its history, and the pockets of prosperity sustained by the tourist dollar, there is a bitter confusion about the place. Where there should be an identity there is instead a sour muddle. Cuzco never yielded gracefully to its ancient conquistadors, and it does not do so now to its modern ones. There is a edginess to the town.

Pickpocketing must be so much a part of the local economy that it would be interesting to sponsor research into what proportion of the city's income derives from larceny; what proportion of police time is devoted to writing down reports of robberies which will never be investigated; and what proportion of the Entel telephone company's profits are due to tourists trying to reach American Express in Lima to give notice of stolen travellers' cheques.

If you have not been robbed in Cuzco, or if you do not at least know someone else who has, you have not travelled.

'I'm looking for a girl in this city,' Christian told us, as we checked in to our barracks-like *hostal*, 'who can massage my back. She must have fingers like – how do you say? – questing rats.'

'Don't you mean velvet mice?'

'No, rats.'

After a few days' sightseeing, we grew tired of ecclesiastical splendours and determined on a new adventure. We must eat guinea-pig.

One of our guidebooks said that a local speciality was 'seared' guinea-pig, which could be found in the suburbs.

Suburbs? Cuzco lies in a bowl, with hills and mountains rising steeply on three sides. Townships of mud-and-cobble streets and tin-roofed houses climb out of the old city in all directions. So where should we look? We decided to split up for the day, try our luck separately, and report back to the *hostal* at dusk.

Ian did not get very far. He was waylaid at the post office by three girls from Argentina. A blond boy, in this of all places, was luck beyond their dreams, and they all but dragged him away.

'They just stared at me while I was queuing for stamps,' he said. 'I looked away. Then, while I was licking the stamps to put them on the postcard, they started giggling and whispering to each other. After a bit, the bravest one came up to me and asked if I was Swedish – and did I want her and her friends to help lick my stamps?

'Then came a wild fit of giggling from the other two. Then they asked me if there was a good café anywhere, which I could show them ...'

Ian seemed to have displayed little fortitude, and ended up tagging along with the girls for the day. 'They invited all of us to the disco with them tonight but I explained that you three were too old for that sort of thing. You'll have to arrange for the man at the gate to let me in late, as they lock up about eleven.

'And guinea-pig?'

'I didn't ask about guinea-pig. These were cultured girls, with taste …' Ian spoke as though guinea-pig was the South American equivalent of fish and chips. 'No. We went to a restaurant.'

'Why didn't you order guinea-pig?'

'None on the menu. But there was a man playing the harp, with no nose …' So much for Ian.

Mick came back without guinea-pig news either. But he had met a couple from Birmingham. They were called Chris and Elaine. They were tourists in Peru, but lived at present in Quito, Ecuador, to which they had recently emigrated.

'We thought we'd try teaching English, but Elaine doesn't like Ecuador much, do you Elaine?'

'It's not what I thought.'

'We used to live in Birmingham. I was in the chauffeuring business and bought out my boss. Made a lot of money with hire cars. But Elaine didn't like it, did you, Elaine?'

'The pits. I had to get away from Birmingham. It's not what it was.'

'I'd had this dream – we both had – of running a pub and restaurant somewhere scenic, so we bought a place in the Lake District, by Lake Windermere. It went well at first, but – well, it was really hard grind and the catering business is …'

'Not what it was,' said Elaine. 'I didn't like it.'

'So I bought this little stone cottage and smallholding in Wales. It was Elaine's idea. We wanted to drop out of the rat-race completely. It was a beautiful situation. We tried keeping speciality goats. But Elaine didn't go for it in the end, did you, Elaine?'

'It rained all the time. It does in Wales.'

'So this is our latest move – to Quito. Marvellous climate, friendly people, but Elaine doesn't really … . Oh I think I mentioned … Now we're taking this little holiday, to think about our next move. Isn't Peru incredible! Mind you, Elaine doesn't like it.'

Mick took them for tea and carrot cake in a vegetarian restaurant run by two Israelis. Elaine didn't like it. It would have seemed provocative, Mick thought, to ask the Israeli vegetarians about seared guinea-pig – kosher or otherwise – so, like Ian, he gave up on that.

John was even less lucky. Taking the guidebook very much at its word, he had climbed the stone-stepped alleys, constructed by the Incas, up into the poorer quarters which surround Cuzco, clinging to the slopes above the city. These, he thought, might be the 'suburbs' of which the book spoke. Soon, he found himself all but lost in a maze of little earth pathways and rickety houses.

Remembering the word for guinea-pig – *cuy* – and remembering how to pronounce it – cwee – John had moved among the populace saying 'Cwee, cwee' in what he hoped was an inquisitive sort of voice. People started setting their dogs on him.

Apparently he had become confused and mistook his way home. So he decided that downhill, towards the lights of the city, must be more or less the right direction and began to take any path or alley that seemed to go that way. The result was that he ended up in a blind alley which led only to a little group of shacks.

Foolishly, John decided to press on – for he knew his general direction – searching for a way through the houses. Weaving through people's backyards, he lost track even of the way he had come.

'I panicked,' he confessed. 'I found myself at the end of somebody's yard, with a straw-and-thorn wall in front of me. People had been peering out at me from inside their houses, and this household suddenly opened their doors. Two huge black dogs came tearing across the yard at me, snarling and baring their teeth. They looked like bears. They made a terrible noise ... I tried to rush the fence. I got caught up in the thorns. The dogs were at my heels. I don't know how I did it, but the strength seemed to come, and I just tore the fence apart' – John showed us the cuts and grazes which proved it – 'and scarpered.

'I don't know how long I ran for. The barking stopped – I don't think the dogs did follow me – but I was vaulting over walls and dodging down alleys so blindly that people began shouting, and new dogs began barking, too. It seemed as though all the dogs on the hillside were alerted, and the whole place sounded like a kennels. Once, three or four mongrels formed into a pack and met me, coming the other way, up a walled alley ...

'I scrambled over the wall, and carried on running. Eventually I found a proper street. The barking had died down. I stopped to get my breath, and saw that the emergency was over. I feel sick now.'

But all was not lost, for Mick had found the name of a restaurant where it was said they served *cuy*. His informant was a man he'd met in the main square who said he was a Swiss stucco-repairer.

The restaurant was called (in the best translation we could manage) The Oven of the Coloured Ladies. We would eat there that night. Tomorrow we would walk up to Sacsayhuaman, the Inca fort which overlooks and guards the city.

The Oven of the Coloured Ladies was a dirty place whose proprietor, head waiter, wine waiter, cook and dishwasher was a Chino-Peruvian who looked like Deng Xiao Ping. Cats peered at us from behind the pillars as we pored over the menu.

There it was! Guinea-pig casserole; seared guinea-pig; guinea-pig with peas and sweet potatoes ... We had hit the jackpot. Deng Xiao Ping was called.

'One seared *cuy*, please, two *cuy* with peas and ...' Deng interrupted.

'No seared *cuy*.'

'Ah. Three *cuy* with peas and ...'

'No. No *cuy* with peas and sweet potatoes.'

'Do you have *cuy* at all?'

'No *cuy* today. Cats eat.'

And we had come so close! Flies danced around the dim light bulb as we studied the menu afresh.

After a bad meal of mushy avocado stuffed with mashed tuna from a tin, John went out to the lavatory to be sick. It was a while before he returned. 'All the plumbing's painted gloss magenta,' he said.

Walking home through the darkened streets, it was surprising to see how many blind-drunk Indians lay around or staggered down the carriageway.

We had noticed this in bars, too. They do not seem to drink much before they are pathetically drunk – 'pathetically' being the word, for most become maudlin, weepy, incoherent or just stupefied. There is neither the aggression nor the jollity that more often goes with alcohol in Europe.

Why? Do they have different metabolisms from us? Or are there layers of melancholy beneath their skins, missing from our psyche, and laid bare by the alcohol?

We were up early next morning, for the climb to Sacsayhuaman.

Cuzco's altitude is about 10,000 feet, and the slightest climb soon begins to tell. The cobbles grew steeper as we passed a gatehouse erected by the tourist board. The officials within were like all the Cuzco tourist board officials: they wore orange mining helmets, blew on little whistles, but seemed to serve no other function.

It was not long before Mick realized that he had left the newspapers he had bought at the gatehouse. It was only fifty yards back, but it was all Mick could do to fetch it. John was still feeling sick.

Ian had gone ahead and met us at the top, with a shout. 'This place is amazing.'

It was. All our woes left us as we contemplated it, lost in wonder.

Vast walls with lookout towers, steep steps and dark, enclosed passages had been constructed at the mountain's edge. Slabs of rock as big as the wall of an English country cottage had been levered into place, keyed into a design in which each stone was of a different shape and size. There were no methodically layered rows of stone: yet, like the patchwork of a jigsaw puzzle, the whole construction added up. The walls stood clean, cool and strong. The intricate geometry worked.

'The Incas had no proper form of notation,' said Mick. 'No writing.'
Then how could they have planned and executed a design like this?
'And they never invented the wheel.'

Then how could they have moved these stones? The thing must have
been accomplished with manic ingenuity. Ruses, dodges and ways round
the problem, now long-forgotten, must have played their part. Only the
bird's-eye view that history affords shows us the obvious short-cuts to
which they were blind. So much cleverness, so much energy, all to bridge
a tiny gap created by the lack of one missing piece in the jigsaw puzzle,
a simple invention, an 'obvious' truth: a thought so basic that – missed
at the outset – nobody ever turned back to notice the gap.

When successor civilizations look back on this, our own civilization,
what 'simple' truths will be seen to have been staring us in the face, yet
we never saw them? What wheel have we failed to invent? What wings
do we possess with which we have never tried to fly?

'Try looking in the obvious places.' In what obvious places have
we forgotten to look? No doubt people will marvel at our ingenuity,
our technical skills. 'The sophistication,' they will say, 'of their
medical surgery! The accuracy of their measurements; the devilish
complication of the technical tasks they could accomplish! Yet they
never realized ...'

Never realized *what*? *What* are we missing? Sometimes I lie in bed
trying to forget all that body of acquired knowledge, the accretion of
ingenuity, the thousand clever ways round the problem, that must be
blinding us to the problem itself.

We stretched out on the grass before the fort. Mick opened his newspaper – a Lima edition of a national paper, three days out of date – and
read aloud.

'In Ica, the populace have raided a lorryload of one thousand seven
hundred and forty boxes of evaporated milk – in a rage because an ex-
Secretary of the PAP was spotted surreptitiously loading four boxes of
the milk into his car, when local people have to queue for two cans per
person, which is the ration.

'With what authority can the PAP claim to be the vanguard of social
change?'

There were other items: one about a scare that there would be
shortages of key products, which had led to panic buying in parts of
Lima. As a result, sugar, rice, milk, oil and kerosene were now in
seriously short supply in much of the capital.

False dollars were circulating in Puerto Maldonado, in the jungle. A
third cocaine laboratory had been found in the Amazon region within
a week. On the back page there was a half-page picture of a hole in the
road, in Lima: 'HOLE IN ROAD SUBJECT OF SUSTAINED PROTEST'.

A hundred peasants had been murdered – whether by Shining Path or by government troops was disputed – in a remote Andean village. There had been another assassination attempt on the Deputy Mayor of Puno. Twelve soldiers had been blown up in Huanaco, and an earth tremor had hit Tacna.

The sun was low in the sky, and we were almost alone. But not quite. Across the grass, beneath the largest of the great stones forming the wall, sat an Indian peasant, in its shadow. She was hawking Coca-Cola and Inca-Kola, which she had carted up from the town in an old plastic bucket filled with cool water. She wore the brilliant crimson and magenta skirts traditional among these women, and the bowler hat.

'Inca-Kola! Cold Inca-Kola!' she cackled across at us, the only tourists. Then, in the sort of pleading whimper that the peasants adopt as a sales pitch: 'Buy from me. Buy from me sir.' ('*Compra-me señor*') she whined, hugging her plastic bucket of Inca-Kola, her words echoing around the ruins of her ancestors.

The night at our hotel was interrupted by a drunk trying to get in at the front entrance. He shook the gate and shouted in Quechua for what seemed like hours. Then he began to weep. When at last the gatekeeper was roused to let him in, he continued to weep. For what seemed like most of the night, the courtyard rang to the sound of a man sobbing uncontrollably, railing against his fate in a strange tongue.

Chapter Twenty-One

Not
Machu-Picchu

It was an hour before sunrise when the drunk finally passed out. Only then could we sleep. And we slept so heavily that we missed the taxi ordered to take us early to the railway station whence – at 6.00 a.m. – the train left for Machu-Picchu. This place, a Wizard-of-Oz-like fortress in the sky, rises from the jungled mountains further down towards the Amazon basin. It was one of the last and most remote haunts of the embattled Incas, and only rediscovered earlier in this century. It is one of the wonders of the world, and the others, who had not seen it, were determined not to miss the chance. There are no roads, just an incredible railway: and a one-day excursion by train from Cuzco is the only way of getting there.

Even after missing our taxi, we so nearly made the train. Mick awoke not long after dawn and we ran the mile or two to the station. The train pulled out just as we sprinted for the platform.

Yet we were determined to catch that train: not because it was the last – in two hours the luxurious 'tourist train' would depart – but because Christian had said that foreigners were not allowed on the early train. It was for peasants only, he said, paying peasant prices, so the authorities forced tourists to take the more expensive diesel-car. He himself would be obliged to do so – pride himself though he did on always getting the best bargain.

It was true that all the brochures and hotel receptions confirmed Christian's story. But we did not believe it. How could you bar someone from a train because of his nationality?

'Try it,' Christian had sneered. 'You will see. You will not be permitted to buy the tickets; and, if you are, the conductor – when he sees you are not peasants – will exile you. I will pass you, excommunicated at some little station, in my air-conditioned train. On the *left*-hand side of the carriage, from which the premium vistas are possible. And I will wave.'

That was a challenge. Mick had met it well, so far, by purchasing the tickets in advance, and speaking such good Spanish that nobody could suspect he was English. Now we had to see whether we would be thrown off.

First, though, we had to get on. We watched the back of our train disappearing up the track. What to do?

All was not lost. To get out of Cuzco and over the rim of mountains that surrounded the city the railway made a laborious succession of switchbacks, shunting backwards and forwards along a track that zig-zagged up the mountainside.

The road was more direct. We reckoned that if we could find a taxi to take us over the top and down to the first station beyond that pass, then we would have overtaken the train and could board it there.

The plan worked. Our taxi driver became so caught up in our enthusiasm to overtake the train that he forsook his own commercial advantage (which surely lay in *not* catching the train) and tore along the trackside roads through the suburbs which cling to the hillside above the city, hoping to catch it even before it reached the top.

But we never gained the ground needed for an orderly boarding of the carriages. Just as the train would screech to a halt to reverse up the next stretch of line – and the guard leap from the last carriage to switch the points behind him, allowing the train to reverse up the 'zag' rather than advance up the 'zig' of the switchback – so our taxi would arrive, seconds too late to board.

Perhaps we were lucky, for we noticed some urchins trying to steal a free ride by boarding in this way. The guard was knocking them off with a stick.

On our instructions, the driver sped ahead, over the top of the ridge, to the next station in the valley below. The place was called Cucuchucha. It was 6.30 when our taxi limped up to the trackside and left us. The driver had suddenly spotted the station from the road and driven straight for it across an intervening field. As a result we had driven into a ditch. It did his front suspension no good at all, but we got the car out.

Anyway, there was no hurry now, for we were well ahead. The village was swathed in a morning mist. It seemed to be unknown for tourists to try to board trains here; and for company we only had a handful of uncomprehending peasants who spoke no Spanish, let alone English. Friendly enough, they shared mugs of hot maize gruel with us as, all shivering, we waited for the train to come down from the top.

It did, dead on time. It was packed with Indian peasants, and we took our chances with them.

At first people stared as we shoved our way among the Indians already crowding the car. Roads reached only part of the way along the route we were travelling, and many of the villages and towns were accessible only by train. There were only two trains a day. So the human pressure upon this, their only line of communication, was intense.

Our train had been filled at Cuzco, its starting point. By Cucuchucha, where we joined it in the dawn mist, there was standing room only. As sun broke through the mist and we rattled past succeeding villages, stopping at each to take on more passengers, the struggle to find a place on board became more intense. Soon it was desperate. Every time we stopped, more peasants would claw and struggle their way in. By mid-morning it was impossible to move and hard to breathe. And the stench was awful.

Our carriage was a cross-section of Peru. We were the only tourists, but there were a couple of middle-class women, a schoolteacher and her daughter, travelling down to Quillabamba (the end of the line). The rest were peasants, labourers and hawkers, dressed in a marvellous assortment of styles. Elsewhere in the world fashions in clothes come and go, and, when they go, disappear to be replaced by something else. But in South America it seemed that each wave that had swept the continent had left, as it receded, a pocket of Indians cleaving to the style – never to abandon it. Society had become a museum of dress, or costume theme-park.

In our carriage were women in bowler hats and men in trilbies. Some of the older women were in the ankle-length skirts, bustled out with yards of petticoat, that their Spanish conquistadors' fine ladies must have worn more than a century ago. A few of the younger men were in the jeans and trainers of North American youth, and the teacher and her daughter were in short skirts and blouses; others wore shabby suits of almost Edwardian vintage.

At each end of the carriage a soldier with a sub-machine gun was riding shotgun (a Machu-Picchu train had been blown up recently by the Shining Path) and these guards were trying to prevent passengers from moving between carriages. Why, it was not clear, and there were exceptions to this rule: hawkers of hot food and drinks seemed to pass freely.

One such hawker got on with us at Cucuchucha. She carried a tray heaped with steaming food and covered in layers of linen to keep it warm. Throwing this tray on to the coupling between two carriages, she hauled herself and her many skirts through the door at the carriage end. A very small boy with a very big flour-sack did the same. There was no room for both him and his sack where he got on, so he perched the sack on the platform at the end of one carriage, and boarded the other.

As we gathered speed, the hawker struggled through to her tray of wares and, balancing it on her head, started to move down the carriage crying '*papas rellenas*' (stuffed potatoes). It was a struggle to move but she seemed enormously powerful, and shouldered her way through, sometimes climbing right over people and possessions.

Somehow she managed to do all this while extracting individual potatoes from the folds of cloth and exchanging them for ten-*inti* notes – giving change where necessary from the dozens of notes she kept neatly stacked in the clefts of all five fingers and one hand. Just to watch this magnificent performance – as triumphant a display of human skill, in its way, as a ballet dancer's or trick cyclist's art – was gripping.

The little boy with the big flour-sack had got into an argument with the soldier guarding his end of the carriage. Quite resolutely, the soldier was refusing to let the little boy cross carriages to be reunited with his sack. He could see it from where he stood, across the platform coupling with the next carriage. He kept pointing, and pleading with the soldier.

'It's my mother's,' he was saying anxiously. 'I am taking it to my aunt in Aguas Calientes. I must have it.' Other people were moving up and down, joining, leaving and rejoining the train at different parts, and there was really no problem about giving the boy access to his sack, but the soldier seemed to have got it into his head that this particular demand had to be resisted. The harder the boy pleaded, the more determined the soldier became to stop him.

It was probably the boy's bad luck that fellow passengers pitched in on his side. Interestingly, the more educated among us (the school-teacher, for instance), who might have been expected to stand up to this ignorant soldier, were more respectful towards him. It was the peasants who gave the soldier the hardest time. The old women, in particular, seemed fearless.

An Indian woman who had managed to wedge herself, her own flour-sack, a heap of woven blankets and three chickens into a corner by the door, tried to argue his case with the soldier.

'Everybody is standing where they can, and putting their parcels where they can,' she told him. 'Why do you stop him fetching his things?'

'Because it is not permitted. My instructions are that each passenger should identify his own belongings and carry them with him.'

'Well that is what this boy is trying to do. He just got separated.'

'He was wrong to be separated. It is not permitted.'

'Well now he wants to do the right thing. Why can't he?'

It is often a mistake to ask a servant of the state to give a reason for a ruling. It causes him to think of one.

'The reason is that this luggage is now ... confiscated.'

'Why?'

Pause. 'Because it was ... unaccompanied.'

At this the little boy burst into tears. It was not his luggage, he sobbed, it was for his aunt, sent by his mother. It was very important luggage.

There were clothes, sugar and oranges in the sack. What would he tell his aunt? She would say he had lost it.

Other passengers now joined the argument. Peruvians are not a particularly outgoing nation: people are, on the whole, rather subdued and the peasants *look* cowed. But they are no great respecters of authority either, and do not seem to bend the knee quickly to men in uniform. 'You animal!' somebody shouted from behind the cover of a pile of stuffed potatoes.

That was too much for the soldier. Feeling beleaguered by hostile forces he reacted as men-in-uniform usually do: he dug his heels right in.

'That boy leaves this train at the next station,' he said. 'Without the confiscated sack.'

There was a flurry of angry voices raised in protest, but the soldier just stood there, and the boy kept up his sobs. This had escalated beyond all reason. The train pulled into the station at a small town called Anta.

The boy was wailing uncontrollably. The soldier shoved him roughly down from the footplate. The boy tried to scramble back on. The soldier lunged at him with the butt of his rifle. The boy screamed and fell back, terrified but unhurt.

The train's whistle blew and we pulled away, passengers muttering angrily.

Suddenly, the peasant woman who had first taken the boy's side levered herself over her belongings, landed on the platform between the carriages, and simply shouldered past the soldier. With one remarkably muscular movement, she picked up the boy's flour-sack, swung it clear of the footplate and launched it from the side of the train.

Nobody cheered – we were taken by surprise. So was the soldier, who just stood there, dumbstruck. And the woman returned to her place.

As we left Anta, the little boy was running joyfully towards his flour-sack. Better to arrive late than empty-handed.

We had been galloping along quite fast – for a Peruvian train – across a wide, flat plain. It was grassy country, open, rather dusty, with willow trees, herds of cattle, and many small villages. Mountains were closing in on us from both sides, cornering us. Yet the track ran on, straight and level. Where were we heading? Where would the track go when the approaching range to our left met the approaching range to our right? Through a tunnel? Surely we could not climb. A sluggish brown river ran by our side, flowing our way. Where would that go? This provided the clue.

Within the carriage it was now bedlam. The day had grown hot, and each village we passed had added a handful more Indians to the train, hurling themselves and their bags at open carriage doors already packed tight with bodies.

To a background chorus of chicks and hens cheeping and squawking (the animals do the squawking in Peru – babies rarely seem to cry, and children are grown up before their time) there came the Andean equivalent of *Cries of London*. 'Pigs' trotters! Pigs' trotters!' one young hawker called. '*Tamales! Tamales!*' (These were balls of thick, dry maize-porridge.) 'Chocolate!' 'Inca-Kola!' 'Hot bread!' 'Spare ribs!' 'Oranges!' 'Pigs' heads!'

'Try the lamb's head soup,' the schoolteacher advised Mick. 'It's very good for headaches. Eat lamb's head soup regularly, and you will *never* have a headache.' But the lamb might, one thought.

Our own carriage was by now so full that some of the vendors were giving it a miss, jumping off at halts or stations, and rejoining at the other end of the car. When the ticket inspector arrived at our end, travelling down, he took one look at the solid wall of bodies packed into the space in front of him, and climbed a steel ladder up the end of the carriage on to the roof. We were travelling at some speed at the time, so it was a relief, a minute later, to see his legs appearing down the stairs at the other end of the car.

A relief in two ways, for Christian had said the inspector would throw us off if we could not convince him that we were peasants. Would he have? We will never know, but there turned out to be a couple of other tourists in other carriages, and they, too, escaped.

The stuffed-potato lady was made of sterner stuff than the ticket inspector. One of the minor miracles of the journey was to see her clambering over people, lurching from seat-backs to flour-sacks to heaps of oranges, her tray of stuffed potatoes (now much depleted) on her head, balanced with one arm, the other arm free to steady herself against the sides of benches or the necks of children, whatever came in handy. Between her fingers was now a greatly enlarged cache of banknotes, neatly folded and somehow sorted accurately into their denominations.

Soon, events came to her aid. For when we reached the edge of the plain, the river we had been following plunged into a gorge between the mountains, beginning a steep drop into the valleys behind them. The railway track followed it. Zigzagging down the mountainside by the same switchback method as it has used to climb out of Cuzco, the train rocked downhill, the river rushing and tumbling beside the track.

While the guard at the back (and, alternately, the driver at the front) jumped down to switch over the points each time the train changed direction, the stuffed-potato lady would jump down herself and sell a few more stuffed potatoes from outside the carriages, through the windows.

We were peering out to marvel at her when something swimming in the river caught Ian's eye.

'John.'

'Yes?'

'If I said I'd seen a small black and white bird shooting the rapids, what would you say it was?'

John swivelled towards the window. His face was a picture of suppressed excitement: 'Black body and white *back*?'

'Exactly.'

'Ian.'

'Yes?'

'Are you having me on? Have you been looking in my bird book without telling me?'

'No, John. I've just seen a torrent-duck, haven't I?'

John could barely speak with excitement. He just made a little squealing noise, and scanned the river wildly.

'Pity, John, that it's gone behind the rocks.'

At that moment the train pulled away. The stuffed-potato lady leaped back up on to the footplate at the last moment. John sighed.

We were descending a magnificent gorge. Through the top of the open carriage windows, towering walls of rock were all the eye could see; no sky was visible, however much you craned your neck. To each side of the gorge clung ferns and flowering shrubs, and around the track lusher vegetation than we had seen for many weeks in the high Andes began to crowd in.

Around the middle of the morning, as we neared the bottom of the gorge, there was a brief and sudden rainstorm, but it remained hot and grew hotter as the track lost altitude.

The schoolteacher near us was talking earnestly to Mick. His ability to strike up friendly conversation never failed him. Partly, of course, it was his fluency in Spanish, but it was more than that.

She was berating the government. 'We are asked to admire them! It's incredible. All they offer us is a 58 per cent pay rise. Just a *tip*! Prices rise by more than that in a month!'

Her attitude to the Shining Path terrorists was simple – the attitude of the 'plain man' the world over. 'Something' should be done about it. 'There are thousands of bereaved households in our country, and the government lets it continue. Banditry flourishes and the country drifts. We've taken fifteen years to drop what it took us two hundred years to climb. It will take a century to get back up, now. Something should be done ...'

The gorge widened out now, quite fast, as we met another, larger river and entered a beautiful valley, broad and fertile, but deep. To each side the mountains towered higher than ever; and behind the first great ridge could be seen a majestic Matterhorn-like peak, clear and white, snow shining and misting from its summit. 'That is Veronica,' said the schoolteacher.

This valley – the valley of the Urubamba River – was cultivated and rich. Trees clung to the slopes, but wherever the gradient was cultivable, Inca terracing could be seen. Much of it was still in use: neat parallel lines, intricately geometrical, swirled with the swirling contours: finger-prints left by a lost empire.

Where the Indians had built new terracing in more recent centuries it was crude, makeshift, by comparison: and the same was true of the little towns that followed the valley. Bold, neat, confident Inca foundations, walls and culverts that looked like architects' drawing, merged into the tin and mud, rough stonework and corrugated iron that later generations had added.

In places the Incas had realigned the river, digging a new course, straight for miles. At a handful of points where there were heads of valleys or sweeps of river which military strategists had wanted to guard, Inca forts clung impossibly to the mountainside, all with their own terracing (to grow food in a siege). The strategy seemed to be a defensive one.

The schoolteacher's remarks about having dropped so fast from what had been patiently built up came back. History, here, seemed (more nakedly than in Europe) a building up and dropping back, in wave after wave. The Spanish, too, had built something magnificent – one thought of the great colonial squares in Arequipa, the baroque cathedrals by the shores of Lake Titicaca, the full-skirted crimson finery that the Indian women still wore. That colonial empire had failed utterly and more spectacularly than our own had yet done.

Perhaps ours would too, in time. But there was something spiritually squalid in the condition of a country where the remnants of not one, but two great cultures squatted, shitting in each other's ruins. The glory was over. Two spectacular failures, one after the other, and now the post-colonial age was failing too.

We pulled into a siding at a little settlement they just called Kilometre 88, and waited. What for? The question was soon answered. From behind us came the hoot of another engine, and we leaned out of the window.

With a second triumphant toot, the tourist train swept past. Through the smoked-glass windows of its two diesel-cars, reclining on cushioned seats, we just had time to see Christian. Worse: he had time to see us. He removed his arm from the shoulder of the girl he was with and waved, as Royalty might wave. But he was on the right, not the left-hand side of the car – from which 'the premium vistas are not possible'. Still tooting, the tourist train slid off into the distance.

Ours was slower. But after Kilometre 88 that was an advantage, for the scenery grew more magnificent by the moment. The Urubamba River was cutting ever more deeply into the mountainside, and the mountains themselves seemed almost vertical. It was like looking from the bottom of a well. They climbed so high that if you leaned as far as you dared out of the window and tried to look up, you might just see sky, but could estimate no top at all to the walls.

The vegetation was now real jungle. Brilliant red flowering trees, orchids, yellow acacias and vines crowded the banks of the Urubamba. Yards from the track, the river leaped from gully to waterfall to rockpool, its roar drowning the whistle of the train.

It was downhill all the way, now. The engines were harnessed only for braking, and filings of hot metal from the brake shoes spat from our wheels as we passed. Leaves and creepers brushed against the carriage roof and children competed to grasp at flowers from the windows.

John's spirits had returned, for he had seen a flock of green parrots, identified a brilliant yellow dove and celebrated the return of the hummingbirds.

John, Mick and Ian were to leave the train at the station beneath Machu-Picchu. They had never seen this, the wildest and most spectacular of all the Inca forts, suspended among the rocks in the sky, curtains of jungle falling at its feet.

I had. The plan, therefore, was for them to leave me on the train. I would ride on, to the end of the line at Quillabamba, and then return when the same train came back early that evening. The others would rejoin at Aguas Calientes, a few miles up the line from Machu-Picchu. That gave them most of the afternoon there, and it gave me the chance to see something new. We would get back to Cuzco quite late that evening.

So off they got at Machu-Picchu, full of expectation. Ian had spotted a blonde on Christian's train. John was in the mood to meet another buzzard or two, while, for Mick, Machu-Picchu was one of the wonders he had come to South America to see.

There was half an hour's delay while a carriage that had been shunted too far and derailed was set to rights in a way that none of us had witnessed before. Railway officials put together a team of labourers – passengers and bystanders – and, to many cries of exhortation from someone who appeared to be a ticket inspector, the carriage was simply pushed sideways in a series of little hops, until manoeuvred into place.

Then Mick, John and Ian left me and, departing, were swallowed up into a shrieking mêlée of vendors of tourist knick-knacks.

*

I sat back to enjoy what was left of our descent into the jungle.

There were no tourists left on our train. As we pulled out of the station and gathered speed down the next loop of the valley, I glanced out of the window at the green bank suspended above the railway. On it, squatting quite daintily on her little haunches, her skirts gathered up around her waist, was a little Indian girl having a pee.

She was about nine. The train – the one down-train of the day to Quillabamba – had rushed out of the cutting and surprised her, bare-bottomed and defenceless.

Nine is such a sensitive age. On her face was an expression of vivid and all-consuming horror. It was unforgettable. It is caught still in my memory, like a single frame from a fast-moving film.

She may have been just a little Indian girl, speaking only Quechua, from a simple village in a remote and isolated culture – but her face expressed the mortification of any little girl from any age in any place anywhere in the world, who has been undone. Just at that moment her affront was boundless: her embarrassment cosmic, epic and international.

Our little train rattled on.

Chapter Twenty-Two

The Student
Electrician

The world began to change again, past Machu-Picchu. The Urubamba emerged from the jungled cliffs in whose folds we had been encased, and the landscape opened out. It was still green mountain all around, but the valley was broader and not so steep. The river had swelled now to a great size, and flowed, yellow-brown and boiling with energy – a combination of volume with violence which I had never seen before – between wide banks cultivated with maize, bananas and mango trees. Some of the hillsides had been cultivated too. Here, man was regaining the upper hand.

Our journey began to grow unbearably hot. The air outside was warmer and damper with each downward loop in the railway track; and, within, it was stifling.

Before long we pulled into a little village called Santa Teresa. This is what I wrote in my notes:

> Santa Teresa – tin roofs – red blossoms – jacaranda, hisbiscus, bou-gainvillea – tiny two-storey wooden houses – balconies on upper floor – mules in street – blackboard in main square for notices – chickens every-where – children running – Restaurant La Primavera – no cars – no roads in or out, only railway – tin-roofed hotel – tiny Banco de La Nación in a corrugated-iron hut – soldier with revolvers – Indian women with white hats and plaited hair – papaya trees laden with fruit . . .

The schoolteacher in the next seat told me about Saint Teresa of Avila, after whom this village was named. She used to levitate, said my companion, 'involuntarily'. It began to happen so often that, annoyed to be distracted from her work, she asked four fellow nuns to hold her down whenever signs of an imminent levitation were upon her.

It was odd to think of Saint Teresa, and of the tin roofs, Indian children and papaya trees in this village to which she had given her name. Would she have liked it? Would she have levitated here? What would the soldier with the revolvers have thought? Would levitation have startled the chickens, or would they, perhaps, have understood?

159

As we whistled and left, a tuneless iron bell on a little thatched-roof church clanged its invitation to Mass. The Indian schoolgirl opposite me was reading a translation of Homer.

What was England like, the teacher asked; was it desert, there? She had heard that it was foggy, but were there trees? Or was it all houses?

Next to the schoolgirl was a young man reading a paperback novel, in Spanish, by Hemingway: *Por Quién Dobian Las Campanas* (*For Whom the Bell Tolls*). There was a look of earnest intensity on the boy's face – fierce, pained almost. And, as the afternoon grew hotter, I lay back and began to doze, dreaming of someone, it was not clear who, not welcoming me home. Awaking, my eyes were already open, gazing at a yellow bird flitting alongside our carriage.

The tops of the hills and mountains were clothed in grey-white cloud, and still it was growing hotter, as we paused at a halt by some tin warehouses. All the trees were in flower, a scrawny cock strutted down the dirt street, and, over in a dusty field, some boys were playing a vicious game of football. Indians were loading fruit into the warehouses, shirtless and sweating – my first sight of these strangely formal people in less than full dress, however threadbare. Others were sitting under trees, sleeping, talking, weaving. What clothes they wore were American in style, colourful. Faces and bodies were shining and greasy, and some of the women wore bandanas. Some slow, jazzy guitar music drifted from a radio somewhere, and there were butterflies.

All the tenseness, all the rawness, all the nervous quality of the mountains had gone from the air. The Andes had been harsh, so brittle and so dry. Here it was damp and warm: here it was limp.

'A storm flood cut the railway line last year,' the schoolteacher told me, 'and they took two months to repair it!' A two-foot green bean, hanging from a tree, whisked past our window, tapping the carriages' sides.

'I have a great admiration for Margaret Thatcher,' the schoolteacher said. 'People wish she would come here. She would make the economy work. She would stop the murders. Our politicians are so ... corrupt. But she is clean, and clever, and hard. Clean, clever, hard ... that is what we need.'

Just as we pulled into Quillabamba, I saw my first boat on the river, a canoe built of straw and reeds. This, surely, was the edge of Amazonia? It started to *rain*.

'The Harrier jump-jet – how does it fly?' I was being politely interrogated by a young trainee electrical student, on the train back.

There had been just enough time in Quillabamba to look at the town, a shabby, friendly place on a hill above the river and railway line. After the rain, everything had steamed gently in the afternoon sun, and we had drunk cold coca tea: an odd, bitter taste, right in the back of the mouth. The women in the market place had sold huge steaming plastic plates of mutton, rice and gravy – 'first course' – followed by more rice, pasta, sweet potato and chicken – 'second course'. Between courses, and customers, they just wiped the plates over with a greasy cloth.

Back at the station there were no tickets: until I discovered that it was the ticket-touts (young boys) who had the tickets and sold them for a small commission. These urchins, in little more than rags, showed the acumen of City jobbers, their eyes shining with the excitement of commerce as they darted from passenger to passenger.

I reboarded the train alongside a man struggling beneath an enormous sack of tangerines which he was taking back to Cuzco. 'Your price, lady?' he had said to the fruit-vendor; interrupting testily, when she had pulled some figure from the air, 'Come, we have no time to wait, lady: your *last* price, please.'

Back on board there was apple juice, which was pear juice, bought from a woman who called me '*tio*' ('uncle'). I watched from the window as we rattled past little graveyards, unfenced but neat, with colourful crosses and bunches of plastic flowers beside them. Here, perhaps, plastic flowers were more of an extravagance than real ones, which hung from every tree above the graves.

We passed a starving dog. No dog starved in the poorer, harsher communities of the high Andes. Every dog was owned. But here where life seemed more comfortable, it also seemed cheaper, blowsier, more casual.

Now we were discussing the Falklands War, the student electrician and I.

'Peru,' he said, proudly 'was very instrumental in trying to mediate in the Malvinas dispute. Did you hear of the role of our President?'

He explained that all Peruvians believed that the islands should not be a British colony, but should be part of South America. But nobody in South America like the Argentinians, and there was some pleasure in seeing them bloodied. However, the issue of colonialism was more important, and he still supported Argentina. Any South American would.

'But the Harrier jump-jet is famous, for this war. I have seen pictures.'

Then he asked me about the pyramids. Had I ever been to Cairo, and seen these pyramids? What were they like? Why did I think the Egyptians had built them? Their structure had always fascinated him, and he believed they might be of some mystical or cosmic significance, 'like the ancient lines and patterns over the landscape at Tacna, here in our country, which can only be seen from aeroplanes. Perhaps they are linked with the pyramids? I have seen pictures, of course, of the pyramids, but I have never seen one. To do so, one day, is my greatest ambition.'

He was a very good-looking boy, part Indian, part Latin, thin and strong with high cheekbones and long black eyelashes. His girlfriend, Rosa, was quietly infatuated, staring speechless at him as he spoke. But he was without evident vanity or selfishness. His hands were very delicate, unscathed by manual labour. Rosa's, by contrast, were already work-worn, though she was only about seventeen.

They shared with me some hot pork crackling they had bought by the trackside. As we spoke, two soldiers with revolvers like the lad in Santa Teresa, moved down the carriage searching passengers and bags. One wore a blue beret, the other a makeshift cap. They searched quietly, almost apologetically. Nobody made a fuss, or even muttered: but nobody liked it. None bowed or scraped or tried to ingratiate themselves with the soldiers. People were embarrassed, the atmosphere tense. But it was soon over.

As they searched, a young woman breast-fed her baby a few yards away from me, seemingly unperturbed. She, too, had bought some pieces of roast pork which she was eating with her fingers. She must have been hungry for she was tearing at the meat with her head, as an animal does, fierce-eyed. At her breast, though, all was tranquillity and calm. The baby sucked with a steady intensity, an expression of utter bliss on its tiny face.

The student electrician had asked about politics in Britain. 'Here,' he said, 'the politicians are greedy for themselves: corrupt. Everybody at the top in Peru – politicians, businessmen, even churchmen – cares only for their pockets, and steals from the ordinary people. Meanwhile, the poor cannot eat.'

The intensity of his views was surprising, especially given that everything else about his attitude and ambitions suggested a quite conventional young man. But Rosa nodded and so did a couple of the other passengers seated within earshot. Nobody dissented.

'This so-called "man of the people", our president, Alan Garcia, is said to have bought his parents – who came from nothing – a mansion, somewhere abroad.' We had heard that story in Lima, first. Nazario in the little village of Llamac had repeated it, too, as though only Llamac knew ... 'And he thinks he can get away with it. The Shining Path will teach him a lesson!'

It was surprising to hear him volunteer that. Often in countries where there is a security problem, people do not speak openly about what worries them most. And it was only moments since the soldiers had come down the carriage, searching. But there were no hushed voices here, and others joined in. Was the Shining Path popular here?

'Not in Lima, or Cuzco. Not on the coast, at all. People hate them there. People in the city are afraid of the countryside. They feel guilt about the exploitation of the poor in the Andes ...'

'But here?'

'Some people do support them. Especially the young people. They are not *part* of the Shining Path. They do not know very much about it. There is no contact. It is secret. The support is a reaction: it is due to resentment. They like the terrorists because they hate Lima. Everybody hates Lima. Even the people who fear the Shining Path hate Lima. Even the older people, who are more ... traditional: they do not support the terrorists' – he used that word: everybody did – 'but they do ... understand.'

He asked me my own opinion of the prospects for the terrorists. It was odd how often one was asked by Peruvians to give a view on the future of their country. As if I knew! Yet time and time again one sensed that the ordinary people felt themselves to be in the dark about events, and vulnerable to them. Foreigners, perhaps, might have heard things which were not known within the country ...

His eyes were alight as he talked of the 'exploitation' of the poor by Lima, and of the struggle of the Andean regions to emerge as self-respecting parts of Peru. But he was vague about what form this exploitation took. Not enough, he said, was spent on roads and railways in the mountains, not enough on schools.

But was Lima not also very poor?

'Only because it is filled with refugees from the rural areas.'

He – his name was Carlos – and Rosa had been taking it in turns to sit on the one empty space on their bench. After the pork was finished, though, Carlos wiped his fingers and sat on Rosa's lap. Rosa went to sleep. Carlos carried on talking with me.

'I am very, very proud to be Peruvian. Everyone here is. We are all interested in our history, and we learn about it. We know that this is a beautiful country. We love the mountains and the sea. We see beauty everywhere – and this is Peru: *our* Peru.

'It is not the same, to hate your government, as to hate your country. Our government is not popular. Our president is not popular. It is many years since there has been a government which was popular or successful, and our presidents, also, usually end their careers in ruins.

'Perhaps we are a very critical people. Garcia says that we are too negative, and in this, at least, he has a point. Perhaps we are not co-operative and democracy is not the best way for us ... but we remain patriotic. All Peruvians remain patriotic. Therefore we do not like the USA.'

And Carlos, too, slept.

'Arrangements' so seldom work, but this one did. At Aguas Calientes, Mick, John and Ian were waiting by the trackside for us. With two women! We were introduced.

'This is Gail. She teaches English in Mexico City, but she's under a cloud due to having had an affair with one of the older pupils.' Gail was a short, skinny, punchy girl from the north of England. She had blonde hair and an almost white-mouse-like blondeness. It was as short as mouse fur too.

'So you're the fascist. Hi.' I was taken aback.

'And this is Michelle. She's the nanny to the British Ambassador in Mexico.' Michelle was quieter, and slightly upper class.

'Gail and Michelle are coming with us. We've all decided not to go as far as Cuzco on the train, but to get off at a place called Ollantaitambo, look for somewhere to stay the night, then make our way back to Cuzco by road. There's a market at Pisac, on the way.'

This sounded an adventure worth trying. But where was Christian?

'Aha! Triumph! He's been trying to chat up Gail all afternoon. He wanted to come with us to Ollantaitambo. But the tourist train doesn't stop there. So he tried to buy a ticket on our train, and they told him that they don't sell tickets for the local train to tourists. So he told them he was a Peruvian – ha! With *his* Spanish! – who had spent most of his life at finishing schools in Switzerland. They told him to piss off.'

Poor Christian. We laughed; and the others related tales of Machu-Picchu. They were bowled over by the place, of course. Everyone is.

As for Aguas Calientes (Hot Waters), where they had had three-quarters of an hour to kill, it was, they said, a shanty town, scratching a living on the edge of the tourist trade around Machu-Picchu.

'There are four or five little restaurants in shacks. One of them,' said Mick, 'is apparently run by someone advertised outside as 'Manuel, Prince Of The Primus ...'

'There *are* warm springs, too. Well, sort of. More a matter of Peruvians cuddling in a hot mud puddle.'

'Ssh! We're the only foreigners in this carriage.'

We were, or nearly, but there was one exception: a Mexican. Mick got talking to him. It turned out that he was a singer of some repute in Mexico City – or so he claimed. His speciality was romantic popular songs of recent vintage, and (he said) he was much in demand for weddings, dinners and even company outings.

'Go on, then,' said Mick. 'Give us all a song.'

It was getting dark outside, and the evening scent of the flowering shrubs brushing past our window was heavy in the air. The heat of the day was over. Some of the passengers were dozing, mothers were feeding their babies, and – the train being less crowded than when we came down – a sleepy calm had descended.

'*Alma, corazón y vida!*' the deep Mexican voice suddenly boomed out. It means 'spirit, heart, and life itself'.

Peruvians looked up, amazed. They were reserved people, and would no more sing in public than an English railway passenger would.

But he sang well, with a dramatic-romantic and rather old-fashioned bass voice. It was a Peruvian song he was singing, the usual sort of thing:

> 'I have the spirit to win you
> The heart to love you
> And the life to spend by your side.'

We English wanted to respond.

'How about "Old Macdonald Had a Farm"?' suggested John.

'Brilliant!' And off we went:

> 'Ee-i-ee-i-o ...
> With a Cluck, Cluck here, and an Oink, Oink there,
> Here a Moo, there a Quack ...'

The Peruvians were stunned at first. But when Mick suggested to a group of them that they could hardly refuse to give us a song from their own country – and be outdone by mere Mexicans and gringos – they took courage.

The song they sang seemed to be known by the whole carriage, who joined in the chorus. It had a rather plaintive sound and made a strange contrast with 'Old Macdonald'. Honour satisfied, we fell back upon the natural talent of the Mexican, who entertained us with song after song.

Few of the lightbulbs in our carriage worked, and it was dark outside. In the cool and friendly dimness I looked across at the Mexican, singing his heart out. He looked just like Michael Cocks. I shut my eyes and was transported back to the House of Commons, not so many years ago ...

It was early 1986, I remember, when I – a junior Conservative Member of Parliament – walked out of the showers and into the Members' Changing Room, to find Michael Cocks standing stark naked in the middle of the floor.

Michael was the Labour Member of Parliament for Bristol South. A large man, with the moustache, demeanour and general aspect of an exceptionally unsqueamish Mexican bandit, he was towelling himself vigorously, and singing as loudly and merrily as it is possible to imagine in that august and oak-panelled place.

It was some months since he had quit as Opposition Chief Whip – the unlucky man responsible for trying to make an undisciplined rabble of feuding politicians speak, vote and behave like a professional army.

'You sound like a happy man, Michael,' I said.

'Happy?' he replied. 'Oh yes, I'm happy. And I'll tell you why. I've been Chief Whip in a government when we had no majority. I've been

Chief Whip through two elections when we had no hope. I've been Chief Whip in a party which wanted to be led but had no leadership, and I've been Chief Whip in a party when we have leadership but nobody wants to be led. And now I've been chucked out by my constituency party in Bristol.

'And you know what? I just don't give a *fuck* any more!' And he resumed his song.

Lying back in the train, I smiled to myself. He's *Lord* Cocks, now. And still singing, I daresay . . .

By now everyone was talking, laughing and trying to join in. But it was we, not they, who had broken the ice. Not for the first time, it seemed that the easy generalizations about the English being reserved and cool, the South Americans hot-blooded and relaxed, were too easy. The Peruvians are not a straightforward people at all; and whatever clichés may be repeated about Latin blood, Indian blood is very mysterious.

Onwards up the pitch-black valley we roared. The river, invisible now, roared beside us. From the exhaust stacks of the two diesel locomotives hauling us, fire and sparks shot up into the night sky, and the stacks themselves glowed red hot.

I climbed the ladder up the end of the carriage (the same one that the conductor had climbed to clamber over the roof) and stood, steadying myself against the metalwork, head and shoulders above the roofline.

I could see the whole train before me, snaking along the valley, drawn by two fire-breathing dragons. The stars were very bright, the river very black, and the wind was on my heels. Was it possible to be happier than this?

At Ollantaitambo we leapt off, shouting and waving goodbye to our Peruvian and Mexican companions. The train whistled impatiently and in panic we chucked our rucksacks out of doors, windows – anywhere – on to the trackside beneath.

Off the train rumbled in a moving pool of its own light, its own sound, its own warmth. The Mexican was still singing as light and sound dwindled down the track.

Quite suddenly, we were in another world. There was only the sound of the river, and the hiss of a kerosene pressure-lamp inside the stationmaster's little house. The quiet seemed to grow, almost threateningly; and, with it, the little night sounds – the rustles and shrieks and distant barking of dogs, a world away from the carriage and company we had just quit.

And it was so dark! Was there ever darkness like this? You couldn't see an inch of ground in front of you. Painfully slowly, we made our way along the little cart track that led the mile or so from the station to the village. Gail fell straight into the ditch and was rescued, screaming and giggling.

And, as our eyes grew accustomed to the dark and our steps grew more confident, we wondered aloud what sort of place it was we were going to, and whether we had been rash to quit that friendly train.

The sound of the river was receding at our backs. Above us, the wind sighed a little in the tall gum trees lining the track, and the smell of eucalyptus hung, sweet and aromatic in the night air.

Chapter Twenty-Three

'Tambo

It was not difficult to find an *hostal* in Ollantaitambo. Ours, the Hostal Tambo, was at the same time the most primitive and the most charming place we ever found to stay in Peru.

Ollantaitambo is a small town, laid out in traditional style. A patchwork of small cobbled streets, neat open water-channels gushing along the middle of each, ran down into a main square. The houses were of stone and mud. Above and behind the town were magnificent Inca fortifications, so well preserved that they could be used today.

And the Hostal Tambo was in keeping with all this. Laid out around a little courtyard filled with sweet-scented flowering bushes, and with scarlet and purple bougainvillea cascading down from the tin gutters to the yard below, the whole establishment had only one tap, which could not be turned off but ran continuously. There was only one lavatory, and chamber pots under all our beds.

In the girls' bedroom were beds with real springs: in our own the more usual metal sheeting with hard mattresses on it. Ian's bed had the habit of gracefully bowing the knee – at the headboard end – down to the ground, when least expected in the night. The effect was rather like that of a camel kneeling; and Ian would slide, head first and feet in the air, into the tin headboard.

When this happened we all started to shake with laughter; and, as any shaking of the bedframe produced the same result as we had achieved in Llamac (the metal sheeting under our mattresses would rumble like the sound effects for thunder in a village-hall pantomime), the entire bedroom was reduced to uproar more than once that night. This 'thunder effect' seemed to be a feature of rural bedding in Peru.

Gail and Michelle were at first horrified at the primitiveness of the *hostal*. We wondered how they had come so far without encountering worse establishments than this, which was at least clean, friendly and pretty. But they soon got used to the place: they were adaptable, like us. We slept well (in between Ian's collapses) and were sorry to leave the next morning.

But leave we must, and early. We wanted to inspect the Inca fort, then find transport by road towards Pisac and Cuzco.

The ruins caused some dispute among us. Gail took a Merseyside view of historical wisdom.

'These,' said John, reading from his guide, 'are the princesses' bath-houses.'

'Why?'

'What do you mean, "why", Gail?'

'Well, what is it about these stone troughs which shouts at you "Princesses"?'

'It says it in the guidebook.'

'How does the guidebook know?'

'They've checked the historical facts before writing it, Gail.'

'How? Did the Incas leave written instructions?'

'No. It's not like that. But ... well – historians learn about how they lived, so they get an idea how everything fits into place.'

'Including princesses? It stands to reason, does it, that these must have been reserved for princesses? Don't you realize that these historians just talk shit? Don't you think some old professor just took a look at this and said. "Oh, these are pretty ritzy bath-houses. They must have been for princesses."'

John sighed, and marched on to a steep flight of outdoor steps. He stopped to consult his guidebook. 'These steps lead to the temple-stone, probably associated with moon-worshipping ceremonies.'

'John.'

'Yes, Gail.'

'You said "moon-worshipping" ceremonies. Why the moon in particular?'

At the foot of the fortifications was a wide stone market-place. Here Indians sold rugs, intricately woven red blankets and ponchos and a woman squeezed fresh orange juice for sale. We fell into conversation with three American girls.

Were they enjoying their holiday, Mick asked.

'Yes and no. One thing wrecks this country. We can't get Pepsi. They only have Coke, wherever you go. We hate Coke. The taste of Coke is obnoxious to us. Jesus, the minute I touch down in Miami, I'm gonna sink five cans of Pepsi. What godforsaken country is this, that they only have Coke?'

Her friend nodded agreement and they continued inspecting the woven blankets, many of them so fine that they might have been the work of a whole year for some Indian for whom the difference between Pepsi and Coke was, perhaps, immaterial. They would be sold to gringos like us for the price of – perhaps – fifty Cokes (or Pepsis).

Ollantaitambo's main square was already alive with transport loading up to head in every direction. There would be no problem about getting to Urubamba (the next town, whose name was the same as the river, on the way to Pisac). So there was time for a breakfast of bread, jam and coffee at a restaurant on the square. Luckily we were hungry, so the meal was hardly spoiled by the proprietress's infant son, who walked up to our table and urinated under it while we were eating.

Michelle asked where the toilets were. A dignified and rather quiet girl, her work as an ambassador's nanny had lent her a certain social command. The question was discreet.

The answer was not. 'There,' said the serving girl, pointing towards a sheet of blue plastic a few feet away from us.

'The door is that way?' asked Michelle, to make sure she had understood.

'No, the lavatory is behind the curtain,' said the waitress; and impatient to be understood, thrust aside the tattered plastic to reveal a hole dug in the floor behind it, with two little platforms for feet to each side. This was about three yards away from our table.

Michelle could not back down now, and showed courage in going through with it. We could see her feet, as the plastic stopped short of the floor. When it flapped open, despite her efforts to secure it, all of us pretended not to notice. Gail, however, decided to wait for something better, and soon we were trooping out to look for transport to Urubamba.

Mick found a *camioneta* – a pick-up truck operating as a rural taxi – and we all jumped into the back. It was standing room only, but fast and cheap. As we gathered speed down a goodish road, Gail screamed loudly with excitement. Indians do not display emotions in this way and people stared. A young man near us in the back looked away in deep embarrassment.

There were no tourists in Urubamba, just the liveliest, most colourful local market you could find. If you wanted hairclips, cheap jeans, goats' heads, herbal remedies or oil-lamps made out of condensed milk tins and Coca-Cola bottletops, this was the place.

Around the square Mick noticed that a few of the doorways had broomsticks sticking, like flagpoles, diagonally from the lintel immediately above the door. On the end of the pole would be a bit of red plastic sheeting, or, sometimes, cloth. He walked through one such door and asked what kind of business it was.

It was a bar. Or, rather, it was the front room of a peasant who would sell you liquor. And there was only one kind of liquor. The red flag was a sign that *chicha* – a sort of maize beer – was on sale. *Chicha* varied from a strongly porridgy substance with the taste and consistency of fizzy, fermented gruel, to something more like sour, milky water, barely alcoholic.

Ian tried some, the woman dipping what seemed to be her only jar into a barrel and handing it to him to drink. There were no tables, no sense of social drinking. It was more like filling up with petrol: you walked in, paid, drank your litre or half-litre, handed back the jar for the next customer and left.

We found a van for the half-hour ride to Pisac. Among the other passengers was a Seventh Day Adventist: an American boy training as a missionary. He would have been good-looking, were it not for his relentlessly unfashionable dress: a door-to-door salesman's pre-pressed trousers, jacket and tie, and heavy-rimmed spectacles. He kept up an earnest conversation with his Indian companions, glancing at Gail (who had fallen asleep on Ian's shoulder, in the back) with a look that told of disapproval and intense longing. He allowed himself to look for about two seconds, and never looked again. At Pisac he walked quickly away.

We found the market which Gail and Michelle had heard was famous, and wanted to visit.

This market was organized entirely with tourist customers in mind. Yet it was very beautiful. A small square, filled with racks of gaily coloured fabrics, hats and jewellery, was dominated by one huge, deep-green tree. It looked centuries old. Spanish moss hung from its branches, and it gave shade to the whole market. Beneath it, three little boys bowled wire hoops with wooden sticks – one so tiny he could not have been walking for long; but he was determined to be part of the gang. He kept falling over, picking himself up and trying again.

You could lift your eyes from this scene to the steep hillside above. It was terraced as far and as high as you could see with the most impressive Inca fortresses we had encountered.

We all walked as far as the bottom gate, up an alley teeming with pigs and piglets dozing contentedly in the afternoon sun. A boy ran out, startling the piglets, and asked if the girls would like mules to take them up.

'Mules,' said Gail. 'Why?'

'Because you are women,' replied the boy.

'No,' said Gail. 'We are tigers!'

The boy laughed, and offered to accompany them free, anyway, as a guide. It worked. They agreed to take him, and set off sightseeing with a free guide who probably knew he would be paid but had the initiative not to insist, at least at this stage.

Later, we all met in a café off the square. You could sit outside, underneath the vines and bougainvillea and inevitable flaps of torn plastic sheeting, in the shady yard behind, served by a little waiter with a nervous cough and a worried expression. We did: and into the yard walked a man and a woman we recognized immediately. They were two of the South African mountaineers we had last seen preparing the ascent of Yerupaja, hundreds of miles away by the shores of Lake Jahuacocha.

They had failed. Shortly after we left, the weather had turned. They had established base camp, waited six days in the snow and wind, learned of the dead New Zealander, and given up. Now they were just tourists, like us.

'Better to have loved and lost,' said the South African.

Is it? If you are going to lose, then perhaps better not to love. The South Africans were putting a brave face on it, but traipsing around tourist markets and Inca ruins was not what they had come for. They had done the sensible thing – nobody could criticize that – and yet . . .

We, who had never entertained ambitions of their sort, thought ourselves conquerors simply for having got from Ollantaitambo to Pisac by *camioneta*.

Finding a bus back to Cuzco took a while. We waited, along with all the local people going the same way, at the iron bridge over the Urubamba. Almost every vehicle that passed – lorries, trucks and buses – would stop and take passengers. But there were always more people than spaces. When a minibus with room to take us finally did stop, we clambered aboard, relieved and tired, and took the last seats.

Just behind us and panting hard, an Indian woman with a live pig on her head shook the driver's door. The pig was so tightly trussed that it was as much a parcel as a pig, but this did nothing to muffle the squeal. It was a small pig – the size, perhaps, of a medium-sized dog, but fat. It must have weighed all of forty pounds, and the woman sweated profusely as she begged the driver to take her and the pig to Cuzco.

He refused. She pleaded. He hardened his heart. And we left, the woman trotting after us over the bridge, with last-minute arguments in favour of including her deployed energetically from the bank on one side of the road.

We began to climb. The route took us over a high pass above the river, and accomplished it gently in a series of zigzags, with hairpin bends to left and right.

After rounding the first of these, an amused shout from one of the passengers had us looking over the side – to where the woman, pig still on head and still squealing, had stormed straight up the hillside, short-cutting the hairpin bend of the road, to meet us again with further arguments for taking her on board. The driver smiled, but shook his head. The woman wailed, the pig squealed, and passengers clucked their disapproval at the driver's unkindness. Without properly stopping, we picked up speed again and drove on.

At the next leg of the pass, the driver had to relent. There would otherwise have been mutiny among the passengers: for there she was again, breathing a little more heavily, perhaps, and soaked a little more completely in perspiration – but pig still firmly on head. She hauled herself on board and squatted in the aisle, placing the pig in front of her. The squeals continued for some time, but eventually died away.

The sun had set and the sky was a clear, pale indigo, fading to gold in the west. We were travelling over dry mountain pasture, cold and bare. Here and there were little rivulets, and just a few lonely clusters of mud huts. It was warm in the bus, but the air from the windows was icy.

Nobody spoke. Some passengers slept, others stared out of the window. The man and woman in front of me tended their child, a little girl.

She was perhaps nine, but a mongol. Her arms and legs were pasty and fat, and her face puffy and slightly misshapen. On one of her hands was a burn – perhaps she had fallen in a fire, for she seemed uncoordinated, or had tried to pick up something hot. This girl was very clean and neat – lovingly dressed, all in ruffles and bows. Her straight black hair had been tied with green ribbon and her little shoes carefully laced. From time to time, her father patted her, as if reassuringly.

By contrast, he and his wife were obviously very poor. Their clothes were shabby but respectable, and their string basket held only some basic provisions, and a frayed blanket. The woman, who was perhaps forty, had dozed off to sleep; her husband awake, was looking after their daughter.

The girl hardly seemed to know where she was, and jerked her head from side to side, whimpering a little sometimes. When she did this, the man, who appeared younger than his wife, cradled the child, folding his arm securely around her, and rocked her a little. He was thin, and his face was careworn and anxious. He looked very tired.

After some time the little girl, too, began to doze. With both wife and daughter sleeping now, the young man looked out of the window, then glanced apologetically at the passengers to each side of him. He glanced at me. 'My daughter,' he said.

Then folding both his arms around the little girl, he smiled, and looked at her with an expression of infinite tenderness.

We found an 'English pub' in Cuzco. It was Gail who told us about it. She and Michelle had rather liked the look of the English barman, Alex, and wanted a second look. So we decided to spend our last night at The Cross Keys.

Against all the odds – and what odds! – the place succeeded in its aim: to create an authentic pub atmosphere. Visually this is not difficult or expensive: the appropriate bar layout, seating and knick-knacks on the wall, all did their job. But it was really Alex who made it work.

Alex was in his mid-twenties, tanned, with fair hair and brown eyes. He had an easy, friendly manner, though his bearing and accent were of a class slightly above what you would expect in a pub barman. He greeted everyone like a long-lost friend, and made a natural double act with the other barman, a darkly good-looking young Parisian with a broken nose, 'from the fourteenth *arrondissement*,' who never spoke, and became more desirable to Gail with every smouldering silence that passed (with him) for conversation.

What was Alex doing in Cuzco? It was the question (he said, with weary good nature) that everybody asked.

'I didn't like mortgage-broking, that's why. I came here for a holiday – one of those 'drop-out-for-the-summer-in-South-America-and-find-yourself' ideas, right? Ran out of money and got a temporary job with the people who own this place. Peruvians. They liked me, I liked them, and they arranged a work-permit – don't ask me how.

'Don't know how long I'll stay. I'm running a couple of little business ventures on the side, now – tourist things – right? Tours and things like that. I'm doing okay ...'

He had a ready smile. There was no sort of edge to him, no sharpness, no obvious conflict. Everybody liked him. Peruvians bought him drinks.

'Being a gringo gives you a certain status in this place – right? – especially if you're local, not a tourist. Gringos come here a lot. I get asked all about Peru – you know, the real situation, behind what the tourist sees – right?'

His family came from Cheltenham, and his father had been an army officer. Had he been to university?

'I did two years' windsurfing, instead. Ended up running a course.'

You sensed that Alex would do well anywhere. Despite himself, he was already a winner, in Cuzco's terms. Before long, he would be mortgage-broking in Chile. Whatever side of himself he had come to South American to escape, the getaway had failed.

We clustered round listening to him and asking questions. The bar had a curious clientele. A couple of hippies, refugees from the 1970s; a failed Austrian poet; and someone with round Trotsky glasses who looked like a dropout from the Baader-Meinhof gang ... otherwise they were Peruvians, the younger set from Cuzco, with a little money. For them, this was the place to be: their way – their only way – of being cosmopolitan.

Suddenly, there was the sound of the door being confidently swung open, banging on the wall. One hand plumped with great assurance on to Mick's shoulder, and another whacked something hard down on to the bar in front of us. It was a guinea-pig's claw.

We turned. Grinning from ear to ear was Christian. He waved to two American girls over in the far corner and they waved back, giggling.

'Grilled guinea-pig – barbecued – on sticks – like kebab. Most delicious! How was yours? This hoof – *hoof*, yes? – is your souvenir to take to London. Give to your wife, John – she keeps guinea-pigs as pets, no? – tell her Christian ate the remainder.' This was ignominy.

Christian introduced us to his latest friend, unusually, a male: Arturo. Arturo was a junior official with the Cuzco tourist board, and looked very proud of his new foreign acquaintance. Christian was giving him the usual tales about his amorous adventures and Arturo was clearly impressed. He had a T-shirt with the word 'THRUSH' printed across the chest.

'It is the name of some birds, I think, meaning like eagle,' said Arturo, shyly. Mick decided against spoiling his evident pleasure in wearing the word.

'It's beautiful,' he said.

Beer at high altitude, especially beer in English-style pint mugs, goes fast to the head. Most of us felt ready to drop; but Ian, Gail and Michelle felt ready to disco. Alex had told them that Cuzco did boast one discotheque, and the three of them headed off to find it. Despite being the owner of a pair of wickedly fashionable size 46 aubergine dancing-shoes, Mick declined to join them, and we said our goodbyes to the Parisian with the broken nose from the fourteenth *arrondissement*, and to Alex.

'Maybe I'll be back in England some day. Who knows?' he said. 'I'll be moving on from here soon. I think. Hey, do any of you happen to know the guy who lived next door to my flat in London?'

Poor Alex, one chuckled – he's been away so long he's getting like the Peruvians, thinking everyone in London knows everyone else . . .

'He's called Crispin Tickell.'

Michelle and I looked separately startled. Crispin Tickell was already a very senior man in the Foreign Office when I worked there after university, and later became British Ambassador at the United Nations . . . As for Michelle, she did know him – through her connections with the British Embassy in Mexico City.

I looked around at the throng of strange people crowding this bar. The air was smoky and the scene took on an unreal air. It was as though this might be just a film set: a saloon-bar in some Wild West town, made from plywood flats supported behind by wooden props. Only

Michelle and Alex, now, seemed properly focused, real people: talking to me about others whom we all knew and who knew us. They were anchors into reality, these third persons: a way of checking our own identities in a bizarre and unreal place.

This bar, after all, was in the Andes. And what was the population of Britain? Fifty-six million? So how was it that we, who had all met Crispin Tickell, should now coincide in Alex's bar in Cuzco?

And why do you encounter your friends by chance in motorway service cafeterias? Why do people introduced at dinner already know half the people you know?

It is as if at certain key points the faceless millions who make up the census figures, cause the traffic jams and constitute crowd scenes, stand momentarily aside so that just a few of us can bump into each other.

As if? But maybe they really do?

Maybe most of the people we think we see do not really exist at all? Maybe they are holograms. Maybe there really are only a few of us, moving amid phantoms. Millions and millions of phantoms.

It would explain why, for instance, as you enter Wales, almost everyone has a Welsh accent, immediately. After centuries of free movement, five hundred yards could never make such a difference.

It would explain why in the 1950s almost everyone was called Rita or Avril, yet now almost nobody is. Fashions in names change of course, but you would expect at least the ones who were Rita and Avril in the 1950s to be here, thirty years on. Or would you? Perhaps they weren't there *then* – they were just holograms, commissioned and materialized to give the era its 1950s' flavour, and afterwards decommissioned, to be replaced by the Traceys and Kevins, Fionas and Henrys who were put in to characterize the 1980s.

It would explain why 'everybody' except you and me has their hair cut in the latest style; and 'everybody' dresses in the clothes that have just become fashionable. What have they done with their other clothes, one wonders. Thrown them away? The answer is that 'they' didn't have any other clothes because 'they' don't exist – any more than the window-dressers' dummies in the windows of the clothes shop. 'They' are, in a grotesquely real sense, the window-dressing of our age. What, I wonder, will 'they' be wearing as the nineties proceed, while you and I carry on wearing out our old clothes?

You and I are almost alone.

How, then, can we tell who the real people are?

We cannot. We can never be sure. The phenomena who seem to be people can walk and talk and squash you in railway carriages. Superficial relationships can be established with them and they can appear to return affection. But it will never come to anything; the hologram – if that is what it is – will disappear from your life. You will call it 'chance' but it is not chance. It has been switched off.

So sympathy is wasted upon these apparitions, for they are not sentient. They experience nothing, but only act as though they did. They could not, for instance, register the idea behind the passage you are reading. You can. That you can, is proof that you are real. Welcome.

At first it is a lonely feeling, to know that there are only a few of us. But one is quickly overtaken by a sense of privilege. One day, perhaps soon, the hologram projector will be shut down without warning, and the few of us left (smiling at one another in recognition) will be assembled for an explanation of why we have been put here, and what it has all been about.

I long to know. I tried to explain these thoughts to Mick and John as the three of us made our way rather unsteadily back across the town to our *hostal*. It was late, but the water-cannon were out in the main square, trundling around and squirting. Whether this was a show of military force to impress the night birds of Cuzco, or just a cheap expedient for watering the grass, was unclear to us: unclear, perhaps, to the soldiers themselves.

Mick picked up a local newspaper left on a bench, and recited extracts as we walked. 'BUS AL ABISMO: 23 MUERTOS' ... Then there was a piece from Lima: 'PARENTS BEFORE COURT': it seemed that a business-man and his wife had mistreated their child of seven, forcing him to dress as a pig and parading him with a sign: 'I AM A STUPID PIG AND EVERY TIME I SHIT AND LIE I GET MADE MORE UGLY'. They even (the report explained) made him wear an egg-box as a snout ...

'Look out Mick!' We just saved him from stumbling across the corpse of a dog in the road. Civic-minded citizens had placed two large rocks, one at its head and one at its paws, to alert pedestrians and cyclists to the danger. But nobody had moved it.

'BREAD RIOT IN URUBAMBA,' Mick read on, 'FOURTH BOMB IN PUNO' ... and we were soon back at the *hostal* rattling the gate to be let in.

Later – much later – Ian's rattling on the same gate woke Mick where it failed to wake the doorman. The disco had not impressed him. 'It was Steely Dan, Fleetwood Mac, and New Riders of the Purple Sage,' he complained. John pricked up his ears: this was his generation. 'No record cut in the last three years, I'd say. The Peruvians loved it, though. Thought it was dead cool.'

'I walked the girls home. They forgot which was their hotel. Took us to the wrong one, but they were sure it was right. They even found their own room – or what they thought was their own room. I said goodnight and started to walk away. Loud scream, then laughing noises. Somebody gabbling in Norwegian. Wrong hotel, wrong room, bedroom with three Norwegian men in it. Thought their ship had come in. We scarpered.'

Dawn found us dragging flour-sacks full of our belongings round and round the courtyard, to get them dirty. Rucksacks look too tempting to thieves, and the morning was the beginning of a new chapter for each of us: time to get our gear sorted out.

Ian, Mick and John planned to fly to Puerto Maldonado, in the Peruvian jungle, and their plane left that afternoon from Cuzco airport.

Puerto Maldonado is a gold-rush town by the banks of the river Madre de Dios (Mother of God), a tributary of the Amazon. It lies at the feet of the Andes, some 500 kilometres away and 10,000 feet down. There was time, before we returned to Europe, to spend a few days in the real jungle – but only if we flew there. Fly? Surely not. A paragraph from our guidebook had caught my eye. There was a road, it said, to this outpost. A bad road, it was true – it could take up to three days to get there – but trucks did run the route regularly. Enquire in Cuzco, it advised, for a passage on the back of a truck. And be prepared for a rough journey.

The temptation was irresistible. It meant arriving in Puerto Maldonado only a day or so before having to leave, by air, for Lima. I would miss the jungle tour that the others planned. But there would be future occasions, surely, to visit jungles ...

So, early that morning, with my rucksack, flour sack, camera and notebook, and a new 'TOYOTA' cap, I set out from the *hostal* gates. There was an element of recklessness in this venture, and, for the first time, I felt nervous.

Chapter Twenty-Four

Onto the Truck

'To Maldonado by truck? Thirty-six hours. Twenty-four if you are lucky. The trucks go from the square near the Coliseum.'

'To Maldonado? By road? There is no road. It was washed away last year.'

'To Maldonado by road? A week, perhaps more. The road is terrible.'

'To Maldonado by truck? They don't go from here. Go from Urcos. They all pass the square there.'

'Two days, señor: or a month if it rains. Good luck. You will need it.'

Strange though it might seem, all these statements turned out to be true, partly true, or true in certain circumstances. Their reconciliation, one with another, was to be the experience of the days ahead, and of a lifetime.

Cuzco lies at the head of a high valley. Around the town and its environs the plateaux and mountains rise far higher. In order to descend from Cuzco down into the Amazon basin it is necessary to cross two great ridges, with another vast and remote valley between them. Only then do you reach the edge – the cloud-capped escarpments, plunging down into the green hills and jungle beyond.

This journey was to take me right up over the top, then down. Finally, it would cross and recross a large river destined to become one of the tributaries of the Amazon itself. The road would follow that tributary down to its confluence with the great Madre de Dios River. Here at this confluence was the town – or port – of Maldonado, navigable down the Madre de Dios into the Rio Madeira, thence into the Amazon, and then all the way to the Atlantic.

The puzzle about where the trucks left from was soon solved. They left from the main square in Urcos, a small town not far away. Transport from Cuzco to Urcos, however, left from the square near the Coliseum.

It was a long, hot walk: past the brewery, with its immaculate

building, high security fences, neat gravel drive and uniformed guards –
quite the smartest industry in Peru. And past the local high school,
where pickets of striking teachers were trying to stop the drift back to
work. The pickets had strung up an effigy of some hated figure within
their profession – the Minister of Education perhaps? the leader of some
breakaway faction? – and pinned abusive notices to the straw body.
You can always tell when a strike is crumbling.

You could not miss the square by the Coliseum. There seemed to be
buses and minibuses everywhere, loading up and heading out in all
directions. Three men, nearby, seemed to be in the process of finding
out for themselves about buses. It seemed best to ask them.

They were as bewildered as me. 'We don't know,' replied the oldest
of them, a man of about fifty. 'We're trying to find transport to Urcos
too. We have never been there.'

He was wearing blue denim dungarees, much patched, a woollen
cardigan with buttons, and a GI-type cap. He had a lined, kind face.

Together the four of us walked around asking bus drivers and passengers, but nobody seemed to know much. After a while the second of
the three companions pointed to a bus bound for Urcos. This was a
man of about thirty, with a long, comic face and a faintly loopy
expression, curly hair and a floppy felt hat – a sort of Peruvian Harpo
Marx.

It was standing room only, but we jumped aboard. The fare was
nominal (though my three friends had to calculate carefully and hard)
and the bus was soon on its way. There was time to study the third and
youngest of the group.

This was a boy of about twenty-five. He was tall for a Peruvian, with
short hair, bad skin and a sore under one eye. He also had a hare-lip
and wore an orange and yellow gas-station attendant's cap, a brown
T-shirt and mauve plastic sandals. He looked even goofier than the other
one – perhaps a little retarded, but not badly. It was noticeable that the
other two were quite patient with him, though they teased him a lot.

Were they rogues? Fortune-seekers? Simpletons? They were friendly
to me, anyway. Where was I going, they asked.

'Puerto Maldonado. People say you can get trucks from Urcos.'

They laughed. 'Maldonado? We are going there too. We also have
heard that it's from Urcos that you go. But we know nothing. No more
than you. Let's look together, in Urcos.'

'How long do you think the journey will take? You see I have to be
in Maldonado within five days – by Wednesday – because I fly from
there on Thursday.'

'Fly? By aeroplane? From Maldonado? To where?'

'Back to Lima.'

'But you can go from here to Lima, direct . . .'

'Yes, I know. But in an aeroplane you see nothing but clouds. I want to see more of Peru; more of the Andes; and the jungle and rivers, too.'

It was the older man who spoke. 'It is just the same with us,' he said. 'We hope to find work in Maldonado, it is true – there is no work here except for policemen and soldiers and thieves – but we are curious to see more of Peru. We have none of us been to the Amazon regions, or Madre de Dios. For us also, this is an adventure.'

There are not many poor countries in the world where a foreigner can tell a group of uneducated labourers that he chooses to travel by the cheapest and most uncomfortable form of transport across desolate country for many days, simply because that is interesting to him, or beautiful – and expect to be understood. But Peru is such a country. These three were pretty near the bottom of the social heap, but there was simply no need to explain. Ask yourself whether their social equivalents in Britain would have as much understanding.

'Perhaps we will travel together,' said the older man. Harpo nodded his floppy hat, and the goofiest one smiled. 'Perhaps we can choose the best from many lorries.'

It did not turn out quite like that. We waited together for three hours in the main square at Urcos. Many others were looking for transport to Maldonado, for we had indeed hit upon the place where everything for the jungle starts; but nobody seemed to agree whether or when transport would arrive.

'In the next three days.'

'Now.'

'At two p.m.'

'In the night.'

'Perhaps never. The road has been washed away, I hear.'

There was nothing to do but wait.

It was a sleepy little town, and the noon sun was hot. Even the vendors of warm, sweet, mauve jelly – a favourite with the children – grew sleepy, hauled their jelly carts into the shadows of the great trees around the square, and snoozed.

A lone gringo quickly became the centre of attraction, for few foreigners came to Urcos. A whole gang of kids formed, following me around and staring. But the novelty faded.

The three companions, meanwhile, played cards. One of them – Harpo – had a flashy cassette player of which he was very proud, but it only had one tape, the sole cassette he possessed.

He demonstrated it to the rest of us. It consisted entirely of noises of a baby crying and gurgling.

'Mine,' he said. 'My child. My little son, Wilfredo. This is to help me remember him, when I am in Maldonado.' He pulled out a grubby pocket photograph album and began to show me pictures of his wife and son.

Walking away to take a stroll around the square I looked back. You could see him still sitting there by the tree trunk in a world of his own, bending over his cassette player, listening to the recorded noises. His face was filled with adoration. It was the last time I was able to speak properly to them.

For the square was suddenly filled with people running. Two big trucks had roared into town. Now it seemed that half the people in Urcos were waiting for transport to Maldonado: and here it was.

There was no time to buy food. I settled for a small sack of oranges and ran, with the others, towards one of the vehicles. It was a high-sided truck of steel and wood construction, but there were ladders from above the wheel arches, up over the side, and people were clambering up. I followed, hauling my bags and rucksack behind me. A youth, who was rather light-skinned for a Peruvian, helped me.

Inside the back of the open truck, a group of Indians had already staked out territory. It struck me as odd that there were not more of them, and it was noticeable that some of those who had clambered on were clambering off again, and heading for the other truck, which was already filled with many more passengers than ours.

But the light-skinned youth stayed, as did a few of the others. He laid claim to an eagle's nest of a lookout on the edge of the roof above the driver's cab. For me there was something more sheltered, on the floor of the back of the truck.

From the security of this position, it became clear why our truck was not more popular. 'The smell!' was the way one man, clambering back down over the side, put it, wryly. Our cargo was diesel oil. Sixty-five 44-gallon drums of it – to be precise – plus four giant cylinders of gas, two babies and twenty-six adults. In that order of importance, so far as loading was concerned.

We simply had to make do as best as we could among the drums and cylinders, which were roped to the floor in the back. And over the whole vehicle hung the heavy, pervasive smell of fresh diesel oil.

That smell – it struck me then, smelling it for the first time, as a bit odd but quite bearable – was to become so burned into the memory that for the rest of my life a whiff of diesel oil will instantly bring back the whole epic journey which lay ahead. Smells can – more, almost than anything. It is filed in my brain under 'JOURNEYS (By Smell)' next to 'molasses' . . .

As a youth I had somehow secured a passage from Jamaica, where my parents were living, by ship to London, for a shilling. The shilling was paid *to* me, not by me. It was my nominal wages as 'supernumerary crew'. The vessel was a leaky old sugar-boat, taking molasses from Milk River in Jamaica, to the Tate and Lyle sugar refinery at Silvertown Docks, in London.

For me the passage was a godsend, as air fares were expensive and I wanted to take my motor scooter, record player and all my LP records. I was on my way to start my first year at Cambridge.

But the voyage took three weeks. The ship was on its last voyage with the company and the engines kept failing. We would drift while they were repaired. Being high summer and on a windless Atlantic, we were followed by an overpowering smell of molasses. It seemed to trap and envelope the entire boat. Nowhere, not the cabins, not the bathroom or canteen, not the outside deck baking in the sun, escaped the smell. At first it was pleasant – exotic even. But as the days, then weeks, wore on, it became sickly and oppressive.

Sometimes you wanted to scream: 'Help! Take that smell away!' When we docked – up the River Thames, in the East End of London off Charlton buoy – I remember leaping from the little outboard motor boat which took us ashore, and running exhilarated through the cool London evening, shaking that smell from my hair, skin and clothes …

But, now, it was diesel, not molasses. No wonder the other truck was twice as crowded as ours. From its top, one of my three erstwhile travelling companions – the older man with the GI cap – waved. Harpo, standing next to him, pointed across to my truck and held his nose in an exaggerated gesture. Then, with a flourish of horns and a revving of engines, we were away.

Nobody enquired about the destination. Nobody checked passports, took a fare or even quoted a price. There was no itinerary and no passenger list. The driver and his mates simply left it to all who boarded our tanker to find out for themselves where we were going. Money would be taken later: for now, it was hold tight – and we were off, the horns echoing through the narrow streets of Urcos as we headed out of town.

The wind as we travelled, fresh and cool on our faces, blew the heat and flies away. Everyone on board talked excitedly or peered out over the edge. There was a sense of adventure in the air, and a sense of speed. The road was good.

This, I thought, peeling an orange and throwing back my head in the breeze, would surely be a quick and easy journey.

Chapter Twenty-Five

Over
the Top

The tarmac lasted for about a mile. It gave way to a broad earth road which ran across the valley Urcos overlooked. Then we reached the other side. The broad road became a narrow road, and we began to climb.

The climb steepened, the road became a mountain track, twisting and turning up the hillside, and the truck began to pitch and roll as clouds of our own dust blew over our heads in a following wind. Looking back down towards the town whence we had come, we could see what looked like a map spread out at our feet. A sack of oranges fell on my head.

I rearranged the oranges and settled down. The truck took a sudden turn and a gas cylinder rolled on to my leg. To stop a repeat of this it had to be wedged tight, which took a while, but had just been satisfactorily accomplished when the lorry hit a series of humps and the oranges fell on my head again.

Shaking the dust from her face and hair and blowing it from the downy head of the baby at her breast, a young Indian mother smiled up at me in sympathy. 'Dust,' she said, in explanatory tone.

'Yes,' I said.

The light-skinned youth clinging to the platform above the roof of the driver's cab was well above the rest of us – stuck, as we were, in a pit of rolling cylinders. From his perch he surveyed our woes.

This boy looked about sixteen and wore a cool pair of wraparound sunglasses which he seemed never to take off. He occupied a secure little cockpit. It was rather like a private box at the opera. Stretched out in the sun and wind (and escaping much of the dust swirling up around the back of the truck), it was hard to avoid the impression that he was posing. Certainly he seemed to have spoken to nobody.

As the truck heaved, I moved to help the woman on the floor beside me – the woman with the little baby. Both of them were threatened by the rolling cylinder. We now managed to secure it with rope.

She looked poor and ignorant and she smelled; but her manner was quiet and she was gentle with the baby. Her green skirt was already stained with oil from the drums and the dust which had adhered to it. By way of a blouse she wore a frayed tracksuit top of blue nylon, bearing the logo 'Addidas' – wrongly spelled and crudely printed so you could tell this was a Peruvian pirating of the syndicated article. But at least the zip worked, and this gave easy access to her breasts, which were much in demand for the baby. Milk had leaked onto the tracksuit around them, and dust congealed on to the milk. To all of this, her baby seemed utterly oblivious. What was the baby's name?

'Caesar Augustus,' she said. She smiled a shy, proud smile.

By hauling yourself up the high-sided wooden slats which enclosed our territory in the cargo hold, you could see out. In this way a check could be made, from time to time during the afternoon, on progress. And progress was more like that of a kite than a motor vehicle, for by four o'clock we had barely moved on the map from where we had been when we left Urcos at one-thirty: we were just two or three thousand feet above the town, that was all.

With every hairpin bend in the track, Urcos grew smaller, far down now in the valley beneath us. From my seat on the floor with my back to the truck's cab, one could see the entire chassis of the truck buckling, twisting, and twisting back again, as it hauled its full load upwards, very slowly upwards.

Urcos was only a speck now. The dirt road we had travelled was a winding string stretching away from our feet, disappearing in the dust.

At various bends beneath us on the track, other trucks could be seen, labouring (like us) up the mountains. Sometimes you could wave from one hairpin bend to the truck on the next one. Once there was a quick glimpse of the three companions who had boarded a different truck at Urcos, waving from their own vehicle, El Ejecutor (The Executive), one bend below us. We left it later, when it appeared to develop mechanical trouble and pulled off the track.

By late afternoon we had reached the top. Urcos, and the great valley at whose head Cuzco lies, shimmered in the haze below, as they would appear from an aeroplane. The Andean ridge across which we were now passing was topped with small snow peaks, but all around us the earth was bare and dry as bone, and the sierra was completely uninhabited. Clouds of yellow dust trailed behind as we picked up speed. The air was very thin and the atmosphere harsh. The sun still burned, but if you put your nose above the wooden sides and into the dusty slipstream, the wind was growing cold, bitterly cold.

The scene in the cargo hold had changed, now. People were unfurling dusty blankets from their baggage and disappearing beneath them. Heads were wrapped, sometimes entirely wrapped, in brightly coloured scarves or squares of wool. Little tubs of grease were appearing from every bag, and people were smearing faces, hands and – especially – lips.

A very slight but perceptible air of apprehension hung over the passengers. As the truck thundered, faster now, over the atrocious road surface, you could stand facing backwards, your own back against the back of the driver's cab, and look towards the tail. From here you could see the whole steel framework of the vehicle distorting now to the left, now to the right, as we lurched over ridges and gullies in the truck.

Within our cargo hold, everything had shaken down to its natural level. No matter how carefully bags, sacks of oranges or bedding had been stowed, pinned and secured, luggage had torn free and was strewn along the base of the hold among the oil drums. And these drums, too, were working loose. The great majority (which were full) moved only imperceptibly, edging their way in a crazy slow-motion dance around each other, crushing belongings caught between them.

With the higher altitude reducing the air pressure outside them, and the heat of the sun expanding any pockets of air within them, the full drums were beginning to weep. From the small plugs on the top end of each, screwed as tight shut as the driver's mate could get them, diesel oozed continuously. At first all of us tried to keep it off our bodies and clothing, but before long it was everywhere. Nobody escaped. The important thing was not to touch your eyes with oily fingers, for, when this happened, it took hours (and much catlike finger-licking and eye-rubbing) before the eye cleared.

By dusk, everyone was coated in diesel.

The empty drums – there were three of them – proved the real menace. They had no weight of their own to hold them down, and ropes would never secure them for long. Like rogue animals, they started to slide and roll among the passengers, and keeping an eye out for them became a constant preoccupation.

The very young and the very old seemed the most peaceful. In the lee of the driver's cab hunched an old man and three old women, completely covered in dust so that heads and arms appeared yellow, and motionless. You could hardly tell they were breathing but from time to time the old women spoke, while the old man chewed coca leaves continuously, his teeth as green as the coca strings hanging from his lips and little piles of ruminated foliage squashed on the metal floor around him. He was in another world, and content.

Caesar Augustus was happy, too. While his mother made what she could of pieces of stale, dusty bread and bits of my oranges, Caesar's milk supply never seemed to fail. Enfolded in her arms, his tiny head pneumatically cushioned against her breast, he looked out smiling. The jarring and knocking of the truck's side was shock-absorbed through his mother's back, double-sprung through the pillows that were her breasts, and arrived *chez* Caesar Augustus as no more than a soothing massage. Supremely selfish, like the old man, Caesar was also supremely happy.

And one other old man had created for himself the last word in in-truck luxury. As well as three spare wheels we also carried one spare tyre: just the outer tyre, minus tube and wheel-hub. A wizened little character, this man had curled himself *inside* its rubber walls, the outer arch of his back against the inner arch of the tyre.

This tyre was not roped down, but drifted with the motion of the truck all around the cargo bed. Like a gentle dodgem car it was deflected from every solid object it met, drifting off in the other direction until it met another obstacle. Curled within it like a foetus within the womb, the old man floated around the truck in his rubber space capsule: secure against all impact and, mostly, asleep.

Ahead of us lay another valley, broader and shallower than that from which we had just climbed. Shadows were lengthening as we bounced down the mountainside into the more fertile country, and our route began to pass fields, huts, sheep and warmly dressed Indians walking by the roadside.

You could clamber on to the cab roof. On one side of it the pale-skinned youth still clung. The other side was now occupied by a fat Indian girl with pimply skin, in a pink nylon woolly stranded with some sort of shiny tinsel wool.

A wooden platform had been constructed above the cabin, ringed with a low rail. This was mostly for light luggage and cargo, but to each side – on the near-side and off-side edges – the box was deep enough for a small man to anchor himself securely in. These were the roof positions of the boy and girl.

In one sense they were the most dangerous seats on the truck, suspended, as they were, out above the front cab. Low trees, overhanging rocks and any brush with the sides of road cuttings were an occasional danger to watch out for; while an accident of any kind – even an exceptionally violent jolt – would find the occupants of these nests in the most exposed position of all.

On the other hand, you could at least see where you were going and anticipate. To be incarcerated in the cargo hold behind was rather like being down in the bowels of a ship. And, should the vehicle turn over or lurch so hard as to launch the entire cargo into the air, passengers in the hold would almost certainly be crushed by flying 44-gallon drums of diesel. The light-skinned youth and I (for I was now with him, talking) could hope to be catapulted clear.

As suspected, he was not Peruvian; but he was not from Europe either. He was a Brazilian and his name was Marcelo. Marcelo was seventeen.

What had at first appeared to be standoffishness or the conceitedness of adolescence (for he had spoken to nobody, and hardly smiled) was more awkwardness. Brazilians are unlike other South Americans: they are unceremonious and quite direct. They do not bother with the courtesies that even the poorest Peruvians usually show; and as the journey continued it became obvious that although Marcelo spoke (besides his native Portuguese and fluent US-flavoured English) pretty fluent Spanish, he found it quite hard to communicate with Peruvians. He was not fair-skinned enough to deserve the allowances made for real gringos. Peruvian fellow travellers judged him by their own standards, and found his rough manner with them irritating.

But it was not intended to be: for Marcelo was rather a sensitive soul, and quite brave. His father was dead. His mother and family were not, however, poor; but he had decided to try travelling all around the continent overland, alone, and on his own resources. Now, after a long journey, he was trying to get home to Rio de Janeiro. He had a strange confidence.

Later, more emerged. For now, we discussed the trip we were sharing. Marcelo had had enough at the sharp end of our truck, exposed to all the elements, and wanted to rest a little out of the wind, down in the cargo bed with the others. I offered him my corner (in so far as, dodging the moving drums, there were any permanent positions at all) in exchange for a turn up in the eagle's nest.

It was noticeable, as he clambered down, how thin his arms and legs were, and how filthy his clothes.

We were running alongside a small stream, and the land was becoming occasionally populated. We had descended steadily from the ridge, so laboriously attained, above Urcos, and were now in a wide and empty valley. We seemed to be coming to a sizeable village – the first since we had left Urcos, five hours (and one massive mountain range) ago. It was twilight.

The place was called Ccata. The extra c did not seem to make any difference in pronunciation; but there was certainly something strange in the atmosphere.

It was not a threatening strangeness: more the feeling of dislocation one might expect if thrown forward or back in time, or if visiting a different but friendly planet.

For a start, this community was extraordinarily isolated. No river traffic or airfield linked it with the rest of Peru; the road was long and difficult; and the whole valley cut off from the outside. Yet here the people were neither poor nor backward. The land was good, the people looked comfortable and the huts and houses (though mud, tin and straw) were solid.

The women's costume here was quite unique. Their dresses or robes seemed simpler than elsewhere but their hats were extraordinary. They can perhaps best be pictured if you imagine those wooden frames which stretch tight the plain cloth on which a tapestry artist works. Held in a horizontal position, like landing-pads for tiny helicopters, these were somehow mounted above the head.

All the women wore them. Whereas the dresses, skirts and petticoats of the Indian women elsewhere in Peru had looked Victorian, and the bowler hats and straw boaters Edwardian, the scene in the mud streets of Ccata was somehow medieval, as the ladies took an evening prom-enade while mules and horses clip-clopped past.

And a second peculiarity stood out in Ccata. Upon every roof chimney was a wire-frame cross, a Christian cross. And, standing astride the pitch of every roof (however mean the hut beneath), was a miniature china bull.

All combined to produce an effect which was subtly bizarre. It would have been possible (it seemed) to have entered this valley asleep, woken to witness this scene, slept again as one left, and felt sure the following morning that it had all been a dream. It would have been an episode such as little Lis may remember – the Indian girl who had woken on Ian's lap, and left it asleep again.

We unloaded one gas cylinder in Ccata, and took on two wooden poles. It took a while to do, and, by the time we headed out of town on a dirt road that was (temporarily) fast and straight, night had fallen and it was getting cold. We stopped a few miles further on while the drivers changed. It grew colder.

There was one driver in charge. He was a small, leathery man in middle age with a kind but authoritative manner. Everyone called him Tio (Uncle) and the squint-lines around his eyes – born no doubt of thousands of hours of tense driving – made him seem indeed like a well-worn but favourite uncle. Tio was a very, very good driver.

He had an assistant who took turns at the wheel. This was a taller, younger man, with less of Tio's confident sense of humour. He looked slightly oriental, and was called – as about one in twenty of his coun-trymen seemed to be – 'Chino'.

Tio and Chino had a drivers' mate, a tall, slim and exceptionally good-looking young man they called Dabit. The b's and v's seem to be completely interchangeable in Peru.

It was Dabit's job to keep the passengers in order, organize the loading, securing and despatch of cargo, and to oversee the finances. Very occasionally he would be permitted to drive, but never when the going was dangerous, which it mostly was.

It was certainly about to become so, for now we crossed a river and began to climb again.

The stars were out and an icy wind punished anybody who put his face above the parapet. So, curling up as tightly as possible in my box-seat, I lay back, face to the sky.

Whatever our truck had started with by way of exhaust mufflers was shot to pieces, and as we wound our way heavenward along a road so white in the moonlight that it seemed like a river threading between the black banks of the hills to either hand, the roar of the engines filled the night and echoed off the mountainside. But it was peaceful, here at the front. Among the bands of bright stars splashed across the sky, you could just discern the Southern Cross.

Swathed now in yards of dusty blanket and hugged against each other, mother and baby in the back of the truck just beneath my perch were armed against the night. She seemed to be asleep; but, after an afternoon's milky slumber, the baby was awake. Just the top of his tiny face and some wisps of soft black hair peeped from the folds of the blanket. His eyes were open.

Caesar Augustus stared unblinking up, as a shower of asteroids sparkled across the night sky.

Chapter Twenty-Six

And Higher
Still

It was not yet time to turn in for the night, though almost everyone was asleep. Our route – another spectacular ascent – passed mostly unseen in the dark. In recollection it is a confusion, half sleeping, half waking, of what seemed in the headlights' glare to be towering gorges, then red canyons and a rushing river; and, sometimes, strange silences as we passed through tall groves of eucalyptus trees. The road was very bad in places and more than once we stopped for the drivers to pace and inspect sections of the track where floods had cut the way, or cuttings had tumbled in on to the road.

Dimly we were aware that we were part of a convoy of trucks whose number seemed mysteriously to have grown from the two which had left Urcos together. Perhaps others were leaving Urcos without picking up passengers (though you never saw a truck without its full complement). Perhaps some had come direct from Cuzco? Certainly two had been waiting in Ccata, and were now part of the convoy whose presence you guessed from the dust which sometimes hung in the still air ahead of us, the twinkling of moving lights from the valley behind us, or the flash of a headlight's beam moving across a rock face high above us, as a truck swung round a bend . . .

And there was the sound, once, of a baby crying. Once we stopped in the biting wind to secure the remaining gas cylinders, which were shifting dangerously again. Passengers worked quietly, cooperatively and always without complaining, and I helped Dabit with the ropes, glad – when it was done – to snuggle down in the lee of the cab, nursing hands numb with cold, as the truck moved off. Then sleep returned.

Who knows for how long? When we awoke, the others were already struggling over the truck's sides. Marcelo was shaking my shoulder. We had reached a place called Ocongate.

The square was full of trucks and travellers. This was a real town; and though it must have been ten at night by the time we reached it, it was a hive of life and commerce.

The town seemed to have no electricity: at any rate the square was illuminated only by scores of kerosene pressure lamps on the vendors' barrows and outside the houses. Their roar and hiss filled the air, and the smell of kerosene mingled with the smells of roasting food and steaming tea: for the whole square had turned itself into a catering effort for the trucks coming into town.

And in they came, one after the other. By now there were at least seven huge vehicles, all fully loaded, and each (at a guess) with between twenty and fifty passengers. Every barrow became a fast-food operation; and in the gloom, lit by patches of warm light, kettles sang, roasting meat spat, and sleepy figures wrapped in blankets clambered off trucks and drifted around the square.

A few of us stood, rather bewildered, wondering why we had stopped, how long we were staying and what to do.

Tio the driver must have seen me, for his co-driver, Chino, came up to me in the darkness. 'The senior driver has asked you if you wish to eat with us?'

At first I did not recognize Chino or understand the invitation: but rather than hesitate, I followed him. All became clear as we ducked our heads for a low door and entered a little shack, brightly lit within. It was filled with wooden trestle-tables and at one of them sat Tio and Dabit. They gestured to me to sit with them. Food followed. This, then, was the trucking equivalent of being invited to the Captain's table!

Tio and Chino were cross-examining me about life in London, but already my mind was far away in space and time. I was back on the *Queen Elizabeth II* returning from New York to Southampton, as a boy who had just finished university.

The university had been Yale, where I had just finished a two-year postgraduate course. I had no scooter to transport this time, but a bigger record player and many more records; and my books now filled two crates. So it had proved cheaper to buy a tourist-class passage on Cunard (where all my luggage went free) than to fly. One might suppose that only first-class passengers got their turn at the Captain's table, but it seemed that lesser beings were sometimes included – I had been lucky.

Or unlucky, as it turned out. I cannot remember anything about the Captain, for it was the girl on my left who talked to me throughout the meal.

She was (unfortunately for her) very, very fat; and (unfortunately for me) very, very lonely. She was called Karen, and travelling from her mother's home in the US to her divorced father in England.

Karen was too unhappy to be good company, and desperation does not make people likeable, only pitiable. She lacked confidence. So I talked to her in a friendly way, and when she suggested a drink after the meal, I bought her one.

Her drink was gin and tonic, and only as I handed her the glass and said 'Cheers' did I register her replying stare, and realize – stupidly late in the day – that she was expecting me to sleep with her. Not for the first (or last) time, what I had intended as civility had been taken as something else. I froze.

It seems silly now, looking back. There were a thousand ways one could have finished one's drink – had another, even – and parted on some light excuse. God knows I was twenty-three and must have learned the niceties by then?

Yet one remembers the little things – her name and address, and exactly where she was standing at the bar – but not quite how or why I had got myself into this, or what was supposed to be the big problem about getting out of it. My friend Francis at university could remember the details of all the shipping cases in International Law – the vessels' names, tonnages, cargoes, provenance and destination – but never the legal principle illustrated by the case. And I, now, recalling myself face to face with that girl on the *QE2*, gins and tonics in our hands, can remember every detail of the scene – but not the reason why I panicked.

The band struck up at that moment, and in my fevered brain I think I must have concluded that I had to dance with her immediately, and then perhaps make love to her straight afterwards – right there in the bar, maybe . . .

I only remember placing my glass unsteadily on the counter and saying, 'Karen, I think I'm going to be sick'; and tearing out of the room, leaving her there; and never coming back; and never daring to speak to her again for the rest of the voyage.

It was despicable. How long did she wait? Why couldn't I have simply . . . It is pointless to wonder.

Yet I sat there in the shack at Ocongate, Tio, Chino and Dabit opposite me as we finished our thick barley soup, mutton stew and sweet tea . . . and wondered again as I have so often since, why?

Outside in the town square, a great honking of horns and roaring of engines announced the departure of most of the trucks. Passengers ran squealing through the dark, looking for children or comrades still tarrying over the mutton stew. It gave the chance to inspect our truck, and other trucks, more closely.

They were almost all Volvos: engine and transmission built in Sweden, chassis and wooden frame added in Lima. There were two vintage Volvos – some fifteen years old – but most were more recent: most, in fact, looked five years old or less. In England our truck would be described as a two-axle, twenty-tonne, rigid lorry.

Every vehicle was well-maintained. Often the bodywork was shabby, and many of the wooden frames had taken quite a beating; the tyres, as everywhere in Peru, were in atrocious shape; but you could see that what really mattered, the mechanical guts of the vehicle, got all the attention they needed. That was vital.

Now drivers were under bonnets, revving engines, adjusting and checking fuel, oil, brakes and wheels. There was real professionalism in this sector at least of Peruvian national life.

As we headed out of Ocongate and began to climb again, huge white peaks, jagged in the starlight, showed their heads above the hills around. It was midnight. Surely we were not going over that ridge now?

We were not. Only a few miles outside the town, in a grove of eucalyptus trees, Tio brought our truck to a halt. Dabit clambered out of the passengers' cab and explained. 'It will be too cold to continue now. We will start again, dawn. We will sleep, now.'

But where? While the truck was still moving you could doze, after a fashion, cramped among sacks and drums: the motion somehow made that possible. But now all was still, that pit of oily bodies, stray oranges and sharp edges were the last place to induce sleep.

My sleeping-bag was a particularly warm one – 'all seasons' – with a hood. I stowed it under one arm and started to climb off the truck, to find a piece of flat earth somewhere nearby.

Five or six brown hands reached up and tugged me back.

The attitude shown towards me by my fellow passengers (all Indians apart from Marcelo) was distinctly odd. That had already become noticeable. There was an element of distrust (any gringo experiences this) and an element of curiosity, too; but mostly they treated me like a domestic pet – an animal, a mascot, a visitor from outer space – to be talked at, laughed at, treated a little warily, but – on the whole – cherished.

'They say,' said Marcelo, 'that the cold will kill you if you sleep outside the truck. Everyone sleeps together here, for warmth. They are making a space for you.'

So they were. The peasant woman who was mother to Caesar Augustus had laid out her blankets in a straight line, sardine-tight, side by side with a row of other women. Now she was vigorously shoving everything eighteen inches sideways, leaving the narrowest of gaps between herself and the wall of the cab. She indicated that this was my sleeping space and waved a spare edge of blanket over it. The blanket was to cover me, her and Caesar Augustus. Marcelo was to lie with his head at our feet, and his legs between our sides, for added warmth.

Looking sidelong at the cool earth and empty sky and longing for the solitude of my own patch, it was clear nevertheless that there was no polite way to refuse this kindness. With heavy heart I clambered back down and snuggled in.

She smelt awful. As her blanket flapped down over my body and face, and the air from her own clothes and body spilled over us, the desire to retch overwhelmed me. How was sleep possible? The toecaps of Marcelo's boots wiggled by my thighs. At least he had kept his boots on!

Somewhere an infant began to cry, but it was not Caesar Augustus, who was on my left shoulder, his nappies unchanged (it seemed) from when we had left Urcos. Somebody coughed. Again that rich, sweet smell wafted over me and I tried to breathe less deeply.

Now the altitude began to bite and a sudden breathlessness gripped me. Squeezed in, longing – and unable – to gulp a great lungful of air, I experienced momentarily the nightmare of a drowning man. The irrational fear of suffocation caused heart to race and breathlessness to grow. A huge desire to kick and shoulder everything aside, throw out my arms and breathe deeply, gripped me. A sharp headache stabbed somewhere just behind my eyes. My retching startled Caesar Augustus who was awake and breathing hard, but deeply, regularly.

Forcing myself to do likewise, the headache receded. Reason returned. It had been a moment of strange panic.

Caesar and I stared up at the Southern Cross, heard a light wind rustling the tops of the eucalyptus trees, and slept.

Chapter Twenty-Seven

And Down the
Other Side

We were moving before sunrise, but our departure had not awoken me. Consciousness dawned, now, as the truck's gears crashed heavily into reverse, its wooden flanks scraping against an overhanging bank.

Eyes opened to a pale dawn sky above, ringed with ice-mountains. From the wheels came a crunching sound. We were driving over loose snow and had reached a bend so tight that the truck could not make it in one. Chino was executing a three-point turn.

Not everyone was coming to life. Still covered in yesterday's dust, oily figures were emerging from under oily blankets and blinking at the Christmas world around us. It was intensely cold; but Marcelo being still asleep gave me the chance to brave the icy wind and establish myself in the crow's-nest above the cab, on the near-side. On the off-side the fat girl in pink was already installed, and conducting verbal hostilities with a man in the back whom – unaccountably – they called Mata-Rata (Kill-Rat). He seemed a quiet fellow; she seemed the aggressor.

He called her La Gorda (Fat One) and his ammunition consisted mostly in variations on that theme. He was too thin, she was yelling, to keep any woman warm. She was too fat, he called back, to feel the cold.

As sentinels on the roof, then, we greeted the dawn, shielding our faces from the headwind as our truck bucked and crunched along a frosty track.

We were (as I later found out) about 16,000 feet up, crossing a pass called Hualla-Hualla. We were higher than the top of Mont Blanc, Europe's highest mountain; this, as it turned out, was the summit of our route. From here onwards it was down the other side: all the way down, almost to sea level, the jungle, the river and Puerto Maldonado.

The sky flushed pink and yellow and, moments later, the sun came up, already the palest lemon. It was numbingly cold. This would be a scorching day.

'Look, Gringo, look!' Tio, who was not driving, leaned out of the passenger-cab window and shouted up at me 'Viscaya!'

I looked. Scurrying under a big boulder was a little brown rabbit-

196

like creature. These are the 'rock-rabbits' or 'conies' that the South Americans call *viscacha*. The Andes are not rich in fauna so the list of animals to spot is short. This shy creature is often spoken of but seldom seen, but the nondescript little thing was rather a disappointment. I hid this, for all the passengers seemed pleased for me that I had achieved such a sighting.

Except for La Gorda. La Gorda was not the protective sort. This woman was under pressure from the rest of the truck. They assumed she was a prostitute. It was not so much disapproval as ribaldry she had to suffer: particularly from the men. She took it well and gave as good as she got, hurling abuse back at any quarter it came from, twice as loud and twice as vulgar as whatever had provoked it. La Gorda was the virago of our company.

But by now the joke had got around the whole truck, and was getting out of hand.

'Who did you sleep with last night, La Gorda?' shouted one of the men. 'Have you slept with the Brazilian yet?'

In reply, La Gorda simply waved a withered, blackened banana she had found among her provisions. Her friend, Rosa shrieked with laughter. 'The *Brazilian?*' screamed La Gorda. 'This banana would be preferable!'

Everyone laughed. La Gorda seized on this success. At last, someone below her in the pecking order: someone she could herself abuse. There would be less comeback from foreigners.

'How would you like to sleep with me, Gringo?' she called, over the heaps of sacks which separated her corner seat from mine.

'Yes, Gringo, yes!' called Rosa from the back. 'My friend is in love with you. Or the Brazilian will suffice. She is a very desirable girl,' Rosa and La Gorda cackled in amusement at their own joke. Some of the passengers began to join in.

'She's cheap, you know,' shouted a woman in a BMW cap. 'Very good value. Better than Brazil.'

'Easier even than the women in Rio!' another chipped in.

Being unable to reply in kind, it seemed best for me to feign complete incomprehension, while Marcelo simply ignored her. After a while, people got bored with the subject. But I noticed, when we stopped at seven for breakfast, that there was some danger of becoming a figure of fun. It was becoming a habit to crack jokes, not all of which made any sense to me but in which the word 'gringo' could frequently be heard, followed by laughter. I disliked this.

Tio sensed as much. We had stopped at a place called Entel Wahia 2, which seemed to be the shack inhabited by the watchman who maintained the telephone company's microwave relay station. You could see this mast at the top of a little peak above us, its disc reflectors turned forwards towards the next mast in the chain (somewhere miles down in the jungle below) and backwards to the previous one (visible on a distant mountain ridge behind us). This was how Entel provided the telephone link across a country whose terrain made transmission lines an impossibility

The shack was filthy. It seemed to serve as a truck-stop kitchen for all the convoys which passed, and by the time we left there were five trucks in the yard. The room was dominated by an ancient kerosene stove. The walls and ceilings were black with kerosene soot.

'Do not be angry at people calling "Gringo", Gringo,' said Tio. 'It is just their name for you. They are uneducated but they are not intending to upset you.'

This was only partly true. What certainly was true was Tio's reminder that the word 'gringo' need not be intended hurtfully. In South America it is often just a convenient tag for someone who is foreign.

Yet it made me realize (for the first time) how racial tags of any kind can irritate, even where they are not intended to put people down. How 'over-sensitive' black or Asian people in Britain often seem to any word which could be, or has ever been, used in a derogatory way – even where its use is nothing but a friendly jest. Yet was that not exactly my own feeling, now?

'Hurry up, Gringo!' someone shouted. My hackles rose. 'We're leaving!'

We all wolfed what was left of the dry bread and pumpkin jam breakfast, washed down with hot water and chicory powder, and followed the others back to the truck.

Now began our great descent. The edge of the Andes – for that was where we were perched – was the edge of a world. This was underlined in a startling way.

We had left the truck stop some four or five miles behind us and were thumping along an undulating track, raising clouds of yellow-white dust in our wake. The mountains were powder-dry. What little grass grew there was brown and withered in the sun. By our shoulders jagged peaks, like iced needles, pierced a hot blue sky. It was a harsh world.

But as we rounded a corner, cries of amazement went up from passengers. For just below us, our world simply ended. A blank sea of blinding white stretched flat below us, as far as the eye could see – and that was more (at a guess) than a hundred miles. It lapped the flanks of the Andes, and our road, snaking down the side simply disappeared into it.

It was clouds. But not the insubstantial grey blur into which English landscapes fade. This was flat and brilliant as a linen sheet. It could have been marble.

Gazing across the slopes around us you saw a mountain world, shining in the sun, floating, disembodied in space. The cloud did not so much shroud, or hide: it amputated. The mountains just stopped, and, if there was another world at their feet, these hillsides knew nothing of it.

Slowly the truck wound its way downward. Looking back up the mountain from which we had come, you could see the road zigzagging through dozens of bends, with tiny trucks on almost every one, each at its own stage of the descent. And this was the scene from which we were about to disappear. The cloud loomed so close, now, that it seemed to touch the side of the truck with its cold breath ... Just one more bend, perhaps – and then what?

From the cockpit above the passenger-cab I whistled with amazement – and noticed someone else as lost in wonder as me. He was clinging to the wooden framework, his body half hung out over the side of the truck, dangerously. He was a boy of about thirteen, small, very thin and wide-eyed. His name was Luceo. He seemed to be alone on his voyage.

Luceo's eyes caught mine, and registered the same excitement. This, then was the Amazon basin, or edge of it, before us.

Suddenly, the cloud was all around us. We were descending through a cool, soft mist. This was our last view of the mountains.

The road was terrible – worse, even, than before. Crawling in the lowest gear, all the trucks (there were nine, now) edged painfully down the pass. The first thing you noticed about the track was how pitted and rock-strewn it was; how gullies had cut their way across it; and how narrow was the carriageway. More than once we had to stop and reverse to get round a corner.

But the second thing you noticed was that it was a magnificent piece of civil engineering. It must have taken years – and lives – to construct. Stone culverts had been built over the river-beds, rock hacked out of the mountainside to clear a passage. Wherever the ground was soft or unstable, foundations of cut stone had been laid. Surveying the whole sweep of the pass, this – the only road link between one of Peru's richest jungle provinces, and the mountains and Pacific coast – was a roadbuilder's dream.

The only other way out from Maldonado was to the Atlantic, thousands of miles down the great Madre de Dios: navigable all the way to the Amazon.

The cloud was not as thick as it had seemed from above, once we were in it. Our truck was the first of the convoy to dive through. Next came El Ejecutor, the truck in which the three who had been my companions to Urcos had last been seen. A spanking new truck called Danny followed. Higher up were Rosa, Elvis and Conquistador. We were beginning to recognize each other now, and spirited banter – and good-natured abuse – flew between passengers whenever one truck came close enough to another.

Marcelo perched perilously by me in the cockpit seat and the two of us did our best to ignore the taunts of La Gorda. She had found an easy target in these two foreigners and was exploiting this for all it was worth. Installed on the other side of the cab roof, she directed a stream of foul language and sexual innuendo across to us, to the amusement of the crowd in the back where the cargo hold became the auditorium, we the stage.

It was a losing battle with this tart, so we ignored her and talked to each other instead.

Marcelo had just finished his schooling. Some of it had been in Boston in the United States, where his father had worked before he died, when Marcelo was thirteen. He lived now with his mother and sister in Rio.

Marcelo did not know what career he wanted. He hoped to be a writer, one day. He had already written a novel, he said, but had shown it to nobody. Alternatively, he might be a poet. He had written poems too. Another possibility was to be a religious mystic – but he had not yet decided which religion. Zen appealed just at present.

Was I knowledgeable about Zen, he asked. No? How about Saint Teresa of Avila? She used to levitate, apparently, and this was something Marcelo was hoping to learn how to do. Oh – and did I smoke grass?

La Gorda's lampoonery had ceased and we were left to ourselves. It was mid-morning and the truck was crawling painfully slowly down the side of the Andes, staying in lowest gear in case the brakes should fail. The mountainside dropped away from our wheels at a gradient that was not far from the vertical, and once, in a ravine below, someone spotted the twisted remains of a truck which had left the road.

The track was just wide enough to take us – but at various small but critical bridges, barely so. These bridges, spanning the sharp little gorges that carried stormwater down from the mountains, were built roughly from stone and wood. Scores had been constructed and beside many was the debris of previous bridges, washed away.

With every shoulder of mountain we passed you would survey the next sweep of mountainside, and gasp. How would the track ahead tackle this cliff – or that gorge – or those sheer rockfaces? Every time, somehow, the roadbuilder had found a way through.

Had he started with an overall plan, able to see how the whole descent would be accomplished? Or had he tackled each new impossibility as he came to it, hopeful that so long as the road continued to descend, it would eventually reach the jungle? Had this recently been a new road, engineered for the provisioning of Puerto Maldonado? Or did it follow the lines of some ancient bridleway?

We were beneath the cloud layer now, and could see for hundreds of miles. White peaks were behind us and ahead was a swirling mixture of low cloud and the green mountain: those were the lower slopes of the Andes, lusher, and garlanded with mist in the romantic manner of a Renaissance painting. We were descending into a great valley, but it was still thousands of feet beneath us.

Our way down, however, was becoming clearer: we had begun to follow a smaller valley, its thin stream cutting through the mountainside and cascading towards the jungle below. Laboriously our track coiled itself along the same path, sometimes taking miles of zigzags to catch up with what the stream accomplished in a single leap.

This gave a good preview of anything on the road ahead: and by the time a truck called Christ The Redeemer reached us coming the other way, we had known of its approach for half an hour.

The little monkey-faced lad had time to prepare his surprise. Luceo wore a mischievous grin that spread from ear to ear. His ears, in fact, were pointed and the overall impression was of an adolescent elf. He seemed to be without companions, but was on friendly terms with everyone – even La Gorda, whose taunts (she had pressed a small dead caterpillar to his trousers) he had endured with good nature.

For some time before Christ The Redeemer reached us, Luceo was to be seen scrabbling around in the bottom of our truck, in the danger zone where loose drums rolled. As the two trucks neared each other, his head disappeared beneath the natural parapet formed by the wooden-slatted side.

Then we rounded a bend and met. Christ pulled over to the shoulder to let us pass. There was only just room, and we edged nervously alongside, then pulled away.

As we did, Luceo leapt up like a jack-in-the-box and loosed a stream of missiles at the passengers on the other truck. He had collected everything that could be thrown – bananas, oranges, bits of bread, plastic bottles – and launched this dizzying bombardment in continuous quick-fire succession.

It took The Redeemer completely by surprise. Luceo managed to hit almost every one of its passengers. By the time they could organize themselves to retaliate, it was too late. We were away, in a cloud of dust and laughter.

Luceo stood up at the back of our truck and everybody cheered. If there had been room between his ears for his smile to be wider, it would have been. It was a grin that all but broke its bounds and parted company with the sides of his face.

'He is an orphan,' Caesar Augustus's mother explained quietly. 'He told me his father and mother are dead and he was living with relatives near Cuzco. He has run away to prospect for gold in Maldonado. He says they will not search for him.'

Though wisps of cloud hung in the air, and the air was damp, the mountainside was still quite barren. Yet here and there were patches of greenery, and these increased. We had travelled all day without passing habitation of any sort but by noon we began to see llamas and sheep.

They looked in poor shape, and the first huts we reached confirmed this: they were mean and dirty, and the people were ragged. Even the chickens looked broken down.

We stopped there for a while. A group of small boys stood some way off and threw mud at us, until Tio chased them away with a stick. My camera drew the attention of a young man who, with female companion and child, had kept silent and rather apart from the other passengers. There was a hurried whispering with her friend, and she came shyly up. Would I take her photograph?

Certainly, I said, but it would not be developed until I returned to Europe. She would never see the photograph.

No, no, she said. She understood that. The photograph was for me to keep, not for her. There were no photographs of her, she explained. She would like there to be. It did not matter if she could not see them for herself.

Fine, I said. With your friend, in front of our truck?

No. She wanted to be alone, standing on a rock.

'Up you get, then,' I said.

But it was not so simple. She wanted to collect all her belongings and place them next to her on the rock. They too, she said, should be in the photograph as they were hers ... Tio sounded the horn impatiently. There was no time for possessions. So she stood on the rock, looking extremely tense, for her photograph.

It is easy to imagine what La Gorda made of this as we clambered back on to the lorry. So this was the gringo's new girlfriend! Was he to marry her and take her to Miami and make a rich lady of her? And was La Gorda herself not good enough for him, then? A joke which appeared to be about the girl's vagina followed, which divided the more from the less vulgar of our fellow passengers. Some of the older ones protested. Most laughed, Luceo the loudest among them.

But it passed, and we jolted our way on into the afternoon. The air seemed to be growing heavier as we lost altitude, and the track, though still steeply downhill, was not so precipitous as before. Our same little valley – the one we had been following for many hours, now –

broadened, and its stream had become almost a river. There were more huts on the hillside and the land grew steadily less dry. Maize had been planted here and there and looked worth harvesting.

As the afternoon wore on, huts, crops and animals increased, and we passed the first bicycle since the market square at Ocongate. 'At Marcapata,' said Chino to me (he had come to ride for a spell in the back), 'there are hot springs. Wonderful hot springs. A miracle. Famous in all the province. Every driver longs to reach Marcapata. There we will stop and swim, and continue our journey marvellously refreshed. It is,' he said, 'a most significant place.'

It wasn't, really: just a hundred huts, a single muddy street, a football pitch with a Peruvian flag on a crooked pole flying above, and the biggest thatched church that has ever been dreamed of, it was virtually a thatched cathedral. But after the desolation through which we had passed, it seemed like Babylon. The huts had corrugated-iron roofs with enormously wide overhanging eaves. It made them look like friendly tin mushrooms. This must be a place where it rained often.

'Quick!' hissed Tio through the wooden slats. 'Climb down and come with us drivers to the hot springs. Do not tell the other passengers. Do not bring the Brazilian.' Poor Marcelo was not popular with the other passengers. The opinion seemed to be that he was only a South American like them, but arrogant like all Brazilians. He committed the crime of acting like a gringo when he was not one.

So Tio, Chino and Dabit set off for the hot springs, with me in tow.

Tio ushered me proudly into the bath-house. 'Look!' he said. 'Isn't it what Chino told you?' I looked.

It was a hut, about fifteen feet square, with an earth floor and a corrugated-iron roof. There was no lighting (the village had no electricity), but as eyes accustomed to the gloom, you could make out the shadowy figures of about fifteen bathers, of both sexes.

They had removed their shirts but modestly, the men either wore their trousers – wet – or, more bravely, stripped to their underpants. The women all kept their skirts on, clinging waterlogged to their legs, and wore brassieres – or what passed for them.

Most of the interior was taken up with a square concrete tank with slime clinging to its sides. It was about twelve feet across, but subdivided (like a window pane) into four square compartments. All were filled to overflowing with steaming, murky water. A strong smell of sulphur hung in the air.

The four compartments were in fact two pairs. Into one of each pair water flowed from two pipes poking through the mud wall. From this primary compartment it then overflowed into the secondary compartment. From these it overflowed into a trough which took the water away, out of the other end of the hut.

Dabit, now stripped to a pair of underpants that looked like an old washing-up cloth, explained. 'There are four sections. Unsoaped men, soaped men, unsoaped women and soaped women. The top sections – one for each sex – have clean water in, where you get wet before washing, or just lie, for pleasure. The lower sections – again, one for each sex – are where you are allowed to use soap.'

In we all went. My purple underpants, purchased in Huaraz, were just the thing. Tio and Chino kept their trousers on.

The water was almost unbearably hot and very muddy. There was no room to move. And yet ... as we trooped, clean, flushed and wet, back to the truck, it seemed that Chino had been right. It *was* wondrous.

'There is no charge,' said Tio. 'The people of Marcapata are pleased to share their miracle, which comes from God, with all travellers. This is a very hospitable village. Famous throughout Peru – perhaps the world.'

After Marcapata the track continued its downward journey, but the drivers faced two new problems. We had almost reached the basin of the great valley that had lain at our feet all day. No longer a rocky mountain track, the road ran over soft red earth, and steep sections were deep in mud. We crawled through these, our heavy load of diesel helping the wheels bite.

We were running a straight course; the track was clinging to the side of the valley, going the same way as the river at the bottom, and gradually descending to join it. It was as narrow as ever, and – with the vegetation closing in – there was nowhere for trucks to pass each other. Just outside Marcapata, our convoy hit another convoy coming the other way.

The logistics were infernally complicated. Neither convoy was travelling closely packed together: each was spread over many miles. Our truck might carry on forward and the oncoming truck reverse for half a mile or so (it was slow) until a point was found where they could pass – by which time two more trucks had caught up with the first, going down. Should the truck coming *up* then be joined by a second, the whole manoeuvre would be wrecked, for most of the passing places were long enough only for one truck to tuck itself in and wait, while others passed.

It took time, but the drivers' tempers were good and eventually we were clear. There was much camaraderie between the crews of different vehicles. Drivers would stop and pass on details of problems ahead and (as we saw later) trucks stuck in the road which we could expect to meet, waiting for help from passing vehicles.

But behind the bantering abuse that flew between drivers whenever two met or passed, there was real rivalry. Shared perils did bring comradeship, but they also brought a keen sense of who was pulling his weight, and who not.

This was brought home when we rounded a bend and found Socrates, broken down by the roadside. In keeping with its name this was an ancient truck, perhaps twenty years old. But it was also too light and low-slung for this track, and overloaded with passengers.

In the hump in the road, between the two wheel-tracks, lay many great boulders concealed in the mud. Often the tracks to each side had been sunk by successive wheels into deep ruts, some more than two feet deep. The whole underbelly of the vehicle, therefore, was as often as not scraping along the crown of the road, its wheels well down in these troughs. They acted like railway lines, taking the control of the steering away from the driver. Once in them you could not get out.

When the crown was mud and gravel, no harm was done: you just ploughed through. But where there were rocks, these might strike the axles or drive-shaft of the vehicle. The faster you drove, the harder they struck – yet if you lost too much speed then you lost the momentum needed to carry you through the worst patches. It was a hair-raising balance to strike. Mostly, drivers had to err on the side of speed, keeping their eyes peeled for rock. But accidents did occur.

One had, to Socrates. The old truck was by the roadside, its passengers and their belongings spread out along the track. Socrates's driver was staring dolefully at a smashed axle.

Our driver was Chino. We stopped. Socrates was going our way. Tio got out and talked to their crew. It seemed they wanted us to tow them to the next village, or to take on some of their passengers, or both. Tio would do neither. He helped nudge Socrates off the road and into a position where other vehicles could easily pass, but that was the limit of it. We were soon on our way again.

As we drew away, it suddenly dawned on me that that the three passengers in the funny hats who had been waving from the stranded truck's crowd, and calling 'gringo', were the three friends from the square in Urcos: the ones who had been travelling with me right at the start, from Cuzco.

How had they got on to Socrates? When last seen they were on El Ejecutor.

I waved back. As we were at that point abandoning them to their fate, their cheery stoicism did them credit.

'We cannot help this truck,' said Dabit. He was riding shotgun above the cab so that he could guide Chino in his truck-passing manoeuvres.

'It is too old and too small for this road. The driver must learn that other people will not tow him every time he has problems.' This seemed a harsh philosophy but it was one that applied generally on this road. People would help others if they could, and especially where that meant clearing or improving the track for other vehicles; but they were quite unsentimental about the casualties.

'There are many, many accidents on this road,' he said. 'On the mountains where we have just come from, trucks often fall off the side and people die. On this section, more often they just get stuck and are delayed for days. Sometimes even weeks. We may reach Maldonado tomorrow. We may wait for a week, maybe more.'

Dabit talked with me as the afternoon lengthened. He was about twenty, slim and striking, tall for an Indian. The girls among our passengers all fancied him: even La Gorda melted a little at his glance. From the way he was scratching it seemed possible that he might be suffering from some sort of venereal disease.

Dabit asked me about the Falklands War and especially about the Harrier-jump jets, which seem to have become a legend extending from the Andes to the jungle in South America. He spoke quite freely, too, about the Shining Path terrorists.

'Eliminate them,' he said. 'They kill us. Why does the government not kill them? All of them. That is the only answer. Kill them.'

Odd, to compare this blue-collar response with that of the young student electrician on the train from Quillabamba. The student had been sympathetic (in an unspecific way) to the terrorists: if only because he knew enough about Lima and the Peruvian establishment to resent the state and its authority.

Dabit's attitude to authority was more respectful. Yet it was the young electrician, not the truck-driver's mate, who had (if they knew it) most to fear from the collapse of order in Peru.

Dabit talked about his job. 'Any young man like me,' he said, 'hopes to be a truck driver, like Tio. A driver earns enough to buy his own truck or minibus one day, if he is lucky. That is what everybody wants: to own his own vehicle. We do not like to be employed by other people.'

When Dabit had gone, Marcelo replaced him. He summarized for me the plot of the novel he was planning. 'I am very much into magic,' he explained. 'My book will tell people how everything is magic. There is magic in trees and plants, and magic in people. Magic is the way the world works.'

'What, then, is *not* magic?' This was to prove a Socratic dialogue conducted in the absence of the Master himself, who was stranded with a broken axle.

'Nothing. Everything is magic.'

'But if everything is magic, then what do you mean by the word? How does saying something is 'magic' distinguish it from anything else?'

'It is a quality. Once you accept its presence, everything changes.'

'No. Marcelo, 'magic' is a *word* with a distinct meaning. It means 'happening by some strange of mysterious force'. If everything happens like that, then how can the force be strange or mysterious? Is it "magic" that when I push this boot' – I gave my right boot (previously removed) a shove, and it fell into the pit of diesel drums – 'damn! when I pushed that boot, it fell. Was that magic?'

'Yes. Anyway, the novel will start with Adam and Eve, and concentrate on teenage problems.' He paused. 'I think' – he glanced candidly into space – 'that one of my difficulties as a novelist is that I am not a good enough writer to write for children, and I have not had enough experience yet to write for adults. Do you have twenty dollars?'

'To spare? Why?'

'Because from Maldonado I have to get 200 kilometres to the Brazilian border, and then reach Rio overland. It is thousands of kilometres and I have only five thousand *intis* for the truck, no more Peruvian money – that is why I am not eating – and ten dollars for transport in Brazil. There are people in Inyapari who might know my mother, and help me. An extra twenty dollars would be sufficient, I think.' He looked anxious. 'I could send it back to you? Or give you my training shoes?'

'Depends how much money I've got left when we reach Maldonado.'

The hot bath at Marcopata had been curiously relaxing. The air was bright, but a little misty now, and heavy. Though damp, it was warm. There were bushes and clumps of grass by the trackside, and the hills were covered in trees. Sleep came upon me: a deep sleep.

I do not know what woke me, but I opened my eyes to a new world. It was twilight and we must have travelled for an hour or more since I had lost consciousness. Huge overhanging trees crowded the track. Ferns from the roadside banks brushed our faces, and leaves and vines swung down above us. Nearby was the sound of a river, rushing. We were right at the bottom of the valley, still following it. To each side the jungle rose almost vertically, hanging green and heavy in the air. Far above us green walls blocked out the sky.

It was very warm, very moist, and the light was soft. All the harshness of the Andes was gone from the air. Huge moths flitted in our hair and, as it darkened, we could see fireflies in the jungle. There were flowers on the trees.

Our headlights created a strange luminous tunnel ahead – a cylinder of light – so that the undergrowth seemed to press from all sides. Above, great candelabras of white flowers hung from the foliage, glowing as if with light of their own. Caught in the beam, a swathe of spiderweb floated across our path, suspended in mid-air like shining gossamer. Tall trees dripped in the mist, giant leaves, ghostly in the electric light, each one standing proud and separate with an identity of its own.

I felt a damp wind on my face and I shivered with excitement as we descended into the black.

'Magic,' I thought, as sleep returned.

Chapter Twenty-Eight

Through
the Air

I dreamed vividly. I was back in West Africa as a student, travelling (as I once did) across the Sahara and then the Zaire jungle, in an old Land-Rover. An incident from that journey was relived exactly, blow by blow, in my dream.

Brent, an American boy from Yale, had been driving. I was on the roof, holding on to the roof-rack for dear life.

I loved this position. The vehicle was crowded, dusty, sweaty and uncomfortable inside, but on top it was all wind and space and solitude – and gave an eagle's view of the passing countryside. We were in northern Cameroon, a country of gentle green and brown hills, straw huts and friendly people. And it had seemed, just at that moment, that there could be no better place to be in the world than on that roof, and no happier youth than I.

But Brent drove faster than an elderly, overloaded jeep and an appalling dirt road allowed. He rounded a left-hand bend too fast: much too fast. The road was cambered the wrong way. The vehicle, which was seriously overloaded, was on the point of turning over.

Brent did the only thing he could. He abandoned the bend and steered straight off the road and over a bank.

The feeling was not of fear, for there was no time for that, but of horror. I remember my arms being almost ripped from their sockets as I gripped the frame of the roof-rack. I remember the vehicle plunging, bucking like a horse, down the bankside; and then I remember seeing a great ditch yawning in front of us.

We took off. The Land-Rover spent a couple of seconds completely airborne – and still I held on – then hit the other side of the ditch.

And stopped. But I didn't. I was launched forward like a missile. I flew through the air – for how far I never checked. But I do remember looking round for the absent vehicle, after landing, and at first being unable to find it.

About the landing I remember nothing. Only lying in the dust, opening my eyes and wondering if I was dead. For some reason I did not want to move – not an inch – and lay quite still, just looking. I saw some African women labouring in the maize field in which I had landed. They too were still, silent, amazed.

One of them began to wail. This stirred me and, gingerly, I moved my neck and looked down at my body. Everything seemed to be there. No blood. I tried moving my legs. They worked. I tried to get to my feet.

Pain ripped through both my shoulders. My arms seemed dead, unable to move. And when I tried to move them, the pain shot back. Yet both arms seemed to be intact.

I had dislocated a shoulder once before and it occurred to me now that this felt the same. That, as it turned out, was all that was wrong with me – two dislocated shoulders, which I fixed later with the help of my comrades (unharmed), the branch of a tree to swing my weight on to, and more pain than I had ever experienced.

For the moment, though, I just had to get up. So, with painful delicacy, I shifted my weight forward on to my knees and arose from the ground as one who had just been praying might do, without the use of arms or hands. It was a clear, warm day; and I distinctly remember feeling the pleasure of the sun on my back, and hearing a bird (which had been temporarily silenced) resume its song.

It was what happened next that still lives so vividly in my mind – and which came flooding back to me in that dream. The African women raised their arms, one exclaiming in wonder, 'Ah! Ah! Ah!' as Africans do; and then bursting into a song-like chant. They were celebrating my survival. I had catapulted through the air, spaceman-style; arrived, unannounced in the middle of their field; and been greeted in song with a small welcoming ceremony. It was natural. Africans just accept things and are glad.

I was born in Africa. In the company of African people, in a little bar-shack later than night, we toasted what was, at least, a significant postponement of my death.

But what triggered this dream? This jungle? This tropical feeling, a whole ocean away? Or was it the sensation of being on the roof? It had all flooded back so clear and warm.

Around midnight everyone awoke as the truck shuddered to a halt in a village square. This was San Lorenzo. Here the huts were on stilts and the roofs were of straw. Metal and bamboo spouts poured water continuously on to rock platforms around the square. The people were ragged, the dogs were crippled, the music and drumbeats were loud, and pigs were everywhere.

Everybody stared at the gringo, some just standing in groups, seemingly transfixed. The gringo was observed without hostility but with a mixture of curiosity and hilarity. It was as if one were a zoo exhibit. If someone had walked up and poked me with a stick, it would have hardly been surprising.

Every second hut had a veranda and a sign: 'Breakfast', 'Lunch', 'Supper', 'Today: CHICKEN', 'SOUP at all hours' 'CHEAPEST in San Lorenzo'. Truck by truck, the convoy ground into town and passengers poured off.

Mosquitoes dived from all sides, and I shared my malaria pills with Marcelo. We ate chicken and rice while bullfrogs croaked from the jungle.

'Here,' said Tio, 'we will sleep until dawn. We have heard that the road ahead is very bad, too dangerous to continue by night.'

On a wooden bench a foot wide on the veranda of a nearby hut, with my anorak rolled up for a pillow, no blanket, and rats running around on the tin and straw over our heads, I slept again. Above, a huge daddy-long-legs struggled, prey to a spider, throttled in the webbing of a thousand strands. Once I awoke with a rat on my chest.

Yet this was a blissful, warm oxygen-rich night. Bats flitted between the huts, frogs sang and night-birds shrieked. The air was alive with mosquitoes, yet there was the scent of flowers in the air too. Nature crowded in relentlessly, powerfully, yet in such sweet profusion.

Sleep had come fast and heavy. It was the night of our second day.

Chapter Twenty-Nine

Down the
River

Chino gave us seven minutes to re-board the truck. Barely awake, still trying to pack clothes and belongings, we lurched out of the village, horn blaring. This was the stretch that Tio had said was very bad.

It was atrocious. All morning we can have covered no more than fifty kilometres. We were still following the river, but we were out of the mountains now and running through foothills. Our track dived steeply up and down, winding its way along, sometimes by the riverside, sometimes hundreds of feet above it.

Everywhere there were waterfalls. Hundreds of streams had cut the road and makeshift bridges had been constructed over each one. It was not so much a road as a running battle between truckers and nature. And we were leading the convoy.

The most common problems lay in the folds in the hillside, deep creases, where the track would elbow sharply in and cross the stream just where the hillside folded. So the stream had to be bridged right at the crux of the bend. The manoeuvring necessary to get the vehicle round would dislodge the branches and rocks from which the bridge was constructed, and flash floods would make matters worse.

All in all, we had to repair or reconstruct seven of these: and dozens more proved a matter of edging gingerly across, passengers peering nervously out over the side as wheels slipped and slid along the edge, stones and earth tumbling into the abyss beneath.

Some were extremely dangerous, but Tio never suggested we dismount. He took the view that if he and his truck were going over, everyone else might as well go too. But he was a skilful driver, and a hero to his crew.

Three times we failed to get up steep, muddy slopes: but each time we succeeded in the end by dint of taking faster and faster runs at the slope until, passengers cheering, we would slither to the crest.

Then we reached a bridge that had completely collapsed. It had spanned a large stream which now roared down the hillside through the wreckage of the old bridge. There was no way round or through for the hillside was steep, the gorge deep and the forest impenetrable. We would have to build a new bridge.

By the time we had inspected the problem from all sides, two more trucks in our convoy had pulled up behind us. Heart of Jesus and View of The Little Virgin of Fatima. Together the three crews and all the passengers set to work.

This was surely as fast a work of major civil construction – accomplished without machinery of any kind – as it is possible to imagine! It took only a few hours. Everyone joined in, dragging branches and foliage down the hillside to the site, where (under Tio's direction) the two great logs which had formed the spine of the previous bridge (one of them quite rotten) were hauled and levered back into place, parallel, like railway tracks across the gulf.

Then came smaller branches laid between them, filling in the gaps. Then as much foliage as we could lay our hands on: the sound of knives and axes and rending tree limbs cracked and crackled through the jungle.

Finally, Tio wanted the whole thing covered in stones and earth. So, with Chino and the other truck crews shovelling out the bankside, all the passengers scraped up handfuls of rubble and threw it on to the bridge. With some fifty people doing so at once, a continuous stream of rubble poured down, until the bed was sufficient and Tio called a halt.

Our truck went over first, everyone holding their breath. This time we could watch from outside. The two key logs swayed and bent alarmingly, and a scattering of dislodged stones clattered down into the stream below. But the thing held. Everybody cheered. Caesar Augustus was handed back up into the truck, wrapped in a blanket.

With its diesel load, ours was the heaviest truck; and all the others crossed without incident. By now our convoy had grown to six vehicles: we still led.

The sun had come out. Brown birds with yellow tails flapped away from our path. The banks were full of butterflies and the scent of flowers was everywhere. Groves of trees which had no leaves at all, but just a harvest of huge scarlet blossoms, lay to each side. Everyone felt happy, confident that one way or another we would surely reach Maldonado now.

Peruvians love practical jokes. The loss of one of my boots, down amid the diesel drums, had been a source of unending amusement to the whole truck; my every attempt to retrieve it brought new laughter, and there were cheers when my final plan – a hook on the end of a stick – did the job. Marcelo got his lost mitten back in the same way: up it came, soaked in diesel, caught by a bent pin on the end of a piece of foliage.

But the new game was throwing things at passing trucks. Fruit, bananas, seed-pods from the trees – whatever came to hand. Unlike in Europe, it was the old men who were the most irresponsible. With age seemed to come increasing mischief rather than dignity, and two or three of the old boys formed a crack cadre of missile gatherers and launchers. These toothless warriors sat along the front of the cargo hold, drinking bootleg liquor they had brought along with them in old beer bottles, cackling, cursing and chewing coca leaves.

There was retaliation, of course. We came under a heavy siege of bananas from a truck called Julius Caesar, heading up to Cuzco with a load of fruit. One wondered how much they would have left by the time they got there. Caesar Augustus looked up briefly from his milk-bar as Julius Caesar passed, but made no comment. His mother had started to knit – a real achievement on the metal floor of a truck which was rocking wildly back and forth. A small tragedy for Caesar and his mother had been the breakage of their thermos flask, when a drum had rolled over their belongings.

By now everything and everyone, except Caesar, was covered in diesel fuel. My clothes and sleeping-bag were hopelessly impregnated, and the stuff was in my hair, too. Luceo, the young runaway, was beginning to look like a monkey who had been dropped into a vat of oil.

And it was Luceo who became our accomplice in the defeat of La Gorda.

Her jokes were beginning to grate. It is always awkward to handle abuse in a strange language. You can sense what is going on, and hear the titters of the audience; but you are not quick or fluent enough to reply. So something had to be done. Marcelo agreed, and Luceo, who enjoyed sport of any kind, was always ready to aid and abet.

La Gorda's most recent and successful joke had been to grab a small, stunted green banana from among the missiles which hit us from Julius Caesar. Sitting (as she was, chuckling fatly away with her friend) on the perch above the driver's side of the cab, she could be seen clearly by those in the back of any truck we were following. So could I, perched on the other side. But we could not see each other, for there was a pile of luggage stacked up between us.

This arrangement enabled her to make obscene gestures in my direction with the banana: apparently so, anyway, for only once did her head actually appear over the top of the baggage to wave the banana, shouting some obscenity or other in my (or Marcelo's) direction. But there must have been more embroidery to the joke than that, to judge by the hilarity from a truck called Christ Saves which ran ahead of us for a while (with 'God' written on one rear mud-flap, and 'Love' on the other). The fact that La Gorda's performance was hidden from me, its object, made it all the funnier for the others.

This gringo now had this woman's measure, as did the younger men in that truck in front, and as did Luceo. Luceo was often himself the butt of her banana jokes, and was now clinging on to the rigging next to me. Together, we had an idea.

The trucks' motors drowned all speech: so, by visual signals, we put into the minds of the men in Christ Saves the idea of writing a love-note to La Gorda, and pinning it to a passing overhanging bough. Luceo pointed exaggeratedly towards her and clasped his heart with his hand; and we mimed a writing motion, and simulated the action of hanging something on the passing boughs.

They soon got the idea, and found from the others in their truck a pencil and notepaper. One wrote out an exaggerated declaration of passion, stood up and spiked it on to a bush to one side of the track. Though La Gorda could see this, she had not been able to see Luceo and me setting it up. However, her abusive yells showed she knew something was going on.

Thirty seconds later our truck passed the same bush. With great skill the diesel-monkey swung himself out from the side of the wooden frame and grabbed the note. A great cheer went up from Christ's passengers. La Gorda's obscenities intensified.

Luceo handed the note to me. I waited. Soon we passed a tree with a spray of orchids hanging down over the truck. I tore off an especially bright blossom, wove it into the love-note, kissed it and, pressing both to my heart, stretched the note longingly out in La Gorda's direction.

Slight though the joke sounds in the recounting, in the accomplishment it proved a huge hit with the passengers. There were cheers from our own truck, and the lads who had sent the note were rolling on the floor. One threw his cap in the air, where it caught on a tree. As our truck passed beneath, I leaped up and caught it, to further cheers.

La Gorda was now confused as to what was going on, and speechless. Luceo, our go-between, delivered the note and the cap.

Her rage was pleasing to see. This incident marked the end of her banana jokes.

It was not long before we stopped again. This time it was to help a truck broken-down in front of us, and blocking the road. The truck (He Who Fights, Lives!) had a broken half-shaft and all we could do, after towing it into the ditch, was to take the driver and his half-shaft on towards Maldonado where he hoped to find a replacement. His passengers were left to pick up rides with other trucks, or fend for themselves.

The half-shaft took some extracting, and the driver smashed the wooden handle of his sledge-hammer while trying. With quiet skill he chopped a section of branch to length, trimmed it quickly and accurately with his knife, and – within minutes – had a handle that was good as new. This time, the half-shaft came out.

After much shunting, we were ready to depart. Just as we did, there came a hooting of horns and revving of motors, and the yellow cement truck, El Caudillo, rounded the corner and roared past. As it bounced away down the track, there was a shout of recognition from among its passengers – 'Gringo!' – and much waving. It was the old gang from Urcos, Harpo still with his cassette-recorder. The oldest of them, though, seemed to have lost his 'TOYOTA' cap.

Soon we were back on the track ourselves. The river was larger now, and, once, a clearing in the trees gave us a glimpse of what looked like an even bigger river, muddy-brown and flat, stretching out over the plain. Could that be the great tributary we were to follow to the Madre de Dios river at Maldonado?

We started to climb a steep little hill, and, after slipping off the track a couple of times and taking another run at it, we saw two Indians walk past. Where they were going was a mystery, for we had seen no huts; but these men looked different from those I had seen in the towns and villages.

They wore few clothes. The older of them, a young man, wore a pair of yellow shorts, sandals and nothing else; the younger, a boy, had only underpants. Their hair was straight and black and quite long, and in one hand the young man carried a length of fishing-line and two quite big fish.

The young man raised one arm, in dignified fashion, but otherwise did not speak or acknowledge us.

Some of the other passengers peered out with interest, and a couple of the old men pelted the couple with orange peel. The Indian passengers in our truck did not seem to speak their language and showed a curiosity towards them which implied no kinship at all – as though they were wild animals.

The forest men took no notice. They were moving at about the same pace as us, but after a mile or so they branched down a path into the jungle and we saw them no more. These were the closest to 'primitive' Indians that we saw. They looked strong and happy.

After night had fallen, the track seemed to level out, and Tio decided to carry on until midnight. Most slept, though Marcelo and I sat up and talked.

In some ways he was a lost – or at least wandering – soul. In others he was assertive and self-confident. His thought and speech were a strange amalgam of cliché – the fashionable phrases and opinions of his generation – and originality.

Since he had started taking my malaria pills, he had often felt sick. He did now.

It was dark and with a long day behind us, Marcelo was going through one of his tentative patches. He told me about his mother and sisters, and college in Boston; and his ideas in setting out on this adventure.

'How did your mother feel about letting you do this?'

'Oh' – hastily – 'I don't have to submit to conventional family discipline like that. Ours is not so much of a family at all, really. I like to think of it as a team . . .' He tailed off.

'But wasn't she anxious about you? Aren't you anxious about her?'

Marcelo said nothing, but he looked very anxious indeed. There was a long pause – perhaps for five minutes or more. Then he spoke.

'I think I thought of this as a sort of pilgrimage, except I am not sure what I have come to find. People talk about great pilgrimages to religious shrines – or even to see other people: spiritual leaders. I had been thinking about making a pilgrimage to visit the Ma . . . Maharashi Yogi . . . or whatever – you know, the one the Beatles went to see.

'These are what people mean by "pilgrimages", I suppose. But I was thinking, when you were asking me about my mother and sisters, that maybe the greatest pilgrimage I can make is . . . is to go home.'

I dozed off to sleep. I was awoken by shouting and the sound of wheels spinning in the mud. We were stuck again.

'*Pico*, Gringo!' Dabit wanted the pick. It was supposed to be on the floor of our cockpit. In the dark I fumbled around my feet. No pick.

'It's not here.'

Dabit called to me to look again. Still no pick.

He clambered up to search for himself. The pick was under my feet. The gringo felt ashamed.

Very late that night, we rumbled into a village called Quincemil.

All was quiet. There was only one street, the main street. It had no margins, no pavement: only a sea of puddles, a morass of mud, and tin shacks. One of them was a little tin-roofed cinema, named after Admiral Grau. By it was parked an ancient Dodge pick-up with the name Cat written proudly across the top.

We drove a little out of the village, and stopped for the night. I decided to sleep on the ground near the truck.

It had been raining and the ground was damp. Dew clung to the leaves of grass. There was a moon behind light cloud, and on the skyline, the low, black outline of distant mountains. Strange sounds filled the night – the little chirps, shrieks and rustlings of forest animals. It was cool, and a gentle drizzle fell on my face.

But I did not mind. Just for a while I was far away, at home in Derbyshire. Marcelo, perhaps, was in Rio.

A nightmare awoke me. I was a Member of Parliament once more. Mrs Thatcher was accusing me of concealing the whereabouts of a pick. I sat bolt upright, ready to protest my innocence, stared wildly into the dripping leaves by my face, realized where I was and fell back into a deep slumber.

This was the night of our third day.

At dawn it was still raining. We breakfasted well in Quincemil. Tio amused all by demanding a dash of spirits in his coffee, before the road ahead. Perhaps he knew that this breakfast preceded a difficult day's drive.

The first stretch was very bad. It had started to rain, and Chino and Dabit had draped a huge, torn old canvas over the whole of the cargo bed, with us under it. This employed the centre pole that ran like a spine from front to back as ridge-pole to a crude tent. It kept us dry, but the feeling of heaving up and down in a black hole, covered in canvas and unable to see out (except through slits between the wooden planks) was close and unpleasant.

The track at this point was straight, flat and waterlogged. There were now eleven trucks in a line, and the whole convoy came often to a halt as one or other of our number became bogged down in the soft mud and deep ruts that opened up every few hundred yards. Trapped in our slave-pit, we could only guess what was happening – or poke our heads out around the sides of the canvas and into the rain.

Then came a major hold-up. A truck ahead of us (Tiger) got completely stuck. For half an hour it roared and slithered, and the truck in front tried to tow it forward; but it became plain that this was only making matters worse. In mud, a heavy load often helps the wheels grip. But in this case the truck, loaded to capacity with crates of beer for Maldonado, was so bedded into a hole in the mud that the weight had become an obstacle to towing it up and out.

People seemed to know what to do. Caesar Augustus was excused and most of the women stayed put, but all the men in the surrounding trucks formed a human chain leading from the back of the stranded vehicle to the grass verge at the edge of the quagmire. There were some 150 men, and the chain was some 150 yards long.

We began to unload the crates of beer, handing each – one at a time – all the way along the chain to pile up on the roadside. The operation was carried out smoothly and at remarkable speed. Brilliant green hummingbirds hovered around us in the drizzle as the job was completed.

After that it was easy to tow Tiger out. The whole process was then reversed, to reload the truck; and within an hour we were on our way again. This answered my curiosity as to why diesel was taken down to Maldonado in 44-gallon drums, rather than in a proper oil tanker with a single reservoir.

Huddled in the back, wishing the rain would stop, and feeling rather sick after taking malaria pills on an empty stomach, Marcelo offered me half of his last piece of food. 'Here, have a piece of this Krishna-cookie. I heard that it's good for your karma, as well as feeding your stomach. But it tastes a bit dry . . .'

It did. But it neutralized the quinine. Then the rain stopped. As the sun came out we pulled into a roadside village – a few huts on stilts, cats, turkeys, a tame monkey and a garish scarlet and sky-blue parrot. Off came the canvas.

Below us lay a great river. Far wider than the Thames at London Bridge, this river was a chocolately mass of swirling currents, fringed with forest banks and low hills. On one muddy shore lay a raft made of logs. Upstream you could not see the Andes from which the river had sprung: only banks of clouds towering into the sky. Downstream the ribbon of brown stretched out towards a flat, green horizon.

But it was the bridge that amazed. The track we had come on had been, for hundreds of kilometres, just that: no more than a track, barely passable at times. Yet here was a magnificent suspension bridge, strung from one hill to another, high above the water – and painted bright orange.

Once again the importance of this road was borne in on me. A bridge like this justified all those miles of cuttings into the rock, all those careful little stone culverts in the mountains. What ailed a national economy which could raise the capital to build this wonder of the Peruvian jungle, yet which was somehow unable to organize a system of linesmen along the road – peasants whose job it was to keep (say) a kilometre each in passable condition, paid by results?

Everyone was proud of the bridge. Tio asked me to take his photograph, standing on it in front of his truck. Then we were away, thundering along through the air, suspended a hundred feet above the water.

Luceo was the most excited of all. He stood with the ridge-pole for support, peering out over the top of the cab towards the new world to which he was running away. What were his thoughts? It half-occurred to me that the ironwork above was rather low, and Luceo's head rather exposed.

A network of orange girders and steel cables was flashing by the side of the truck. Yet it was not the steel which caught the eye, but the gossamer hanging upon it. Huge forest spiders had filled each square in this network with their webs. There must have been tens of thousands. Each web was constructed upon the same principles of suspension as the bridge.

After the rain, the webs themselves were strings of tiny water droplets, and these were catching the evening sun, shining so bright that the metalwork to which they were strung faded into the background.

Everything transient, everything fine, everything delicate, shone boldly forth. What was permanent, what was strong – the iron upon which this whole fantasy was supported – faded into the background, just a dull margin to a bright show. The luminous spider webs were like an artist's drawing – an idea, delicately pencilled in free style by eye on to paper. The idea shone forth.

The bridge was the application of the idea: the heavy work of the civil engineer, clothing genius with concrete and iron.

And then something made me look up. Luceo was standing well clear of the top of the truck: and his head was flying towards a low girder. In his excitement he had not seen it.

There was no time to shout. I knocked him sideways as the girder rushed over his temples, missing his forehead by inches. It would have killed him instantly. It would have killed him as surely as an iron beam smashes the gossamer of a spider's web.

Just for a moment, the cheeky grin left Luceo's face, and he sat, shaking. What would they have done with the body? Would anyone have been informed?

Chapter Thirty

And into Maldonado

The scenery was changing. Trees were taller, the river wider and slower. On one side were wide mud beaches; on the other, vast boulders stood half submerged. Two condors wheeled above us, and brightly spotted guinea-fowl scuttled through the undergrowth. Now there were people by the roadside, and many fine huts on tall stilts.

Over this shimmering green landscape, the sun looked different: fuller, oranger and softer than before. In the Andes it was an intense point of light, the palest of yellows into which you could hardly look. Now it hung more heavily in a sky which itself had taken on weight. You could feel the vapour in the atmosphere.

The track was improving: soft red earth which could almost call itself a road. Black ants – so big that we could see them from the truck-top – patrolled the verges, as a condor swept its lazy river patrol.

The trees were of every shape and colour, busy with vines, orchids and huge ants' nests made of mud. The curtain of little hills from which the river issued gave a perspective on the jungle. When the jungle is flat and the trees close above your head, you cannot stand back and survey. Here, we could. We could see hillsides of trees. We could see primary forest, as it appears in a child's geography book.

But for how much longer? With the improvement of the road, we started to notice sections of forest thinned of all the great trees. By the side of the track were piles of timber on which the lumberjacks placed notices bidding for transport from any passing truck with capacity to spare. '¡Look!' said one, next to a crude drawing of two eyes: '¡Cargo for Sicuani!'

The mountains behind us – so vast and frightening when we had been among them – seemed to recede very fast on to the horizon. Already they were just a cold purple margin to an enclosing foreground of green.

This was the last leg of our journey.

Marcelo's mellow homesickness from the night before had receded. Like all of us, he was excited. Like Luceo, he was apprehensive. For them this was just the beginning.

For Marcelo, Puerto Maldonado would be the start of a difficult journey towards the Brazilian frontier. The map suggested that there was hardly a road at all: or, if there was, not one on which it was easy to pick up transport like this. He faced the prospect of walking as far as eighty miles. He thought he could.

For Luceo it would be the beginning of life in a new world. It became clear that we were nearing the prospecting shanty town they call Mazuco. As the road broadened, whole villages of huts on stilts opened out to each side. From some homesteads came the sound of new music – different rhythms from those sad, chilling mountain songs: jazzy, lazy rhythms with different instruments. It was Amazon music, gold-diggers' music. Luceo's eyes widened.

Mata-Rata (Kill-Rat) was gathering together his proprietary pest-control products and setting up his portable stall. He had been an exceptionally quiet passenger; whatever aggression was in his nature must have been reserved for rodents. But now his homemade travelling display case became a centre of interest among us. His stall was lined with a venomous range of artillery. Huge rat-traps, delicate mousetraps and poisonous powders of every kind. There were mosquito-repellents and patented fly-bite balms. There was even a rat-bite antidote whose virtues Mata-Rata explained with careful pride to La Gorda.

One of the more raucous women enquired whether Mata-Rata could supply anything for the rat, should it be bitten by La Gorda. This caused great merriment.

La Gorda took it all in her stride. She, like Luceo, was to alight (if La Gorda could do anything so delicate) at Mazuco. Her relationship with the local populace was already being forged, as she leaned from the side of the truck hollering her obscenities at the Indians labouring in the fields. Some replied in a kind and more than once she dodged missiles in the form of yam fragments and cassava roots, but most looked rather taken aback. La Gorda was ready for Mazuco. Was Mazuco ready for La Gorda?

Probably. This was a gold-rush town. Spread out along one broad street, the shanties and offices, general stores and 'hotels' (their tariffs scrawled on to painted boards outside) straggled to left and right.

Here the cars had steel padlocks on their boots, bonnets and even – in a couple of cases – doors. Trucks, pick-ups, mules and donkeys jostled for space on the road. Turkeys – which we had never seen in the mountains, but which here seemed to be all the rage as domestic fowls – scrabbled and gobbled in every ditch. People and movement, noise and colour were all around.

We pulled in beside a truck with tigers on its mud flaps. Rocky – The Zurda Of Gold, it was called.

'MINERAL WORKERS WANTED', said a sign outside a long, low bungalow with an overhanging tin roof. '500 *intis* per day. ¡No documents! Malaria preventatives required.' Luceo's eyes lit up. Outside the Mineral Bank Of Peru hung a notice: 'We Always Buy Gold Including Sundays and Public Holidays'. His eyes widened further.

I was climbing back up as he was taking down his one small bag. We passed – so to speak – on the rigging. Clinging to the side, I held his arm to steady him as he swung his bag down to the earth. As he reached the ground his hand gripped mine, and he just held on.

Perhaps it was only for a second. He stood there and looked up, squeezing my hand tight, and his eyes were filled with tears. Then he let go.

We left. Everybody waved from the truck; and our new friends, who seemed like old friends, whom we would never see again, waved back from the Mazuco throng into which they were disappearing: a tight-knit team, dispersing never to be re-formed. Even La Gorda waved and exchanged parting obscenities. Mata-Rata threaded his way into the crowd, his fine display stall all set out with remedies and poisons: the new Pied Piper of Mazuco.

The truck behind us was called ¡Always With You Oh Lord! As we pulled away, something ricocheted off the side of the truck, having narrowly missed my shoulder. I spun round. It was a green banana. From the hurly-burly we were leaving behind came a cackling shriek – it was La Gorda. We stopped a little way out of the town at an army road-block. Forms were handed round to complete, and the literate passengers helped the illiterate to fill them in. 'Driver?' enquired the form.

'Put Tio,' Chino instructed us all. 'because he is known. He has helped people. People help him.'

Shortly after that, we stopped again. It was dusk and this was the evening of our fourth day.

We were coasting towards the end of a chapter: a chapter not just in my own life but in the lives of almost all the passengers on our truck.

On the morning of our fifth day – Wednesday morning – we would arrive at Maldonado, very early, and I would find only a note at the Aero-Peru office:

> We have gone to the jungle for 4 days with Victor's brother. And we shall be leaving his address (on this card) at 7 a.m. on Thursday. If we don't see you here by Wednesday night we'll see you at the airfield. Hope this finds you as it leaves us: confused – Mick, John & Ian.

Marcelo and I would walk through the streets of Maldonado where the world travels on motorized tricycles with parasols, and the road signs are sponsored by Coca-Cola – to the shouts of 'Gringo!' from all the little children.

We would go down to the banks of the great, swirling brown Madre de Dios river, and we would strip naked and wash, standing with the cool river eddying jaw-high, while the clay (and heaven knows what kinds of worms) squelched between our toes; then lie on the grass in the sun to dry. And drink Coke at the Kiosko Virgen del Chapi.

And I would see him off, diesel-soaked knapsack on his back, walking into the distance along a dusty track in the midday heat with his Brazilian passport, my twenty-dollar bill and very little else in his pocket.

'Did you know,' he would be writing to me a year later, 'that slavery is still common in these parts of Brazil? Every now and again an exasperated guy in chains shows up there, in the towns . . .'

But that was still to come. Now it was evening.

'Maestro!' called Tio to the cook in the grass-roofed restaurant-on-stilts into which we had all trooped for an evening meal. This was a tiny settlement, surrounded by jungle.

It was the beginning of our last overnight stretch to Maldonado. We ordered chicken soup, potatoes and rice, and the proprietor's wife moved round the tables lighting candles and oil-lamps, for there was no electricity. Mosquitoes darted through the flames.

Everyone was happy. The hut was full of soft flickering light, and laughter. Until now the whole journey had been tinged with an anxiety. Few voiced it, everyone shared it: anxiety that we might not get there at all. Now we knew we would.

But there would be a long wait before the food was ready. So I walked away from this little island of lamps and humans, away from the light. I walked into the edge of the forest. I walked for some distance. I became part of the gathering darkness.

A night-bird, with a strange, long shriek on a rising cadence, was calling. The faint glow of sunset was fading, and his hour had come. Fireflies were flashing and the air was still. A hundred small rustlings pierced the dusk.

And I stood, silent, among the trees in this forest. Just stood. The worst of our journey, and the best too, and they were the same, were over.

Where was Luceo? And where is he as I write this now? And Fortunato – is he fishing high up on that lake at Jahuacocha? This was a good time for trout.

Did Señora Fernandez, weeping on that bus to Huaraz, ever find her lost bag? Did anybody claim that little retarded boy with the placard in Puno? Was Tomasina, the Indian girl's tiny baby, destined to live? And what lay in store for Caesar Augustus? Was Socrates still stuck?

What would happen to Marcelo? Would he reach Rio safely? Would Nazario ever leave his village of Llamac? Would La Gorda take to the life of a Mazuco madam and would she prosper here? Is Saul the schoolteacher in Chiquian still on strike? Has he found his soul, temporarily mislaid? Does the little girl in the Huaywash mountains still remember meeting the men from the moon?

Does Lis remember Ian or had this been, for her, all just a dream?

What had it been for me?

I looked into the trees towards where I knew the mountains were. It had been a red sunset, now only a dull glimmer in the west. The whole range of the Andes would be there, clear and black, a sharp silhouette, very low, very hard, along the western horizon. Far away now.

And the great Amazon basin stretched before me to the Atlantic, vast and anonymous. I yearned to see it.

I stood there for I do not know how long, thinking of the places I had been, and of the forest. How unknown to me was this place!

By now it was dark. To the sound of the night bird I made my way back towards the lights.